NORTHROP FRYE
on Culture and Literature

NORTHROP FRYE
on Culture and Literature

*A Collection
of Review Essays*

Edited and with an Introduction by

ROBERT D. DENHAM

The University of Chicago Press

Chicago and London

TO SCOTT AND KRISTIN

The University of Chicago Press, Chicago 60637
The University of Chicago Press, Ltd., London

© 1978 by The University of Chicago
All rights reserved. Published 1978

Printed in the United States of America
82 81 80 79 78   9 8 7 6 5 4 3 2 1

NORTHROP FRYE is University Professor at the University of Toronto. His many works include *The Educated Imagination, The Well-Tempered Critic*, and, most recently, *The Secular Scripture: A Study of the Structure of Romance*.

ROBERT D. DENHAM is associate professor of English and chairman of the department, Emory and Henry College. He is the author of *Northrop Frye: An Enumerative Bibliography* and numerous scholarly articles.

Library of Congress Cataloging in Publication Data

Frye, Northrop.
 Northrop Frye on culture and literature.

 Includes index.
 1. Books—Reviews.   I. Title.
Z1035.A1F78   028.1   77–12917
ISBN 0–226–26647–8

CONTENTS

The reviews collected here are examples of a creative mind confronting other creative minds. This alone is enough to recommend them. But while they begin as reviews, they always move in the direction of the essay; thus their significance lies in what they have to say not only about a group of important thinkers, poets, and novelists, from Cervantes to Char, but also about the foundations and direction of Frye's own thought. Frye once remarked that "the end of book reviewing is the beginning of criticism proper" ("On Book Reviewing," *Here and Now* 2 [June 1949]: 19). The reviews in the present volume testify to the appropriateness of the observation, at least as it applies to Frye's own work, for a number of sentences and paragraphs from the works reprinted here were later to find their way into *Anatomy of Criticism*.

The selections come from an extraordinarily energetic period in Frye's career. The earliest, on George Orwell, appeared the year before *Fearful Symmetry* (1947) was to chart a new direction in Blake studies, and the latest, on Samuel Beckett, was published only a few years after the *Anatomy* (1957). The essays were written, then, during the decade that Frye was also writing one of the most influential books of literary theory in our time. The achievement is all the more impressive when we consider that during these years Frye published more than one hundred other essays, reviews, and contributions to books.

Fourteen of the selections come from *The Hudson Review*, the journal to which Frye was a regular contributor from 1951 to 1960. For these essays, I have retained Frye's own titles. Five were published in *The Canadian Forum*, which Frye was associated with as a contributor and managing editor for twenty-five years. He wrote more than one hundred separate pieces for the *Forum*, the little monthly "whose good natured hospitality," he once remarked, "helped so many Canadians learn to write" (*The Bush Garden*, p. vii). Of the remaining selections, one appeared in *The Griffin*. The other, on Frazer, was originally a radio talk, later published in the CBC series, *Architects of Thought*.

As a lecturer and essayist, Frye is well known. Eight of his fifteen books began as public lectures; three are collections of essays. But in book form, the work of Frye the reviewer is available to us only in *The Bush Garden* (1971), the bulk of which reprints the annual surveys of Canadian poetry Frye wrote for *The University of Toronto Quarterly* from 1950 to 1960. These, however, represent but one side of his contribution as a reviewer of more than three hundred books over the course of twenty-five years. The aim of making conveniently available a selection of Frye's other reviews is to represent in still another way his achievement as a thinker and a man of letters.

I express my deep appreciation and thanks to Professor Frye for consenting to let me make this collection. I thank also the editors of *The Hudson Review*, *The Canadian Forum*, and *The Griffin* for granting permission to reprint material which first appeared in the pages of their journals. Some of the paragraphs in the Introduction appeared originally in *The South Carolina Review*, *Canadian Literature*, and *The South Atlantic Bulletin*, and in my *Northrop Frye: An Enumerative Bibliography* (1974). I wish to thank the editors of these publications for permitting me to use this material again.

INTRODUCTION

I

The decline in the admiration for continuity is
one of the most striking differences between the
Romantic and the modern feeling.
The Modern Century

In one of the few places where Northrop Frye reflects upon the
sources and development of his intellectual life, he says that
"the sense of continuity in memory" was necessary for the
growth of his own creative and critical work. Like his
preceptor Blake, Frye observes, he unconsciously arranged his
life to be without incident, adding that "no biographer could
possibly take the smallest interest in me."[1] While some future
biographer might look upon Frye's life differently, no one can
dispute "the sense of continuity" that pervades his thought. It
is especially apparent in what he has written since *Fearful
Symmetry* (1947), Blake being the most formative influence
upon his thinking. But even in his earliest essays, which were
on music and opera and ballet and film, we discover the roots
of many ideas which were to be developed in *Anatomy of
Criticism* (1957) and in the fourteen books which have followed.

In his first published essay Frye refers to the opposition
between realism and convention, the two poles which were to
figure importantly in many of his later mental diagrams. He
speaks here also of the *mythological* framework of Wagner,
thus using the word which points toward what was to become
a central interest.[2] And in his second published work, we
discover in a discussion of music—the structural principles of
which later provided some of Frye's chief metaphors for
explaining literary structure—an analysis of melody and

harmony, rhythm and pattern. Tucked away here unobtrusively, then, are the two principles which, translated into
mythos and *dianoia* almost twenty years later, were to stand as
the backbone of the *Anatomy*.[3] Frye's first piece of literary
criticism is a defense of Spengler against the attacks of
Wyndham Lewis.[4] As several of the essays in the present
collection make clear, the formative influence of Spengler on
Frye's thought began early, and, as if imitating the rhythm in
Spengler's vision itself, he has returned to *The Decline of the
West* as least once each decade since the publication of this
defense.[5] Many such evidences of continuity are apparent
when we look at Frye's work as a whole, placing the essays of
the 1930s and 40s alongside his most recent work and considering the issues and themes which have occupied him over the
years.

The continuous vision gives Frye's work as a continuous
form, stretching before us like those encyclopedic works which
have captured his own imagination. In *A Map of Misreading*
Harold Bloom remarks that Frye's myths of freedom and
concern are a Low Church version of Eliot's Anglo-Catholic
myth of Tradition and the Individual Talent, but that such an
understanding of the relation of the individual to tradition is a
fiction. "The fiction," Bloom says, "is a noble idealization, and
as a lie against time will go the way of every noble idealization. Such positive thinking served many purposes during the
sixties, when continuities, of any kind, badly required to be
summoned, even if they did not come to our call. Wherever we
are bound, our dialectical development now seems invested in
the interplay of repetition and discontinuity, and needs a very
different sense of what our stance is in regard to literary
tradition."[6] This remark contains more than a hint of the
anxiety of influence. But regardless of whether one agrees with
Bloom's projection about what our development "seems" to
involve, it is mistaken to suggest that Frye has failed to observe
the "interplay between repetition and discontinuity." In words
that could stand as a motto for theories of misprision, he says
that "the recreating of the literary tradition often has to
proceed . . . through a process of absorption followed by

misunderstanding."[7] Even if Frye's ultimate allegiances are to a continuous intellectual and imaginative universe, to order rather than chaos, to romance rather than irony, he cannot be accused of having turned his back upon the discontinuities in either literature or life. Nor should we let Bloom's remark deceive us into thinking that in the 1960s Frye began suddenly to summon continuities as a bulwark against the changing social order. The central principles in Frye's universe have remained constant over the years. In reflecting on his work since the mid-fifties, Frye says that it

> has assumed the shape of what Professor Jerome Brunner would call a spiral curriculum, circling around the same issues, though trying to keep them open-ended. . . . Emerson, as we know, deprecated what he called a foolish consistency, but there is always one form of consistency which is not foolish, and that is continuity. With some people continuity takes a revolutionary and metaphoric direction: a philosopher may repudiate everything he has written up to a certain time and start afresh. Even so, I doubt if he can start afresh until he discovers the real point of contact with his earlier work. With me, continuity has taken a more gradual direction, not because I insist that everything I have said earlier, in *Anatomy of Criticism* or elsewhere, must be "right," but because the principles I have already formulated are still working as heuristic assumptions, and they are the only ones available to me.[8]

The gradual direction of this continuity is perhaps best illustrated by Frye's views on the social context of criticism. Although he is frequently seen as one of the old New Critics, closer, say, to Eliot and Brooks than to Arnold and Burke, the breadth of Frye's critical theory does not permit such pigeonholing. When Frederick Crews launched his attack several years ago against what he saw as the prevalent tendency in criticism to renounce "methods that would plainly reveal literary determinants,"[9] he singled out Frye as the chief advocate of the doctrine that critics should not stray from literature in developing their fundamental principles. Claiming that such a position was "intellectually indefensible,"

Crews went on to object to the entire enterprise outlined in *Anatomy of Criticism*—a book he saw as symptomatic of critical "anaesthesia." He advanced, in fact, two distinct complaints. On the one hand, he offered an apology for using "extra-literary" hypotheses: thus Frye became his whipping boy for failing to see that criticism cannot be autonomous. On the other, he objected to the academic knowledge industry and the irrelevance which, he felt, criticism of Frye's variety supported: thus his charge that Frye had not properly conceived of the function of art.

A number of other readers have had similar misgivings about Frye's work,[10] suggesting that he shows an unqualified reverence for the literary text, that his critical system always points inward and thus neglects the relationship of literature to life, that his attention to questions of form and convention necessarily precludes all interest in questions of value, that he emphasizes disinterested study at the expense of engagement. This view of Frye, however, is a caricature, resting as it does upon half-truth, and it should be corrected by taking a close look at what Frye has, in fact, been saying about these issues throughout his career.

A formidable amount of Frye's writing, especially in recent years, has been devoted precisely to those issues which critics like Crews have accused him of slighting or neglecting altogether. Even in the *Anatomy*, where Frye's primary concern *is* with the formal nature of literature, we see his willingness to confront such questions as the role of literature in society, the ethical ends of art, and the social function of criticism. These issues are but a part of a much larger concern—what might be called a general theory of culture. Because of the popular conception of Frye as an exclusively formal theorist, this aspect of his work has been slighted or, as in the case of critics like Crews, overlooked. "As some of those who write about me are still asserting that I ignore the social reference of literary criticism," Frye says in his preface to *The Stubborn Structure*, "the subtitle [*Essays on Criticism and Society*] calls the attention of those who read me to the fact that I have written about practically nothing else."[11] He could have said the same about

The Critical Path, a book published a year later and subtitled
An Essay on the Social Context of Literary Criticism.[12] The
social reference of criticism, in short, forms an important part
of Frye's work, as can be seen from the essays in the present
collection.

But even in *Anatomy of Criticism*, where Frye's gaze is
primarily centripetal, it is clear that he neither endorses the
view that criticism is finally autonomous nor accepts the idea
that literature is aesthetically self-contained. In the Tentative
Conclusion he speaks of the necessity for critics becoming
"more aware of the external relations of criticism as a whole
with other disciplines," of the "revolutionary act of consciousness" involved in the response to literature, and of the
obligation of criticism to recover the social function of art. It is
hardly honest, he says, for criticism "to shrink altogether from
[these] larger issues."[13] In confronting the larger issues, Frye
examines a number of alternatives the critic might take,
rejecting some and trying to reconcile others to his Romantic
view of the imagination. His approach is not altogether
systematic, but he does want to indicate that each of the four
kinds of criticism in the *Anatomy* (historical, archetypal,
ethical, and rhetorical) is related to a wider area of humanistic
concern.

Frye first expands the reference of "historical criticism" to
mean not just the codification of the heritage of the past but
the recreation of the past in a new context. "The preoccupa-
tion of the humanities with the past," he says,

> is sometimes made a reproach against them by those who
> forget that we face the past: it may be shadowy, but it is all
> that there is. Plato draws a gloomy picture of man staring at
> the flickering shapes made on the wall of the objective world
> by a fire behind us like the sun. But the analogy breaks
> down when the shadows are those of the past, for the only
> light we can see them by is the Promethean fire within us.
> The substance of these shadows can only be in ourselves,
> and the goal of historical criticism, as our metaphors about
> it often indicate, is a kind of self-resurrection, the vision of a
> valley of dry bones that takes on the flesh and blood of our

own vision. The culture of the past is not only the memory
of mankind, but our own buried life, and study of it leads to
a recognition scene, a discovery in which we see not our past
lives, but the total cultural form of our present life. It is not
only the poet but his reader who is subject to the obligation
to "make it new." [*AC*, pp. 345–46]

A historical criticism which sees art only in terms of the past
must therefore be balanced by a sense of the contemporary
relevance of the past. Such an approach, Frye claims, can lead
to an expansion of our perspective in the present. This view has ·
been anticipated in the Polemical Introduction, where he has
said (1) that in historical criticism, we study literature "as we
do the stars, seeing their interrelationships but not approaching them"; and (2) that historical criticism, therefore, "needs
to be complemented by a corresponding activity growing out
of tropical criticism" (*AC*, p. 24). He does not mean that the
critic should use art to support social or political causes; at
least criticism cannot be based on these ends, for they lead to a
moral or revolutionary perspective which slights the present in
favor of the future. "As soon as we make culture a definite
image of a future and perhaps attainable society, we start
selecting and purging a tradition, and all the artists who don't
fit (an increasing number as the process goes on) have to be
thrown out" (*AC*, p. 346). Thus, just as an uncorrected
historical criticism can lead to a deadening reverence for the
archaic, so an uncorrected ethical criticism can lead to a
futurism based on indoctrination. Both approaches are provincial, and neither, according to Frye, is anchored in the
present in any positive way.

Frye is led, therefore, to reconsider the implications of
ethical criticism as he has defined it in the second essay. There,
in his discussion of fourth-phase symbolism, he maintains that
art in its archetypal aspect is an ethical instrument. It becomes
more than an object for aesthetic contemplation because,
archetypally, it is a product of civilization, "a vision of the
goals of human work" (*AC*, p. 113). "In terms of his moral
significance," Frye says in the second essay, "the poet reflects,

and follows at a distance, what his community really achieves through its work. Hence the moral view of the artist is invariably that he ought to assist the work of his society by framing workable hypotheses, imitating human action and thought in such a way as to suggest realizable modes of both."[14] As attractive as this view is for Frye, he finally rejects it because it represents art as "useful and functional," serving the external goals of truth and goodness (*AC*, pp. 112–15). Thus he is led (in the second essay) from the archetypal phase, where poetry is related to civilization, to the anagogic phase, where it is "disinterested and liberal and stands on its own feet" (*AC*, p. 115).

In the Tentative Conclusion, Frye raises the issue again, and his solution turns out to be the same, though formulated in somewhat different terms. Beginning with Arnold's axiom that "culture seeks to do away with classes," he says:

> The ethical purpose of a liberal education is to liberate, which can only mean to make one capable of conceiving society as free, classless, and urbane. No such society exists, which is one reason why a liberal education must be deeply concerned with works of imagination. The imaginative element in works of art, again, lifts them clear of the bondage of history. Anything that emerges from the total experience of criticism to form a part of liberal education becomes, by virtue of that fact, part of the emancipated and humane community of culture, whatever its original reference. Thus liberal education liberates the works of culture themselves as well as the mind they educate. . . . No discussion of beauty can confine itself to the formal relations of the isolated work of art; it must consider, too, the participation of the work of art in the vision of the goal of social effort, the idea of complete and classless civilization. This idea of complete civilization is also the implicit moral standard to which ethical criticism always refers.[15]

There are two poles of reference in this passage, the imagination and society, and Frye is unwilling to let either of them be his ultimate norm. If society becomes the goal of criticism, then art becomes subservient to morality or to one of the practical sciences, and the detached imaginative vision Frye seeks is lost. Thus, he adds, "the goal of ethical criticism is transvaluation, the ability to look at contemporary social values with the detachment of one who is able to compare them in some degree with the infinite vision of possibilities presented by culture" (*AC*, p. 348). On the other hand, if the aesthetic norm is given priority, the social function of criticism withers. Thus he appeals to archetypal criticism to right the balance. "We tried to show in the second essay," he says, "that the moment we go from the individual work of art to the sense of the total form of the art, the art becomes no longer an object of aesthetic contemplation but an ethical instrument, participating in the work of civilization. In this shift to the ethical, criticism as well as poetry is involved" (*AC*, p. 349).

But Frye also argued in the second essay that both ethical and aesthetic norms must ultimately give way, at the anagogic level, to a self-contained literary universe where the critic is a model of Arnold's disinterestedness, freed from all external goals. Reflecting on this leap, however, he remarks (in the Conclusion) that he was perhaps merely restoring "the aesthetic view on a gigantic scale, substituting Poetry for a mass of poems, aesthetic mysticism for aesthetic empiricism" (*AC*, p. 350). Thus, to right the balance once more, Frye appeals to the critical approach of his fourth essay, the argument of which, he says, "led to the principle that all structures in words are partly rhetorical, and hence literary, and that the notion of a scientific or philosophical verbal structure free of rhetorical elements is an illusion. If so, then our literary universe has expanded into a verbal universe, and no aesthetic principle of self-containment will work" (*AC*, p. 350).

These are sweeping generalizations, yet they illustrate Frye's concern to establish, on the one hand, an autonomous conceptual universe while insuring, on the other, that this universe is not isolated from culture, society, and humane letters. "I am not wholly unaware," he says, "that at every step of this argument there are extremely complicated philosophical problems which I am incompetent to solve as such" (*AC*, p. 350). Not the least of these, one might say, is how criticism can be both disinterested and engaged at the same time. Or, one might ask, what is criticism really, the study of self-contained literary form or the relation of literature to social value? Frye's system, of course, will not easily permit these kinds of questions to be asked, for he conceives of criticism as a dialectical axis, having "as one pole the total acceptance of the data of literature, and as the other the total acceptance of the potential values of those data" (*AC*, p. 25). This dyadic framework permits him to pursue practically any critical problem he wants, depending on whether his gaze is centripetal or centrifugal—to use the language of the second essay. His primary interest in the *Anatomy* is centripetal, the inward gaze toward the structure of literature itself. Much of his other work, however, is directed outward toward the social context of literature. In the final analysis, Frye does not see "detachment" and "concern," to use his familiar terms, as contradictory at all; he sees them simply as contrary, that is, as different in emphasis and direction. This is why he can say that

> seeing literature as a unity in itself does not withdraw it from a social context: on the contrary, it becomes far easier to see what its place in civilization is. Criticism will always have two aspects, one turned toward the structure of literature and one turned toward the other cultural phenomena that form the social environment of literature. Together, they balance each other: when one is worked on to the exclusion of the other, the critical perspective goes out of focus. If criticism is in proper balance, the tendency of critics to move from critical to larger social issues becomes more intelligible. Such a movement need not, and should not, be due to a dissatisfaction with the narrowness of criticism as a discipline, but should be simply the result of a sense of social context. [*CP*, pp. 24–25]

This passage comes from a work published a decade and a half after the *Anatomy*, but it represents what Frye is reaching for in the Conclusion to the earlier work. And the application of the principle expressed here, in such later works as *The Critical Path* and *The Modern Century*, and in a number of individual essays should dispel the view that Frye's work represents a mypoic commitment to the disinterested study of literary structure.[16]

Another way of describing Frye's view is to see it as a combination of poetics, which separates literature from other areas of verbal expression, and rhetoric, which does not. Frye himself uses this traditional distinction in *The Well-Tempered Critic*, a book which seems consciously intent on giving a kind of moral and philosophic rationale for the *Anatomy of Criticism*. In the last chapter of the later book, he returns to the distinction, first made toward the end of the theory of modes in the *Anatomy*, that literature can be viewed from one of two principal perspectives, the Aristotelian or the Longinian. The difference between the two, according to Frye, is whether art is seen fundamentally as product or as process. He describes the difference by appealing to a series of opposing concepts: classical versus romantic, aesthetic versus psychological, hieratic versus demotic, artifact versus expression, imitation versus creation, and the like. From the perspective of poetics, Frye says, *poeta* and *poema* are assumed to be embedded in a context of *nature*, whatever concepts or metaphors a critic uses to discuss them. In the Aristotelian tradition, nature has reference to the physical order, or to structure and system. In the Longinian tradition, it refers to the total creative process.[17]

But when *poeta* and *poema* are seen in the context of experience, rather than nature, we leave the province of poetics and enter the realm of rhetoric—the area where authors' intentions, direct appeals, moral value, evidence, and truth become important considerations. And in this area, Frye argues, criticism, like literature, can also be discussed in terms of either product or process, either detachment or participation. The critic, therefore, "is concerned with two kinds of experience. First, he has to understand and interpret the experience which forms the content of the work he is reading. Second, the impact of the literary work on him itself is an experience, 'an experience different in kind from any experience not of art,' as T. S. Eliot puts it" (*WC*, p. 128). Frye wants to balance the two conceptions of criticism which derive from the two contexts of experience. The disinterested critical response, he says, is fundamental, but never an end in itself (*WC*, p. 140); for the ultimate aim of "literary education is an ethical and participating aim" (*WC*, p. 142).

The reconciliation of the two poles of Frye's critical axis is accomplished, as suggested above, by his Blakean view of the imagination. The schema just outlined is, after all, a dualistic one. And since Frye is looking for a more unified conception of criticism than any approach that splits off the intellect from the emotions, nature from experience, beauty from truth, and aesthetic from social value, such a dualism for him is inadequate. His solution is to say that these opposites are "inseparable, two halves of one great whole which is the *possession* of literature" (*WC*, pp. 144–45). Perhaps this should really read "possession *by* literature"; for when we ask what it means to "possess" literature, our answer can only be that it means finally to affirm Frye's view of the imagination and his conception of the central place of art in culture. He defines culture as "a total imaginative vision of life with literature at its center. . . . It is, in its totality, a vision or model of what humanity is capable of achieving, the matrix of all Utopias and social ideals" (*WC*, p. 154). And he defines literature as "a total imaginative form which is . . . *bigger* than either nature or human life, because it contains them, the actual being only a part of the possible" (*WC*, p. 155). To speak of culture and literature in these terms takes us directly to the heart of Frye's critical system. To put it in the language of the second essay of the *Anatomy*, it takes us to the highest of the five critical phases. "When we pass into anagogy," he says, "nature becomes, not the container, but the thing contained" (*AC*, p. 119). To possess literature, in other words, means really to be possessed by it, and this happens at the highest level of imaginative experience. Frye puts it this way at the end of *The Well-Tempered Critic*:

> Literature, we say, neither reflects nor escapes from ordinary life: what it does reflect is the world as human imagination conceives it, in mythical, romantic, heroic and ironic

as well as realistic and fantastic terms. This world is the
universe in human form, stretching from the complete
fulfillment of human desire to what human desire utterly
repudiates, the *quo tendas* [that is, anagogic, "where you
should be going"] vision of reality that elsewhere I have
called, for reasons rooted in my study of Blake, apocalyptic.
. . . Some religions assume that such a world exists, though
only for gods; other religions, including those closer to us,
identify it with a world man enters at death, the extremes of
desire becoming its heavens and hells; revolutionary philosophies associate it with what man is to gain in the future;
mystics call it the world of total or cosmic consciousness. A
poet may accept any of these identifications without damage to his poetry; but for the literary critic, this larger
world is the world man exists and participates in through
his imagination. It is the world in which our imaginations
move and have their being while we are also living in the
"real" world, where our imaginations find the ideals that
they try to pass on to belief and action, where they find the
vision which is the source of both the dignity and the joy of
life. [*WC*, pp. 155–56]

However strongly Frye emphasizes the principle of autonomy in the introduction to the *Anatomy*, his conception of
criticism is always broad enough to include the dialectically
opposite emphasis: the moral and social reference of criticism
and the centrifugal aspect of literary meaning. Each of the
four types of criticism in the *Anatomy* is continually qualified
or corrected by the succeeding type, the result being a breadth
of reference which permits Frye to discuss literature in both its
poetic and its more-than-poetic contexts, both of which are
ultimately subsumed under the most expansive of all his
critical categories, the visionary imagination.

The fact that Frye has devoted himself in recent years to
subjects less strictly literary than we find in the theoretical
concerns of the *Anatomy* and in the practical concerns of, say,
his books on Shakespeare and Milton does not represent the
birth of some new interest—as the essays in the present
collection will bear witness. *The Well-Tempered Critic* is one
of his efforts to mark the intimate relationship between literary

style and social meaning. Much of his writing in the past decade has been in the same vein, reaching out across literature into areas of social concern. It would be a mistake, of course, to lump all of these recent writings together: such works as *The Modern Century* and the essays in part 1 of both *The Stubborn Structure* and *Spiritus Mundi* are completely different in emphasis. But there is a similarity among them in that the focus of Frye's attention is on what could be called a criticism of culture—an analysis of the social, moral, and philosophic aspects of the products of culture. The same can be said of a number of essays in the present collection, most of which were written before *Anatomy of Criticism*. The breadth of vision in Frye's work has been there from the beginning; it is perhaps what leads Hayden White to call Frye "the greatest natural cultural historian of our time."[18]

The most extensive of Frye's recent essays in cultural criticism is *The Critical Path*, a book which stands as an example of his conviction that criticism must ultimately take a centrifugal direction. It is the logical outcome of the conclusion to the *Anatomy*. Frye himself refers to it as continuous with his other work—a rewriting of his central myth (*CP*, p. 9).

Frye's method in *The Critical Path* is implicit in his claims that the process of interpreting the social myths of culture is "very similar to criticism in literature" and that "different forms of critical interpretation cannot be sharply separated, whether they are applied to the plays of Shakespeare, the manuscripts of the Bible, the American Constitution, or the oral traditions of an aboriginal tribe. In the area of general concern they converge, however widely the technical contexts in law, theology, literature or anthropology may differ" (*CP*, p. 123). This aptly describes the main assumption on which the book is based, namely, that while the literary critic is not qualified to handle all the "technical contexts" of culture, he is especially prepared, particularly if he is an archetypal critic, to interpret the cultural phenomena that form the social environment of literature. "The modern critic," he says, "is a student of mythology, and his total subject embraces not merely literature, but the areas of concern which the mythical language of construction and belief enters and informs. These areas constitute the mythological subjects, and they include large parts of religion, philosophy, political theory, and the social sciences" (*CP*, p. 98).

The book treats a far-ranging body of such topics, including such things as the difference between oral and writing cultures, Renaissance humanism, the critical theories of Sidney and Shelley, Marxism and Democracy, the idea of progress, advertising and propaganda, social contract theories and conceptions of Utopia, contemporary youth culture, McLuhanism, theories of education, and so on. What holds these apparently unrelated subjects together is the dialectical framework of Frye's discussion. Whatever issue he confronts, it is always set against the background of what he sees as the two opposing myths of Western culture, the myth of concern and the myth of freedom.

The myth of concern comprises everything that a society is most concerned to know. It is the disposition which leads man to uphold communal, rather than individual, values. It exists, Frye says, "to hold society together. . . . For it, truth and reality are not directly connected with reasoning or evidence, but are socially established. What is true, for concern, is what society does and believes in response to authority, and a belief, so far as a belief is verbalized, is a statement of willingness to participate in a myth of concern. The typical language of concern therefore tends to become the language of belief" (*CP*, p. 36). A myth of concern has its roots in religion and only later branches out into politics, law, and literature. It is inherently traditional and conservative, placing a strong emphasis on values of coherence and continuity. It originates in oral or preliterate culture and is associated with continuous verse conventions and discontinuous prose forms. And it is "deeply attached to ritual, to coronations, weddings, funerals, parades, demonstrations, where something is publicly done that expresses an inner social identity" (*CP*, p. 45).

The myth of freedom, on the other hand, is committed to a truth of correspondence. It appeals to such self-validating criteria as "logicality of argument or (usually a later stage) impersonal evidence and verification." It is inherently "liberal," helping to develop and honoring such values as objectivity, detachment, suspension of judgment, tolerance, and respect for the individual. It "stresses the importance of the non-mythical elements in culture, of the truths and realities that are studied rather than created, provided by nature rather than by social vision" (*CP*, p. 44). It originates in the mental habits which a writing culture, with its continuous prose and discontinuous verse forms, brings into society.[19]

The way Frye uses this broad dialectic of freedom and concern is illustrated by his treatment of two classic defenses of poetry, Sidney's and Shelley's. Placing Sidney's view of poetry against the background of Renaissance humanism, Frye concludes that Sidney accommodates the role of the poet to the values of a reading and writing culture, to the norms of meaning established by writers of discursive prose. "The conception of poetry in Sidney," he says, "is an application of the general humanist view of disciplined speech as the manifestation or audible presence of social authority" (*CP*, p. 66). For Sidney, "what is most distinctive about poetry is the poet's power of illustration, a power which is partially an ability to popularize and make more accessible the truths of revelation and reason" (*CP*, p. 67). In other words, poetry is not qualitatively distinct from the other verbal disciplines. What actually occurs in Sidney's view of poetry, according to Frye, is that the original characteristics of the myths of freedom and concern are interchanged. "The myth of concern takes on a reasoning aspect, claiming the support of logic and historical evidence; the myth of freedom becomes literary and imaginative, as the poet, excluded from primary authority in the myth of concern, finds his social function in a complementary activity, which liberalizes concern but also . . . reinforces it" (*CP*, p. 75).

In Shelley's defense, on the other hand, we return to a conception of poetry as mythical and psychologically primitive.

Shelley begins by neatly inverting the hierarchy of values assumed in Sidney. . . . Shelley puts all the discursive disciplines into an inferior group of "analytic" operations of reason. They are aggressive; they think of ideas as weapons; they seek the irrefutable argument, which keeps eluding them because all arguments are theses, and theses are half-truths implying their own opposites. . . . The works of imagination, by contrast, cannot be refuted: poetry is the dialectic of love, which treats everything it encounters as another form of itself, and never attacks, only includes. . . . This argument assumes, not only that the language of poetry is mythical, but that poetry, in its totality, is in fact society's real myth of concern, and that the poet is still the teacher of that myth. . . . In Sidney's day, it was accepted that the models of creation were established by God: for Shelley, man makes his own civilization and at the center of man's creation are the poets, whose work provides the models of human society. The myths of poetry embody and express man's creation of his own culture, rather than his reception of it from a divine source. [*CP*, pp. 94, 95–96]

There is no denying the fact that Frye's sympathies lie on the side of Shelley, for they both believe that the language of literature represents the imaginative possibilities of concern. And both of them are opposed to the constrictive view of Sidney which makes the critic an evaluator and which makes poetry subservient to whatever established framework of concern an elite society happens to be championing at the moment. To say that literature contains the imaginative possibilities of concern means, for Frye, that it displays "the total range of verbal fictions and models and images and metaphors out of which all myths of concern are constructed" (*CP*, p. 98). Frye's conclusion is that, while Shelley's (and his own) view of poetry takes us back to the areas of concern expressed in primitive and oracular mythology, the critic's approach to the values expressed by a myth of concern must derive from the myth of freedom. "The critic *qua* critic," Frye says, "is not himself concerned but detached" (*CP*, p. 99).

The merging of freedom and concern, however, is what produces the social context of literature. If there is a central thesis to *The Critical Path* it is the dialectical tension Frye seeks to establish between the myths of freedom and concern. This tension comprises his own central myth, as it were, and the cultural phenomena he examines throughout the book are interpreted from the perspective of this tension. A corollary to the tension is the necessity for a pluralism of myths of concern, which can only occur in societies with open mythologies.

> The basis of all tolerance in society, the condition in which a plurality of concerns can co-exist, is the recognition of the tension between concern and freedom. . . . Concern and freedom both occupy the whole of the same universe: they interpenetrate, and it is no good trying to set up boundary stones. Some, of course, meet the collision of concern and freedom from the opposite side, with a naive rationalism which expects that before long all myths of concern will be outgrown and only the appeal to reason and evidence and experiment will be taken seriously. . . . I consider such a view entirely impossible. The growth of non-mythical knowledge tends to eliminate the incredible from belief, and helps to shape the myth of concern according to the outlines of what experience finds possible and vision desirable. But the growth of knowledge cannot in itself provide us with the social vision which will suggest what we should do with our knowledge. [*CP*, pp. 108, 109–10]

This is where Frye's view of the social function of criticism comes in, for the literary critic—at least Frye's ideal critic—is prepared to see that myths of concern in society are like those in literature in that they represent the range of imaginative possibilities of belief. Frye will not be cornered into accepting the Kierkegaardian "either-or" position. He wants the best of both possible worlds: the detached, liberal, impersonal values of the "aesthetic" attitude which Kierkegaard rejects and the values of commitment which come from the primacy of concern. In a passage that echoes some remarks on Dante in the present collection, he says: "If we stop with the voluntary self-blinkering of commitment, we are no better off than the 'aesthetic': on the other side of 'or' is another step to be taken, a step from the committed to the creative, from iconoclastic concern to what the literary critic above all ought to be able to see, that in literature man *is* a spectator of his own life, or at least of the larger vision in which his life is contained" (*CP*, p. 129).

This is Frye's answer to how man can be detached yet joined to the community of concern. It is an answer in which the visionary imagination, once again, becomes the ultimate criterion, for only in the world of imagination can the tension between freedom and concern be properly maintained. It is out of this tension, Frye concludes, "that glimpses of a third order of experience emerge, of a world that may not exist but completes existence, the world of the definitive experience that poetry urges us to have but which we never quite get. If such a world existed, no individual could live in it. . . . If we could live in it, of course, criticism would cease and the distinction between literature and life would disappear, because life itself would then be the continuous incarnation of the creative word" (*CP*, pp. 170–71).

The doctrine of the imagination being proposed here takes us back to the Blakean ideas set forth in the second essay of the *Anatomy*. If we "stand back" from *The Critical Path*, as Frye urges us to do in looking at literature, we cannot help but observe that the twin values of detachment and concern are, in fact, the same values adumbrated in the *Anatomy*; for throughout that work Frye seeks to hold in tension an ethical or social criticism, which is forever extended toward the myth of concern, with a detached and disinterested criticism of literary structure and convention.

II

The imagination recreates nature.
Fearful Symmetry

The keystone in Frye's critical theory is his doctrine of the imagination. This itself distinguishes his poetics from the positions of those who find the source of their general philosophic principles in (1) the nature of "things" (for example, Plato and Aristotle, who use "imitation" as the basic term for their discussion of art) and, in (2) operations or processes (for example, Horace and Tolstoy, who use "poetic effects" as their basic term). Rather, Frye's emphasis on the imagination aligns him with the tradition of those, such as Kant, who have located the source of their general principles in the human understanding or in the faculties of the mind and who use the word "imagination" as their basic term for discussing art.[20] This is not to say, however, that Kant's aesthetic views are the source of Frye's conception of the imagination;[21] its chief source is the Romantic tradition, mainly Blake. Like Blake, Frye understands the imagination as both a creative and perceptive faculty. His fullest discussion of the topic appears in a fellowship lecture, "The Imaginative and the Imaginary," presented to the American Psychiatric Association (1962).[22] Here he equates the imagination with the "creative force in the mind." What it has produced is "everything that we call culture and civilization. It is the power of transforming a sub-human physical world into a world with a human shape and meaning" (*FI*, p. 152). "Imagination creates reality,"[23] Frye says: it creates culture out of nature; it also produces literary language.[24] The most important thing it creates is not the surface texture of literature but its deeper structures and designs.

Frye is careful to emphasize this point. It is the structuring power of the imagination, in fact, which distinguishes his understanding of the imaginative faculty from Coleridge's. In the well-known passage in chapter 13 of the *Biographia*, Coleridge speaks of the imagination as a vital, recreative force which struggles to idealize and unify. Frye often uses the same kind of language to describe the imagination;[25] yet Coleridge, in Frye's view, did not actually believe in the power of the imagination to create the total structures of literature, even though he talks, almost obsessively, about the imagination as the creative force which is able to make one thing out of many. Coleridge "intended the climax of the *Biographia Literaria*," Frye says

to be a demonstration of the "esemplastic" or structural nature of the imagination, only to discover when the great chapter arrived he was unable to write it. There were doubtless many reasons for this, but one was that he does not really think of the imagination as a constructive power at all. He means by imagination . . . the reproductive power, the ability to bring to life the texture of character-ization and imagery. It is to this power that he applies his favorite metaphor of an organism, where the unity is some mysterious and elusive "vitality." His practical criticism of work he admires is concerned with texture: he never dis-cusses the total design. . . . Coleridge is in the tradition of critical naturalism, which bases its values on the immediacy of contact between art and nature that we continuously feel in the texture of mimetic fiction.[26]

Because the imagination "is the constructive power of the mind, the power of building unities out of units" (*SeS*, p. 36), the designs it creates are most obvious in undisplaced literary works—those which are most formulaic. "What the imagina-tion, left to itself, produces is the rigidly conventionalized" (*SeS*, p. 36). And since literary works displaced in the direction of the plausible move toward realism, where formulaic struc-tures are less rigid, the context of the imagination can be seen as occupying a space opposite that of the context of realistic, representational, or displaced literary works. In *The Secular Scripture*, in fact, Frye appropriates Wallace Stevens's use of the word *imagination*, meaning "the shaping spirit, the power of ordering which seems so mysterious to the poet himself, because it often acts as though it were an identity separate from him."[27] Thus, while the imagination, by means of displacement, does produce credibility and lifelikeness, it also produces "total design"; and this is its most important power for Frye.

One of Frye's readers argues that his views on the imagina-tive and the imaginary "establish the fact that for Frye imagination is a constructive faculty as opposed to a perceptive faculty" and that it "is *not* primarily an *originating* faculty."[28] But this is to misunderstand Frye's view, especially those ideas on imaginative perception which he has taken over from Blake's theory of knowledge. In Blake's view of reality, the imagination, which transforms the nonhuman world (Nature) into something with human shape and meaning (Culture), is opposed to the commonsense view of Locke in which the perceiving subject is separated from the perceived object. Frye agrees with Blake. Sometimes he speaks of two basic modes of apprehending reality, as in the *Anatomy*, where the scientific mode which perceives an objective nature is opposed to the poetic mode which perceives a transformed one. Sometimes he speaks of three basic modes of perceiving the world: (1) the egocentric perception of the unreal world of reflection and abstract ideas, which he calls the world of memory; (2) the ordinary perception of the world we live in, called the world of sight; and (3) the imaginative perception of the world we desire and want to create, called the world of vision (*FS*, p. 26). Whether there are three orders of perception, or only two, is not so important for understanding Frye as is his conviction that there are different kinds or levels of perception and that these depend, as they did for Blake, on differing ways men can apprehend the relationships between subject and object. As a perceptive faculty, the visionary imagination is common to all men:

> [Blake's] "All Religions Are One" means that the material world provides a universal language of images and that each man's imagination speaks that language with his own accent. [*FS*, p. 28]

> What makes the poet worth studying at all is his ability to communicate beyond his own context in time and space. . . . It is here that Blake comes in with his doctrine that "all had originally one language, and one religion." If we follow his own method, and interpret this in imaginative instead of historical terms, we have the doctrine that all symbolism in all art and all religion is mutually intelligible among all men, and that there is such a thing as an iconography of the imagination. [*FS*, p. 420]

> Neither the study of ritual nor of mythopoeic dreams takes us above a subconscious mental level, nor does such a study, except in rare cases, attempt to suggest anything more than

a subconscious unity among men. But if we can find such impressive archetypal forms emerging from sleeping or savage minds, it is surely possible that they would emerge more clearly from the concentrated visions of genius. . . . A comparative study of dreams and rituals can lead us only to a vague and intuitive sense of the unity of the human mind; a comparative study of works of art should demonstrate it beyond conjecture. [*FS*, p. 424]

Art, therefore, demonstrates the universality of the human imagination, a belief reinforced by Frye's conviction that all men, whether creators (artists) or creatures, are motivated by "desire." He does not use the word in a biological or psychological sense. He means simply that all men have some conception of a "world" they want to live in—some mental model of an imaginatively possible experience. "Desire," he says, "is part of imagination" (*FS*, p. 27). It is "the impulse toward what Aristotle calls *telos*, realizing the form that one potentially has. . . . It works dialectically, separating what is wanted from what is not wanted" (*FI*, p. 152). Thus, while all men are limited in nature, their desire is infinite: "in the imagination anything goes that can be imagined. . . . In the human world the imagination has no limits" (*EI*, pp. 29, 30).

If all men possess the imaginative faculty because of the teleological impulse, they do not possess it to the same degree. As the titles of several of Frye's works put it, the imagination must be educated; it must develop. And it is the artist who develops the perceptive power of the imagination into a constructive one. The artist "catches and trains the objects of his vision: he can put human imagination into them, make them intelligible and responsive" (*FS*, pp. 41–42). Therefore, only those who have the "energy"—another Blakean concept which Frye often identifies with the imagination—to train themselves to see clearly, to pass "through sight into vision" (*FS*, p. 25), possess imagination as a structural power. "The artist is *par excellence* the man who struggles to develop his perception into creation, his sight into vision" (*FS*, p. 26).

The imagination, then, is a universal perceptive faculty for Frye,[29] but it varies among men according to the degree they can create the forms of culture from their perceptions. Not all men, obviously, are artists, but all men, for Frye, can at least educate their imaginations into a constructive or creative awareness. The unity of the human mind makes it possible for them to perceive the universal forms of the imagination. Frye has had his own vision, as it were, of the total order of words produced by the imagination. What this vision looks like—"the iconography of the imagination," as he puts it—is the entire elaborate map of cyclical and dialectical structures in *Anatomy of Criticism*.

III

In critical theory there is no such thing as private symbolism.

The Stubborn Structure

In *The Critical Path*, Frye remarks that his theory of literature was developed from an attempt to answer two questions: What is the total subject of study of which criticism forms a part? and How do we arrive at poetic meaning? (*CP*, pp. 14-15). The second essay of the *Anatomy*, "Ethical Criticism: Theory of Symbols," addresses itself to the latter question. Frye's starting point is to admit the principle of "polysemous" meaning, a modified version of Dante's fourfold system of interpretation. Once the principle is granted, he claims, "we can either stop with a purely relative and pluralistic position, or we can go on to consider the possibility that there is a finite number of valid critical methods, and that they can all be contained within a single theory . . . " (*AC*, p. 72).

Frye develops his argument by first placing the issue of meaning in a broader context:

> The meaning of a literary work forms a part of a larger whole. In the previous essay we saw that meaning or *dia-noia* was one of three elements, the other two being *mythos* or narrative and *ethos* or characterization. It is better to think, therefore, not simply of a sequence of meanings, but of a sequence of contexts or relationships in which the whole work of literary art can be placed, each context having its

characteristic *mythos* and *ethos* as well as its *dianoia* or meaning. [*AC*, p. 73]

Context, then, rather than meaning becomes the organizing principle, and the term Frye uses for the contextual relationships of literature is *phases*. The word *ethical* in the title of this essay does not derive from the meanings which *ethos* had in essay 1: Frye is not concerned here to expand the analysis of "character" found there. The word refers rather to the connection between art and life which makes literature a liberal yet disinterested ethical instrument. Ethical criticism, Frye says in the Introduction, refers to a "consciousness of the presence of society. . . . [It] deals with art as a communication from the past to the present, and is based on a conception of the total and simultaneous possession of past culture" (*AC*, p. 24). It is the archetype which provides the connection between the past and the present.

Unlike the three other essays in the *Anatomy*, Frye's theory of symbols is oriented toward an analysis of *criticism*. "Phases" are contexts within which literature has been and can be interpreted: they are primarily meant to describe critical procedures rather than literary types, which is to say that the phases represent perspectives from which to analyze meaning.

"Symbol" is the first of three basic categories Frye uses to differentiate the five phases, the other two being *mythos* and *dianoia*. Like many of Frye's terms, *symbol* has a broad range of reference. In the second essay it is used to mean "any unit of any literary structure that can be isolated for critical attention" (*AC*, p. 71). This broad definition permits Frye to associate the appropriate kind of symbolism with each phase and thereby to define the phase at the highest level of generality. The symbol used as a sign results in the descriptive phase; as motif in the literal phase; as image in the formal phase; as archetype in the mythical phase; and as monad in the anagogic phase.

In an early essay on the nature of symbolism, Frye says that "wherever we have archetypal symbolism, we pass from the question 'What does this symbol, sea or tree or serpent or character, mean in this work of art?' to the question 'What does it mean in my imaginative comprehension of such things as a whole?' Thus the presence of archetypal symbolism makes the individual poem, not its own object, but a phase of imaginative experience."[30] Archetypal symbolism, which emerges as one of the central themes of the essays in the present collection, works in two directions for Frye. On the one hand, just as he demonstrates in *The Critical Path* that the language of myth and symbol enters and informs all verbal culture, so in these essays he uses what he has learned about symbolism as a literary critic to understand and interpret texts in philosophy, psychology, history, and comparative religion. On the other hand, he sees these disciplines as informing literary criticism itself. Thus, he can approach Toynbee's *Study of History* from the centrifugal perspective, seeing it as "an intuitive response based on an imaginative grasp of the symbolic significance of certain data." The book can be read, then, not as a factual chronicle which is trying to prove something by its massive accumulation of data but as a grand imaginative vision. Similarly, Frye approaches Frazer's *Golden Bough* as if it were an encyclopedic epic or a continuous form of prose fiction. Its subject, he says, is really "about what the human imagination does when it tries to express itself about the greatest mysteries."

But Frye also works in a centripetal direction. Cassirer, Spengler, Frazer, Jung, and Eliade are themselves students of symbolism, whose works provide us with a grammar of the human imagination. Cassirer's symbolic forms, like those found in literature, take their structure from the mind and their content from the natural world. And Frazer's expansive collections of material, because they give us a grammar of unconscious symbolism on both its personal and its social sides, will be of greater benefit to the poet and literary critic than to the anthropologist. Thus, *The Golden Bough*, like Jung's *Psychology of the Unconscious*, becomes primarily a work of literary criticism. Similarly, Eliade's studies in *Religionsgeschichte* are especially important for the literary critic because they provide a grammar of initiatory and comparative symbolism.

The two perspectives—the centrifugal and the centripetal—
do not finally move in opposite directions in Frye's work. They
interpenetrate, to use his familiar metaphor. In his review of
Jung's *Psychology of the Unconscious*, Frye develops a view of
criticism which makes its way later, some of it verbatim, into
his account of the archetypal phase of symbolism in the
Anatomy. But this is not to say that Frye is a Jungian. His view
has always been that criticism needs to be independent from
externally derived frameworks, or from what he calls, in his
review in this volume of books by Allen Tate and Herbert
Read, "determinisms." "Critical principles," he says in the
Anatomy, "cannot be taken over ready-made from theology,
philosophy, politics, science, or any combination of these"
(*AC*, p. 7). Yet Frye himself, as the reviews here bear ample
witness, has appropriated a number of concepts from other
disciplines, especially from psychology and anthropology. In
the second essay of the *Anatomy* they appear as ritual and
dream.

Ritual and dream represent the *mythos* (narrative) and
dianoia (meaning) of archetypal symbolism. The archetypal
study of narrative, Frye says, deals with "the generic, recurring, or conventional actions which show analogies to
rituals: the weddings, funerals, intellectual and social initia-
tions, executions or mock executions, the chasing away of the
scapegoat villain, and so on"; whereas the archetypal study of
dianoia treats the generic, recurring, or conventional "shape"
of a work, "indicated by its mood and resolution, whether
tragic, comic, ironic, or what not, in which the relationship of
desire and experience is expressed" (*AC*, p. 105). Frye treats
archetypal criticism in the third essay. In the second, his aim is
to show the relationship between ritual and dream, neither of
which, of course, is literary, to a single form of verbal
communication. This form is myth, which explains the title of
the fourth phase. From the perspective of the mythical phase,
we see the same kinds of processes or rhythms occurring in
literature that we find in ritual and dream. There are two
basic patterns, one cyclical, the other dialectical. Ritual
imitates the cyclical process of nature: the rhythmic movement

of the universe and the seasons, as well as the recurring cycles of human life; and literature in the archetypal phase imitates nature in the same way. The dialectical pattern, on the other hand, derives from the world of dream, where desire is in constant conflict with reality. Liberation and capture, integration and expulsion, love and hate are some of the terms we apply to this moral dialectic in ritual and dream. The same pattern, when it is expressed hypothetically, is to be found in poetry. Archetypal criticism, Frye concludes, is based upon these two organizing patterns (*AC*, pp. 105-6).

Frye's indebtedness to contemporary anthropology and psychology is apparent in these distinctions, resonating as they do with the language of Frazer, Freud, and Jung. But Frye is careful to emphasize the distinction between the aims of criticism and those of these other disciplines. The critic, he says, "is concerned only with the ritual or dream patterns which are actually in what he is studying, however they got there" (*AC*, p. 109). Some archetypal critics, he adds, do not recognize this, having been misled into searching for the origins of the ritual elements of literature. His point is not that such studies have no place in criticism but that they belong on the descriptive rather than the archetypal level. What is at stake here is distinguishing clearly between the history of literary works and the genre to which they belong. Frye apparently has his eye on scholars such as Gilbert Murray, who maintained that in tragedy there survives an ancient ritual involving a combat between the old year–spirit and the new; or F. M. Cornford, who extended Murray's thesis to Greek comedy, arguing that the basic pattern of the Aristophanic play can be directly traced to primitive seasonal rituals, such as the Combat, Sacred Marriage, and Beanfeast. Frye is not saying that Murray and the Cambridge anthropologists were wrong, even though it may be incorrect to assume that a given Greek play actually descends from a ritual libretto. He is saying, rather, that for the archetypal critic the question is irrelevant. On the other hand, Frye would not deny that a Greek play could have been conditioned by standard patterns of ritual or that its conventions were determined by

actual performances. What is at issue, in other words, is not
the dependence of a given play upon an actual performance,
but simply a parallelism between narrative and ritual patterns, or between the conventions and genres of literature and
those of ritual ceremony. As Frye says in his essay on Frazer in
this book, "Frazer's ritual is to be thought of as something
latent in the human imagination."

Frye's position on the application of psychology to literature
is similar: the archetypal critic will not want to confuse
biography with criticism. The repetition of a certain pattern in
Shakespeare's plays may be studied in various ways. "If
Shakespeare is unique or anomalous, or even exceptional, in
using this pattern, the reason for his use of it may be at least
partly psychological" (*AC*, p. 111); and critics may, at the
descriptive level, resort to psychological theory in attempting
to explain it. The archetypal critic, however, can pursue the
problem only when the same pattern is recognized in Shakespeare's contemporaries or in the dramatists of different ages
and cultures, in which case convention and genre become the
important considerations (*AC*, p. 111).

To see archetypal criticism as concerned with the social
aspects of poetry is to emphasize the relationship of the
individual poem to other poems. But this is only half of what
should properly be emphasized, for a poem is also a "part of
the total imitation of nature that we call civilization" (*AC*, p.
105). What does it mean to say that civilization is a total
imitation of nature, an idea which recurs frequently in Frye's
work? He himself refers to it metaphorically as "the process of
making a total human form out of nature" (*AC*, pp. 105, 112).
He means that as civilization develops, the natural world is
transformed from the nonhuman into something with human
shape and meaning. This process is given direction by desire.
Because man is not satisfied, for example, with roots and
caves, his civilization creates "human forms of nature" in
farming and architecture.[31] This kind of desire, Frye says,

> is thus not a simple response to need, for an animal may
> need food without planting a garden to get it, nor is it a

simple response to want, or desire *for* something in particular. It is neither limited to nor satisfied by objects, but is the
energy that leads human society to develop its own form.
Desire in this sense is the social aspect of what we met on the
literal level as emotion, an impluse toward expression which
would have remained amorphous if the poem had not
liberated it by providing the form of its expression. The form
of desire, similarly, is liberated and made apparent by
civilization. The efficient cause of civilization is work, and
poetry in its social aspect has the function of expressing, as a
verbal hypothesis, a vision of the goal of work and the forms
of desire. [*AC*, pp. 105-6]

Criticism on the archetypal level, therefore, is concerned
not just with genre and convention. Because it views the
symbol as a natural object with a human meaning, its scope is
expanded to include civilization. And from this perspective,
poetry becomes a product of a vision of the goals of human
work.

This broad conception of criticism depends upon Frye's
broad view of verbal culture. "Is it true," he asks, "that the
verbal structures of psychology, anthropology, theology,
history, law and everything else built out of words have been
informed or constructed by the same kinds of myths and
metaphors we find, in their original hypothetical form, in
literature?" (*AC*, p. 352). His answer is—indirectly in the
Anatomy and directly in much of his other work—that it *is*
true. But even in the *Anatomy* Frye steps back from the details
of his literary theory to sketch the broad outline of his
metacritical universe. It does not come until the fourth essay,
and it has a special purpose at this point in the book: Frye
wants to indicate the place which rhetorical criticism has in his
system as a whole. But it recapitulates the broad view of verbal
culture that appears throughout his writing—a view based on
the age-old division of reality into three categories, described
variously as thought, action, and passion, or as truth, goodness, and beauty. In this division, Frye says, "the world of art,
beauty, feeling, and taste is the central one, and is flanked by
two other worlds. One is the world of social action and events,

the other the world of individual thought and ideas. Reading
from left to right, this threefold structure divides human
faculties into will, feeling, and reason. It divides the mental
constructs which these faculties produce into history, art, and
science and philosophy. It divides the ideals which form
compulsions or obligations on these faculties into law, beauty,
and truth" (*AC*, p. 243). The special terms Frye uses throughout the *Anatomy*—*mythos*, *ethos*, and *dianoia*—fit neatly into
the triadic schema. *Ethos*, as Frye defines the term, stands at
the center, flanked on one side by the verbal imitation of
action (*mythos*) and on the other by the verbal imitation of
thought (*dianoia*). Similarly, the poetic symbol finds its place
in the framework midway between event and idea, example
and precept, ritual and dream—all of which are used in the
second essay to define the phases of symbolism.

Such a broad view of verbal culture explains why Frye can
say in the essays that follow that Eliade provides us with a
"grammar of comparative symbolism" and Frazer, with a
"grammar of the imagination." It is obvious, then, that Frye
frequently receives both delight and instruction from other
disciplines. The issue is not whether extraliterary influences
can be found in his critical theory. They are abundant. The
issue, rather, is the function they perform. This, in turn,
depends upon the principles he uses to establish criticism as a
discipline in its own right.

In *The Critical Path*, where Frye discusses the relationship
of criticism to other disciplines, he says: "I have always insisted
that criticism cannot take presuppositions from elsewhere,
which always means wrenching them out of their real context,
and must work out its own" (*CP*, p. 16). The question thus
becomes defining the "real context" of criticism; and Frye's
answer essentially is whether or not literary meaning is
conceived of in intentional or nonintentional terms. He says
that when he first began to write on critical theory, "all
meaning in literature seemed to be referred first of all to the
context of intentional meaning, always a secondary and
sometimes the wrong context. That is, the primary meaning of
a literary work was assumed to be the kind of meaning that a

prose paraphrase could represent. This primary meaning was called the 'literal' meaning, a phrase with a luxuriant growth of semantic tangles around it" (*CP*, p. 15). Placing poetry in this literal or intentional context is to see poetic meaning as "related to some verbal area of study outside literature" (*CP*, p. 16). This is a familiar New Critical dictum, but it lies at the heart of his distinction between an autonomous criticism and one dependent upon the presuppositions of another discipline. Literature, in short, is different from other kinds of verbal expression in that it is nondiscursive, nonintentional, non-descriptive. And a criticism which does not begin with this assumption, in Frye's view, will inevitably move outward into some other discipline for its conceptual presuppositions.

His argument against deterministic approaches is much less absolute in *The Critical Path* than in the *Anatomy*. We find, for example, that he does not condemn all biographical approaches as deterministic—only those which assume that biography is the "essential key" to poetic meaning (*CP*, p. 17). Moreover, only "some" centrifugal methods are "badly motivated" (*CP*, p. 14), and documentary approaches must be used by the centripetal critic with "tact," not banned altogether (*CP*, p. 18). Frye, therefore, admits into critical discourse the contributions of other disciplines as long as the nonintentional rather than the intentional view of poetry is primary. Studying literature in the context of other literature means we will be less likely to capitulate to some "extraliterary schematism" even though other disciplines interpenetrate the literary context.

The choice of metaphors used to describe the relation of one subject to another is, Frye says, "a fateful choice" (*SM*, p. 106). His own choice of "interpenetration" avoids the determinism implicit in such vertical metaphors as "founded upon" and in such horizontal ones as "connected" or "united." The first "means that we have to get something established in another subject 'before' we can study literature, which of course means that we never get to study literature at all"; whereas the second means that by trying to build bridges between different subjects we destroy their individual contexts

(*SM*, pp. 106–7). There should be no problem, then, in understanding Frye's relation to someone like Jung. "I am continually asked about my relation to Jung," Frye says, "and especially about the relation of my use of the word 'archetype' to his. So far I have tended to resist the association, because in my experience whenever anyone mentions it his next sentence is almost certain to be nonsense. . . . it seems strange to overlook the possibility that the arts, including literature, might just conceivably be what they have always been taken to be, possible techniques of mediation, in the strictest sense of the word, ways of cultivating, focusing and ordering one's mental processes on the basis of symbol rather than concept."[32] Which is the reason that Frye can say in one of the reviews collected here that Jung's work is "a grammar of literary symbolism which for all serious students of literature is as important as it is endlessly fascinating."

IV

> I have never been very clear about the shape of the history of literature apart from the shape of history in general.
> > "Reflections in a Mirror"

> The imaginative element in works of art . . . lifts them clear of the bondage of history.
> > *Anatomy of Criticism*

Frye has "always suffered from acute historical consciousness," according to William Rueckert; he has "freed himself from history in order that he might, from within and by means of the timeless coordinates of his system, reenter history, properly, powerfully equipped to study it, cope with it, move around in it, and protect himself from being so mercilessly victimized by it."[33] History, for Frye, is the direct verbal imitation of *praxis*—the world of events—just as philosophy and science are the primary or direct verbal imitations of *theoria*—the world of images and ideas. History, therefore, is set over against poetry, which is the secondary imitation of action (*mythos*) and of thought (*dianoia*). As Frye says, "the historical is the opposite of the mythical" (*FI*, p. 55). This is true, however, only as it relates to what Frye calls the "historian proper," that is, the historian who "works inductively, collecting his facts and trying to avoid any informing patterns except those that he sees, or is honestly convinced he sees, in the facts themselves" (*FI*, p. 54). Frye's historical consciousness has been influenced not so much by the historians proper as by the metahistorians—those whose accounts of human action are carried along by the comprehensive mythical patterns they impose upon their material. When such patterns occur, the distance between the historical and the poetic tends to collapse. Frye observes that "there are romantic historical myths based on a quest or pilgrimage to a City of God or a classless society; there are comic historical myths of progress through evolution or revolution; there are tragic myths of decline and fall, like the works of Gibbon and Spengler; there are ironic myths of recurrence or casual catastrophe" (*FI*, p. 54). The study of such metahistorical patterns becomes especially appropriate for the literary critic because the informing principles behind them are akin to those of poetry and myth. This is why Spengler has been a formative influence on Frye's thought. "If *The Decline of the West* were nothing else," he says, "it would still be one of the world's great Romantic poems" (*SM*, p. 187). The reason for Spengler's appeal, then, is the poetic imagery upon which his vision of history is constructed. Frye is drawn toward the work of Toynbee and Vico for the same reason.

Metahistorians such as Spengler and Vico are important for Frye not simply because he can read their expansive narrative patterns in the same way that he reads the plots of an epic, novel, or historical romance, thereby demonstrating the resemblance between the metahistorical and the poetic. They are important also because of the ways in which they enter and inform his own critical theory. The most obvious influence of Spengler is found in the theory of modes in the first essay of the *Anatomy*, which is Frye's theory of literary history. A mode is "a conventional power of action assumed about the chief characters in fictional literature, or the corresponding attitude

assumed by the poet toward his audience in thematic literature" (*AC*, p. 366). Frye defines the modes broadly in terms of
the ethical elements, or *ethos*, of literary works. The latter
category, an expansion of Aristotle's "character," refers to the
relationship, on the one hand, between a hero and his society,
and, on the other, between a writer and his audience. The
constant term, then, in Frye's definition of both fictional and
thematic modes is *ethos*, though the meaning in each case is
different, since the point of reference is either the hypothetical
characters or the author-audience relationship. "Fictional"
works are those in which the characters are internal, existing
primarily as functions of plot, and a "fictional mode" refers to
the power of action which a character possesses.

This distinction enables Frye to classify fictional works
according to the position of the hero on a *spoudaios-phaulos*
continuum, beginning with the hero as a god and ending with
him as inferior to ourselves. He then develops an elaborate
pattern through which his five modes (myth, romance, high
mimesis, low mimesis, and irony) have cyclically moved.
"Such modes," Frye says, "tend to succeed one another in
historical sequence" (*AC*, p. 366). The subtitle of the first essay
is "Historical Criticism," but Frye does not use the label
conventionally. His concern is not to show that literature is
related to particular social and political events but to suggest
that the five modes correspond to the five epochs of both
Greco-Roman and Western European writing.

Frye argues, for example, that there is a noteworthy correlation between myth and premedieval works and between
romance and the literature of the Middle Ages; and this
correlation is seen as continuing through the high-mimetic
development of the Renaissance, the low-mimetic of the
nineteenth century, and the ironic of the twentieth. The most
explicit indication of the correlation between mode and period
is in Frye's discussion of thematic modes, where he uses the
words *mode* and *period* synonymously. He speaks of the
"literary Platonism of the high mimetic period"; he practically
equates the low mimetic with Romanticism (*AC*, p. 59); and
he refers throughout to the various modes as "epochs" and

"ages." Frye's point is not merely that literature, on a linear scale of modes, "has steadily moved its center of gravity down the list" (*AC*, p. 34) but also that the modal paradigm is cyclical. "Our five modes," he says, "evidently go around in a circle" (*AC*, p. 42). In Kafka and Joyce, for example, tragic irony moves toward the emergence once more of the mythical mode. A similar movement can be observed in the comic modes, where works such as science fiction frequently try to imagine "what life would be like on a plane as far above us as we are above savagery. . . . It is thus a mode of romance with a strong inherent tendency to myth" (*AC*, p. 49). Historical criticism thus refers to the sequence of modes, their movement being a circular succession rather than a strictly linear progression.

The idea of recurrence derives chiefly from Spengler, whose theory of the organic growth of cultures Frye summarizes in his essay on Toynbee and Spengler in the present collection. For Spengler,

> cultures behave exactly like organisms: they grow, mature, decline and die; and they all last about the same length of time. The culture to which we belong is a "western" one, which had its spring in the Middle Ages, its summer in the Renaissance, its autumn in the eighteenth century, and began its winter with the French Revolution. Previously there had been a Classical culture which went through the same stages. The heroes of Homer correspond to those of our own age of chivalry; the era of the Greek city-states to our Renaissance, and the last glories of Athens to our age of Bach and Mozart. With Alexander the "civilization" phase of world-empires begins, for Alexander corresponds to our Napoleon.

This view is analogous to Frye's theory of the parallel phases in cultural history. "I have never been very clear about the shape of the history of literature," he says, "apart from the shape of history in general."[34] Frye acknowledges that Spengler "provided the basis for the conception of modes" in the first essay (*SM*, p. 113), but it is not so much Spengler's cyclic view that is important for him as it is Spengler's conception of

organic cultural growth and aging. In fact, while the seasonal
metaphor might lead us to call the parallel phases "cycles," it is
inappropriate, according to Frye, to call Spengler's view of
history a cyclical one.[35] Frye prefers to say, simply, that
literary modes tend to move toward or return to earlier forms;
thus, he avoids the fatalistic overtones which have frequently
been sounded by cyclical theories of history. Spengler helped
Frye see that the linear, progressive view of history was dead,
that recurrence is best understood as organic rhythm, and that
cultures age rather than decline.

Angus Fletcher, who has written the most illuminating
account of Frye's theory of history, recognizes both the
diachronic and the synchronic thrusts of the first essay.
"Theoretical networks like the *Anatomy*," remarks Fletcher,
"are always called 'antihistorical,' since they openly resist the
uncontrolled evolution of [the] historically changing cityscape,
on which they impose a simpler, reductive, more efficient
system of intercommunication." Fletcher challenges this view,
arguing in general that the *Anatomy* does present an intelligible view of history and, in particular, that the theory of the
first essay is not "too schematic or rigid to allow for actual
human history."[36] He concludes that Frye's theory of modes is
"no less a type of history for combining induction and
deduction,"[37] even though the deductive framework of Frye's
modes does emerge as a utopian informing pattern. Such an
informing pattern is clearly present in the first essay (as it is
present in all of Frye's work), creating what Frye calls, in
"Nature Methodized" in the present volume, that "final unification of material which is the mark of a completely realized
[literary] history."

Fletcher alludes several times to various critics—they remain unnamed—who claim that Frye's modal system denies
"the fluid texture of history."[38] His rebuttal is twofold. On the
one hand, he claims that the first essay

> can be described as a prolegomena to a more meticulous
> periodization of literary history, and it remains deliberately
> rough, without giving up the hope that each mimetic phase

could be distinguished and analyzed in great detail. The theocentric basis of medieval thought could be closely handled, to test its bearing on romance; the courtly cult of the prince in the Renaissance could be related to the methods of high mimetic; the rationalism of modern science to the canons of low mimetic; and so on, through much subtler inquiries than these. In principle there is no reason why Essay I could not form the basis for a freely conducted practical investigation of historical fact.[39]

In other words, the deductive foundations of Frye's view of literary history can be tested, revised, and completed by a series of inquiries into historical fact. This is his immediate answer to the objection that Frye is not writing a properly detached, inductive literary history.

On the other hand, Fletcher argues that a purely inductive history is impossible anyway and that by using a metahistorical plot to develop his view of the literary past Frye is simply engaging in a procedure followed by any other historian. To be sure, some historians are more universalizing and theoretical than others. But the notion that there is a purely inductive history, Fletcher suggests, is a chimera. Frye, then, is no less a historian for engaging in speculative or philosophical historiography, the kind of history where, in the words of Isaiah Berlin, "the pattern, and it alone, brings into being and causes to pass away and confers purpose, that is to say, value and meaning, on all there is. To understand is to perceive patterns."[40]

The difference between the inductive "historian proper" and the deductive metahistorian is a distinction which Fletcher, drawing on contemporary historiographers, suggests is untenable. Hayden White makes the same point in observing that critics of historiography as a discipline have gone "so far as to argue that historical accounts are *nothing but* interpretations, in the establishment of the events that make up the chronicle of the narrative no less than in assessments of the meaning or significance of those events for the understanding of the historical process in general."[41] White, himself a historian, believes that although Frye wants to support the distinction between proper history and metahistory, "on his own analysis of the structures of prose fictions, he must be prepared to grant that there is a mythic element in 'proper history' by which the structures and processes depicted in its narratives are endowed with meanings of a specifically fictive kind." White, in fact, finds Frye's ideas about pregeneric plot structures (romance, comedy, tragedy, and satire) useful in "identifying the specifically 'fictive' element in historical accounts of the world."[42]

The diachronic thrust of the first essay appears to have raised more questions than its synchronic thrust: Tzvetan Todorov claims that Frye's modes are theoretical, not historical,[43] and Fletcher refers to those who believe the first essay is historically naive. Some of the force is taken from these objections, however, not only by those critics, such as Robert Foulke and Paul Smith, who have found Frye's modal scheme to be genuinely useful[44] but also by those, such as Fletcher, who believe that the diachronic elements in the first essay rest firmly in a tradition of interpretation followed by many historiographers. With Hayden White we come full circle, for here is a historian who finds in a literary critic a model for analyzing, not literary history, but historical interpretations in general. White's work offers an excellent example of the uses to which others have put Frye's ideas and of the ways thinkers continue to engage him in dialogue—a dialogue which has moved far beyond the ironic provincialism Frye saw in the criticism of the 1940s and 50s.

As a number of the reviews in the present volume make clear, Frye's view of history is an integral part of his continuous vision of culture, which is a vision, as already said, that does not make radical distinctions among the verbal products of culture. What most attracts Frye's interest are the metaphors which historians, in seeking ways to make sense of history, have projected upon the flux of human events. Toynbee and Spengler are the primary examples in the essays that follow, but Frye's attention to such metaphors also emerges in his review of the books by Niebuhr and Löwith. Where they are absent, as in the case of Dobrée's history of eighteenth-century British literature, the historian's account suffers. Dobrée covers the subject (a revealing. metaphor itself), but what one misses in his book, Frye says, "is the final unification of material which is the mark of the completely realized history, in whatever field." Such final unification, however, may frequently take forms which, from Frye's perspective, are unacceptable because deterministic or one-sided. Thus, just as he rejects progressive views of literature, which manifest themselves in the cult of the original, so he rejects those attitudes toward history which are based solely upon metaphors of growth-toward-perfection. At the other extreme, Frye has little use for ironic views of history, especially the deterministic one described in several places in the pages that follow as the Great Western Butterslide: "the doctrine of a coordinated synthesis in medieval culture giving place, at the Renaissance, to a splitting and specialized schizophrenia which has got steadily worse until it has finally landed us all in that Pretty Pass in which we are today."

Frye's own view of history is founded upon an organic and rhythmic metaphor of cultural aging. Its philosophical foundation, like that of Spengler's own analogical schema, is Romantic, which means that the reality of time, life, and history are to be discovered "by feeling, intuition, imaginative insight, and, above all, by symbolism" (*SM*, p. 180). But its ultimate source is once again Blake, who believed that history, like our daily sense experience, has to be ordered by the imagination. For Blake, as well as for Frye, "history is imaginative material to be synthesized into form" (*FS*, p. 29).

V

It is the task of the public critic to exemplify how a man of taste uses and evaluates literature, and thus show how literature is to be absorbed into society.
Anatomy of Criticism

Most of the reviews in part 2 of the present volume are essays in practical rather than theoretical criticism. The separation between theory and practice, however, does not exist as a sharp distinction in much of Frye's work. *Fearful Symmetry*, ostensibly a work of practical criticism, is laced throughout with theoretical issues. At some places in this book it becomes difficult, especially in retrospect, to determine whether the theory exists for the commentary, or vice versa. And since poetry and criticism at the anagogic level are often indistinguishable for Frye, it is not surprising that his commentary on Blake merges into his theory of criticism. Nevertheless, the difference between the theory of criticism and the application of the theory is a distinction Frye himself makes in referring to his own work.

After completing *Fearful Symmetry*, he began a study of *The Faerie Queene*, but the work was never completed, developing instead, as he tells us in the preface to the *Anatomy*, into a theory of allegory. This, in turn, directed his attention toward much larger theoretical issues, the culmination of which, after more than a decade, was the *Anatomy* itself. "The theoretical and practical aspects of the task I had begun," he says, "completely separated" (*AC*, p. vii). And he speaks of the need for a volume of "practical criticism, a sort of morphology of symbolism," to complement the "pure critical theory" of the *Anatomy* (*AC*, p. vii). Frye's critical theory is seldom "pure," insofar as his continual reference to specific works suggests, at least, the general shape a more detailed commentary would take. Conversely, his commentary on individual writers and works is, at the same time, theoretical —as it must be for any critic, since all critical methods include theoretical assumptions, even if only implicit ones. Nonetheless, we can classify most of Frye's criticism into two broad categories, depending upon whether his aim is primarily to develop a method for doing practical criticism or whether he is actually engaged in specific interpretation, explication, or commentary on individual writers.[45]

Frye has produced a substantial body of this latter kind of criticism. In *Fables of Identity* he examines a number of specific works and writers, even though this book is hardly the sequel, he says, that he had in mind when he wrote the

Anatomy (FI, p. 1). It contains discussions of *The Faerie Queene*, Shakespeare's sonnets, *Lycidas*, Blake, Byron, Emily Dickinson, Yeats, Wallace Stevens, and *Finnegans Wake*. Frye has written two books on Shakespeare, one on Milton, still another on Eliot. Moreover, a large amount of practical criticism is included in his other volumes of selected essays: *The Stubborn Structure* (especially part 2); *Spiritus Mundi* (part 3); and *The Bush Garden*, a collection of his essays and reviews on Canadian writers.[46] His book on English Romanticism (1968) contains long essays on Beddoes's *Death's Jest-Book*, Shelley's *Prometheus Unbound*, and Keats's *Endymion*. The list of such studies is lengthy.[47]

The practical criticism is by no means single in aim or approach. Frye can analyze poetic texture with the best of the New Critics. He can use his discussion of individual works as a means for defining literary periods, the procedure followed in his book on English Romanticism and his essay on the "Age of Sensibility" (*FI*, pp. 130–37). And he can provide interpretative commentary on individual passages. Yet none of these practices is typical of Frye's approach. More often than not he is concerned not with detailed commentary on individual poems but with the whole of a writer's work.[48] "The great merit of explicatory criticism," he says, "was that it accepted poetic language and form as the basis of poetic meaning. On [this] basis it built up a resistance to all 'background' criticism that explained the literary in terms of the non-literary. At the same time, it deprived itself of the great strength of documentary criticism: the sense of context. It simply explicated one work after another, paying little attention to genre or to any larger structural principles connecting the different works explicated" (*CP*, p. 20). Frye's own sense of context, however, is not that of documentary or historical criticism. The following passage, in which Frye recounts his reaction to deterministic and exclusively rhetorical approaches, spells out clearly the kinds of contexts he has in mind:

It seemed to me obvious that, after accepting the poetic form of a poem as its primary basis of meaning, the next step was to look for its context within literature itself. And of course the most obvious literary context for a poem is the entire output of its author. . . . Every poet has his own distinctive structure of imagery, which usually emerges even in his earliest work, and which does not and cannot essentially change. This larger context of the poem within its author's entire "mental landscape" is assumed in all the best explication—Spitzer's, for example. I became aware of its importance myself, when working on Blake, as soon as I realized that Blake's special symbolic names and the like did form a genuine structure of poetic imagery. . . . The structure of imagery, however, as I continued to study it, began to show an increasing number of similarities to the structures of other poets. . . . I was led to three conclusions in particular. First, there is no private symbolism. . . . Second, as just said, every poet has his own structure of imagery, every detail of which has its analogue in that of all other poets. Third, when we follow out this pattern of analogous structures, we find that it leads, not to similarity, but to identity. . . . I was still not satisfied: I wanted a historical approach to literature, but an approach that would be or include a genuine history of literature, and not simply the assimilating of literature to some other kind of history. It was at this point that the immense importance of certain structural elements in the literary tradition, such as conventions, genres, and the recurring use of certain images or image-clusters, which I came to call archetypes, forced itself on me. [*CP*, pp. 21–23]

The convictions outlined in this passage determine the way Frye characteristically approaches literature. As a practical critic, he typically seeks to place individual works within the context of a writer's entire canon and to relate them, in turn, by way of generic and archetypal principles to the literary tradition—what he calls the total order of words. Frye's practical criticism, therefore, is contextual, using the word in both the senses just mentioned. His conception of the total order of words is not unlike Eliot's belief (in "Tradition and the Individual Talent") that the literature from the time of Homer has a simultaneous existence and composes a simultaneous order. More than once Frye echoes this belief, arguing that the literary tradition operates creatively on the poet as a craftsman (*AC*, p. 17; *CP*, p. 23). But he goes beyond Eliot in attempting to identify the conventions that permit the poet to create new works of literature out of earlier ones.

When we consider the writers to whom Frye has devoted the most attention, another characteristic of his practical criticism becomes apparent: his romantic sensibilities and his predisposition to the forms of romance. He refers to Coleridge's division of literary critics into either Iliad or Odyssey types, meaning that one's "interest in literature tends to center either in the area of tragedy, realism, and irony, or in the area of comedy and romance." "I have always," he says, "been temperamentally an Odyssean critic" (*NP*, pp. 1, 2). In another context he remarks, "Romance is the structural core of all fiction" (*SeS*, p. 15). This helps to explain the prominence which Blake, Spenser, Milton, the later Shakespeare, Shelley, Keats, William Morris, and Wallace Stevens assume in Frye's literary universe.

Moreover, these are writers whom he locates in the "central tradition of mythopoeic poetry" (*FI*, p. 1), the primary tendencies of which, Frye says, are Romantic, revolutionary, and Protestant. There is a note of parody here, directed against the Classical, royalist, and Anglo-Catholic pronouncements of Eliot, but Frye means to be taken quite seriously. Despite his disclaimers about preferring one of these traditions to the other (*FI*, p. 149), there can be no question about the locus of his deepest sympathies. He is convinced that the prejudices of modernism are still with us, and, thus, much of his practical criticism is part of a larger effort to right the balance. He sees the Catholic, Tory, and Classical emphases of modernism as a "consciously intellectual reaction" to the Romantic tradition (*FI*, p. 149). The "most articulate supporters" of the reaction, he says,

> were cultural evangelists who came from places like Missouri and Idaho, and who had a clear sense of the shape of the true English tradition, from its beginnings in Provence and mediaeval Italy to its later developments in France. Mr. Eliot's version of this tradition was finally announced as

Classical, royalist, and Anglo-Catholic, implying that whatever was Protestant, radical, and Romantic would have to go into the intellectual doghouse. Many others who did not have the specific motivations of Mr. Eliot or of Mr. Pound joined in the chorus of denigration of Miltonic, Romantic, liberal, and allied values. . . . Although the fashion itself is on its way out, the prejudices set up by it still remain. [*FI*, 149]

This passage comes from an essay on Blake and is a part of Frye's argument that Blake must be seen in the context of his own tradition. And the "fashionable judgments" about this tradition, he says, have consisted mainly of "pseudo-critical hokum" (*FI*, p. 149). Frye has written a great many pages about the Romantic tradition in an effort to rescue it from these "fashionable judgments." He sees Romanticism as "one of the most decisive changes in the history of culture, so decisive as to make everything written since post-Romantic, including, of course, everything that is regarded by its producers as anti-Romantic" (*FI*, p. 3). Although his polemic against the prejudices of modernism is couched in the language of value, belief, and intellectual commitment, his several essays toward a definition of Romanticism approach the issue from a different perspective.[49] "What I see first of all in Romanticism," he says, "is the effect of a profound change, not primarily in belief, but in the spatial projection of reality. This in turn leads to a different localizing of the various levels of that reality. Such a change in the localizing of images is bound to be accompanied by, or even cause, changes in belief or attitude. . . . But the change itself is not in belief or attitude, and may be found in, or at least affecting, poets of a great variety of beliefs" (SS, p. 203). In other words, Romanticism as a literary phenomenon represents a profound change in poetic imagery and an equally profound modification of the traditional idea of four levels of reality, that background or "topocosm" against which images are portrayed. The significance Frye attaches to Romanticism as a revolutionary cultural movement has important consequences for his practical criticism. This emphasis, along with his preferring comic and romantic forms (most fully analyzed in *The Secular Scripture*), and his liberal and Protestant sympathies, goes a long way toward explaining the selection of those writers whose works he has discussed in some detail. Yet even when the selection lies in the hands of some book review editor, Frye's essays have a way of circling back to the same central affirmations. In his review of Sir Herbert Read's *The True Voice of Feeling*, he says that Romanticism is an attempt "not to know essences . . . but to create them, or rather to liberate them. To express the true voice of feeling is, in fact, one of the central liberating processes of human life, and it arises as part of our heritage of freedom, in opposition to the classical view of a prefabricated nature and an art which is merely 'a grace added' to life: a plaything'." The liberating vision of life is a recurrent theme in the reviews collected here, expressed sometimes in terms of what is present, as in Frye's remarks about Don Quixote's final acceptance of innocence, and sometimes in what is absent, as in his critiques of the elitist views of Wyndham Lewis and the anti-Romantic ones of Pound.

VI

> [The] contrast of similarity and identity is one of
> the most difficult problems in critical theory.
> *The Critical Path*

In his essay on Eliade, reprinted below, Frye says that "poetry, as distinct from discursive language, uses the language of identification, based as it is on metaphor, which is a relation of identity." Frye's conception of identity is one of his most important critical insights. It came to him during his study of Blake, yet it did not become fully articulated until twenty years later. In the *Anatomy*, the principle of identity is a part of Frye's theory of symbols, coming at the end of the second essay in his discussion of simile and metaphor. Here he is not so much interested in the rhetorical uses of these figures as he is in the modes of thought which underlie them. These are analogy and identity, principles which represent the two processes by which the imaginative power of the mind trans-

forms the nonhuman world (Nature) into something with
human shape and meaning (Culture). This is the point where
we begin to see the strong influence of Blake. In one of his
autobiographical essays, Frye recounts the intuition that came
to him as he was contemplating the fact that Milton and Blake
were connected by their use of the Bible: "If [they] were alike
on this point, that likeness merely concealed what was individual about each of them, so that in pursuing the likeness I
was chasing a shadow and avoiding the substance. Around
about three in the morning a different kind of intuition hit
me. . . . The two poets were connected by the *same* thing,
and sameness leads to individual variety, just as likeness leads
to monotony" (*SM*, p. 17).

Blake opposed his own view of reality to the commonsense
view of Locke, who conceived of subject and object as only
accidentally related: the subjective center of perception exists
at one pole; the objective world of things at the other. In order
to classify objective things, one points to their resemblances.
Thus, Locke's "natural" epistemology was based on the principles of separation and similarity. And the process of perceiving similarities, according to Blake, must always move
from the concrete to the abstract. Thus, in what Blake calls
"Allegory" or "Similitude" we have a relationship of abstractions. Frye's illustration of these Blakean terms is as follows.
"The artist, contemplating the hero, searches in his memory
for something that reminds him of the hero's courage, and
drags out a lion. But here we no longer have two real things:
we have a correspondence of abstractions. The hero's courage,
not the hero himself, is what the lion symbolizes. And a lion
which symbolizes an abstract quality is not a real but a
heraldic lion. . . . Whenever we take our eye off the image we
slip into abstractions, into regarding qualities, moral or intellectual, as more real than living things" (*FS*, pp. 116–17). Now
what Blake opposes to the natural view of Locke, or to
similitude in this sense, is the imaginary or visionary view of
"Identity," the literary form of which is metaphor.

The process of identity, according to Blake, "unites the
theme and the illustration of it" (*FS*, p. 117). There are two

kinds of identity perceived by the imagination. When Blake
says a thing is identified *as* itself, he means to point not to its
abstract quality but to its experienced reality. He calls this
reality its "living form" or "image." And all of Blake's images
and mythological figures, according to Frye, "are 'minute
particulars' or individuals identified with their total forms."[50]
In the second kind of identity things are seen as identical *with*
each other. Here the Lockean view is turned upside down,
since the perceiving subject is now at the circumference and
not the center of reality. All perceivers, since they are identical
and not separate, are one perceiver, a perceiver who in Blake's
view is totally human and totally divine. Blake's image for
this, in Frye's words, is "the life of a single eternal and infinite
God-Man," in whose body all forms or images are identical.[51]
Thus, in the imaginative world of Blake, things are infinitely
varied, because identified *as* themselves; at the same time, all
things are of one essence, because identical *with* each other.

In the *Anatomy*, Frye associates analogy with both descriptive meaning and realism and identity with poetic meaning
and myth—a separation based on Blake's distinction between
Locke's natural epistemology and his own imaginative one.
But the relationship as it is developed in the *Anatomy* is more
complex than this. The conception one has of simile and
metaphor depends upon the level of criticism he is engaged in;
so that the meaning which metaphor has for a critic at the
descriptive level will be different from its meaning at the
anagogical.

At the *descriptive* level, metaphor and simile have the same
function. To say "A is B" or "A is like B" is to say only that A is
somehow comparable to B. "Descriptively," as Frye says, "all
metaphors are similes" (*AC*, p. 123). On the *literal* level, both
metaphor and simile are distinguished by the absence of a
predicate. A and B are simply juxtaposed with no connecting
link, as in imagistic poetry. "Predication," Frye says, "belongs
to assertion and descriptive meaning, not to the literal structure of poetry" (*AC*, p. 123). At the *formal* level, where images
are the content of nature, metaphors and similes are analogies
of natural proposition, thus requiring four terms, two of which

have some common factor. Thus, "A is B" or "A is like B" means at the formal level, that A:X::B:Y, where the common factor is an attribute of B and Y. "The hero was a lion" is Frye's example, and we recognize in this illustration that formal metaphor is close to what Blake meant by the abstract similitude. In the *archetypal* phase, the metaphor "unites two individual images, each of which is a specific representative of a class or genus" (*AC*, p. 124). Dante's rose and Yeats's rose, while symbolizing different things, nevertheless represent all poetic roses. Archetypal metaphor is thus related to the concrete universal, and its Blakean analogue is the first kind of identity, identification *as*. Finally, at the *anagogic* level the most important analogical principle is metaphor in its radical form. To say that "A is B" means not that they are uniform or that they are separate and similar but that they are unified. Since literature at this level is seen in its totality, everything is potentially identical with everything else. This, of course, corresponds to Blake's second kind of identity, identity *with*.

"A work of literary art," Frye says, "owes its unity to this process of identification *with*, and its variety, clarity, and intensity to identification *as*" (*AC*, p. 123). His own interests direct him most often to search out the former of these analogies. The world of mytholigy lies at the center of his predilections, and this is the world of implicit metaphorical identity: to speak of a sun-god in mythology is to say that a divine being in human shape is identified with an aspect of physical nature. On the other hand, the world of realism, which lies at the periphery of Frye's own interests, is the world of implicit simile. To say that something is "lifelike" is to comment on its "realism," a term Frye once referred to as that "little masterpiece of question-begging" (*FS*, p. 420). So important is the principle of identity to Frye that he sometimes quite explicitly uses it to distinguish poetry from discursive thought or to define the formal principle of poetry.

Analogy and identity, then, are the two important concepts by which nature and human forms are assimilated. Analogy and simile establish the similarities between human life and nature, whereas identity and metaphor show us an imaginative world where things attain a human, rather than merely a natural, form. "If we ask what the human forms of things are," says Frye, "we have only to look at what man tries to do with them. Man tries to build cities out of stones, and to develop farms and gardens out of plants; hence the city and the garden are the human forms of the mineral and vegetable worlds respectively."[52] Frye applies the principle of radical metaphoric identification in the third essay. In the second, what he wants to emphasize is that the radical form of metaphor "comes into its own" in the anagogic phase. Both anagogy and radical metaphor, as principles of literature at the highest imaginative level, show us a poetic world completely possessed by the human mind.

Apocalyptic reality is for Frye, as it was for Blake, reality in its highest form. It is what the human imagination can conceive at the extreme limits of desire. Frye's conception of apocalypse is based upon a disjunction between the phenomenal and noumenal worlds, between what is perceived by sensory perception and what is apprehended by the reach of imagination, or between the "fallen" and "unfallen" worlds. Apocalypse is synonymous with the latter of these categories, and it has been represented variously as the Revelation at the end of the Bible or the Paradise at the beginning, to use the Christian metaphors; or as the Golden Age, to use the image of classical antiquity. It is only in the apocalyptic world, according to Frye, that nature can be humanized and man liberated —and both are achieved at the same time by the principle of radical metaphor. "This is apocalypse," says Frye, "the complete transformation of both nature and human nature into the same form."[53]

Identity is a central principle of literary structure for Frye, and in a number of places he has described the various forms which the drive toward identity takes. In comedy, for example, "there is plural or social identity, when a new social group crystallizes around the marriage of a hero and heroine in the final moments of the comedy. There is dual or erotic identity, when the hero and heroine get married. And there is individual identity, when a character comes to know himself in a way he did not before."[54] But in recent years, Frye has been much more intent on making clear that the drive toward identity is a process engaged in by readers as well as by literary characters. There are recognition and self-recognition scenes in life as well as in literature; the latter, he says, have much to do in helping us in the journey toward our own identity. In *The Secular Scripture* Frye makes clear that the highest form of self-identity comes from one's vision of the apocalyptic world, the original world from which man has fallen, a world of revelation and full knowledge which exists mysteriously between "is" and "is not" and in which divine and human creativity are merged into one.[55] In such a state, the distinction between subject and object disappears in favor of a unified consciousness. In poetry, identity-with, as opposed to identity-as, means that the poet and his theme become one. The religious analogue of such a relation is the symbolic act of communion. Another analogue is the relation between lovers, who, like poets, identify themselves with what they make. In the present volume the relation is best expressed in the essay on Beckett, where Frye says that artists like Beckett and Proust

> look behind the surface of the ego, behind voluntary to involuntary memory, behind will and desire to conscious perception. As soon as the subjective motion-picture disappears, the objective one disappears too, and we have recurring contacts between a particular moment and a particular object, as in the epiphanies of the madeleine and the phrase in Vinteuil's music. Here the object, stripped of the habitual and expected response, appears in all the enchanted glow of uniqueness, and the relation of the moment to such an object is a relation of identity. Such a relation, achieved between two human beings, would be love. . . . In the relation of identity consciousness has triumphed over time.

For Frye, such a relation is the singular way of regaining, in literature and life, the paradise which has been lost.

VII

Both Mr. Fletcher and Mr. Hartman emphasize
the fact that my work is designed to raise questions
rather than to answer them, and that my aim is
not to construct a *Narrenschiff* to keep future
critics all bound in by the same propositions, but
to point to what Mr. Fletcher calls the open vistas
and Mr. Hartman the still closed doors in the
subject.

"Reflections in a Mirror"

Altogether, Frye's work represents one of the most impressive achievements in the recent history of criticism. He is "probably the most influential critic writing in English since the 1950's," according to Walter Jackson Bate. "Certainly, in the English-speaking world," he says, "Frye's importance since 1957 (the date of his *Anatomy of Criticism*) is unique."[56] Murray Krieger remarks that Frye "has had an influence—indeed an absolute hold—on a generation of developing literary critics greater and more exclusive than that of any one theorist in recent critical history."[57] Frank Kermode, in reply to a 1965 questionnaire, says that the *Anatomy* is the one book, published within the previous decade, that he finds himself returning to most often, adding that Frye has "the best mind in the business except for William Empson's."[58] Harold Bloom observes that Frye "has earned the reputation of being the leading theoretician of literary criticism among all those writing in English today."[59] And the editors of a recent anthology of modern criticism refer to Frye as an "indispensable" critic, linking him with Eliot, Pound, and Richards as the "major" critics of our age. "More than any other modern critic," they say, "he stands at the center of critical activity."[60] These are typical expressions of the respect Frye's work commands. His importance as a critic need not be argued. Although many have disagreed with him, especially with his attempt to formulate a comprehensive and systematic theory of criticism independent from value judgments, few within his own field have ignored him.

How are we to assess Frye's achievement? It is, of course, too soon to suggest with any authority how history will come to judge his work, which, after all, is still in progress. But we can indicate the spirit in which his criticism should be assessed, taking our clue from a suggestion in his "Letter to the English Institute," written on the occasion of the conference devoted to his work. "I should want the discussion," he says, "to be as uninhibited as possible. . . . I have no itch to demonstrate that my views are 'right' and that those who disagree with me are 'wrong'. . . . Nor do I wish to correct others for 'misunderstanding my position': I dislike and distrust what is generally implied by the word 'position.' Language is the dwelling-house of being, according to Heidegger, but no writer who is not completely paranoid wants his house to be either a fortress or a prison."[61] This is more than a politeness demanded by the occasion, for in the house that Frye has built there *is* room for all manner of critical views. One of his first principles is that critical systems are judged neither right nor wrong but complementary. They interpenetrate, to use a spatial metaphor from the letter just quoted. "Literature itself is not a field of conflicting arguments," he says, "but of interpenetrating visions. I suspect that this is true even of philosophy, where the place of argument seems more functional. The irrefutable philosopher is not the one who cannot be refuted, but the one who is still there after he has been refuted."[62]

What Frye says here about literature and philosophy can be applied to criticism as well. His own work "is still there" after all the objections have been raised. The farther back from the whole of his work we stand, the less important these objections tend to become. This means that the value of Frye's work depends finally on distancing ourselves from the local complaint and the particular debatable issue. It is from this perspective—one having to do with Frye's conception of criticism as a whole—that a provisional assessment can be made. First, Frye's work is of practical value, a system of terms and doctrines and a method which can be used to answer one kind of critical question. Second, his criticism is a creative and aesthetic achievement in itself: it has final as well as instru- mental value. And third, his writings taken together form what might be called a metacriticism, reaching far beyond literature itself in an effort to account for and defend all the products of human culture. In this respect, Frye provides a meaningful apology for the humanities and a way of doing criticism on a grand scale.

To say that Frye's criticism is practically valuable is to say that the theory can be applied to good advantage in interpreting literature. But we must recognize what his system can and cannot do. It is clearly of limited value in helping to determine all the formal relations which combine to produce *particular* literary works. He offers guidance in rhetorical analysis only at the median level of generality. In discussing a comic work, for example, the total form of comic action is more important for him than whether or not a given work manifests every phase of the total form. Thus, his concern is not to determine what makes an individual comedy a special kind of poetic whole but to see how it relates both to other comedies and to an ideal comic form. He characteristically moves away from, rather than into, the literary work, and thus he emphasizes the thematic, narrative, and archetypal similarities among literary works rather than the explication of single texts. The question is not whether one approach is better than the other. They are simply different. And for his own kind of critical study Frye has provided a powerful set of analytical tools. The evidence for this is not only his own work but the growing number of critics who have found his general approach, his special categories, and his method of criticism genuinely useful. As Meyer Abrams puts it, "The test of the validity of a theory is what it proves capable of doing when it is put to work. And each good (that is, serviceable) theory, as the history of critical theory amply demonstrates, is capable of providing insights into hitherto overlooked or neglected features and structural relations of works of art, of grouping works of art in new and interesting ways, and also of revealing new distinctions and relations between things that (from its special point of view) are art and things that are not art."[63] Frye's critical theory is valid on all three counts.

Those who have found Frye's work to be the New Criticism writ large, while correctly discovering some important influences, have committed the error of misplaced emphasis. My own view is that Frye will be seen historically as having moved far beyond the New Critical assumptions because he is primarily interested in asking questions different from those of the New Critics. And there is value in this, insofar as Frye's universalism has helped to deflect criticism from a myopic organicism to a wider view of literature. It is frequently said that the New Criticism, for all its contributions to formal analysis, reduced criticism to explication or at least tended to see close analysis as the preeminent critical task. Despite a degree of caricature in this judgment, it is nevertheless true that Frye has helped us to see that there are other ways of talking meaningfully about literature. This is to say not only that a pluralism of critical methods should prevail but also that Frye's work, as a healthy corrective to the New Critical emphasis, helps insure that a pluralism will prevail.

Pluralism is not the same thing as Frye's vision of complementary critcal methods. He talks too often about the archetypal approach as the one way for breaking down barriers among critics and about a syncretism of interpenetrating views for us to label him a critical pluralist. But he has attacked provincialism on many fronts and thus has helped to extend the range of critical questions that may be legitimately asked. At a time when realism and irony dominate the literary world he has reminded us that a complete "iconography of the imagination" must account for myth and romance as well, that comedy is as deserving of critical attention as tragedy. A large measure of Frye's practical value depends finally on his opening up the critical world to questions previously slighted and to literary works frequently neglected; and on his providing us with some excellent analytical tools and an extensive glossary of concepts to better accomplish one kind of critical task.

Frye's ideas have had far-ranging consequences. An entire generation of literary critics has found his work to be useful and challenging. The practical effect of his criticism, however, extends far beyond its application to individual literary texts, having influenced the nature of the curriculum and provided models for entire educational programs in the humanities.[64]

Moreover, his work has helped determine the kinds of material, both literary and critical, that gets anthologized in textbooks, and his presence has even been felt by a group of Canadian writers—sometimes called the "Northrop Frye school" of poets.[65]

To say that Frye's criticism is an aesthetic achievement refers not merely to the wit and stylistic charm that grace his pages but to the fact that his *oeuvre* is itself an object for aesthetic contemplation. His complex conceptual structures are as intricately designed and as resonant with allusive meaning as many literary works. George Woodcock remarks that *Anatomy of Criticism* is "a great and intricate edifice of theory and myth whose true purpose is in its own existence; it has the same ultimate effect as buildings like the Angkor Wat or the Sainte Chapelle, which were built to exemplify religious truths and which survive, when their message is forgotten or derided, as objects whose sole meaning to modern man lies in their beauty. . . . [Frye] has exemplified more effectively than Wilde himself the latter's argument that criticism is primarily a creative process, leaving its masterpieces to impress and move by their skill and grandeur long after their subjects have ceased to interest us."[66] Woodcock dismisses too easily the practical value which a whole generation of critics and teachers has found in Frye's work,[67] and he overstates his case by using such expressions as *true* purpose and *sole* meaning. But he is surely correct in calling attention to the creative genius in Frye, a genius we associate more closely with artistic accomplishment than with discursive judgment.

It is significant that Frye labels one of his forms of prose fiction the *anatomy*. This extroverted, intellectual, and often satiric form is born of a thematic interest, replete with catalogs and diagrams, encyclopedic in scope, and reliant on the free play of intellectual fancy; like its forerunner, the Menippean satire, it "presents us with a vision of the world in terms of a single intellectual pattern" (*AC*, p. 310). All of which seems to describe quite well Frye's magnum opus itself, even without the title's calling it to our attention. Many readers have felt that the *Anatomy*—with its own oracular rhythm, aphoristic manner, associational logic, with its cyclical and epicyclical designs—is in part, at least, a narrative to be unraveled or a design to be contemplated. "I should call *Anatomy of Criticism*," says Frank Kermode, "a work of sixth-phase Symbolism. . . . Certainly it would be reasonable to treat this as a work of criticism that has turned into literature. . . . As literature it has, if I may be permitted to say so, great value."[68] Other readers have made similar claims. Graham Hough maintains that the *Anatomy* is not so much a treatise providing us with usable critical tools as it is a work of literature in its own right: "Frye has written his own compendious *Golden Bough*. . . . It is itself poetry." Harry Levin sees the *Anatomy* as a book we may set on our shelves beside Yeats's *A Vision*. And Rene Wellek remarks that Frye's work is "an elaborate fiction."[69] While each of these readers commits the fallacy of misplaced emphasis (reducing Frye's work to something less than it is), there is nevertheless a strong aesthetic interest that radiates from all his writing.

The clearest expression of this interest is in the schematic structures Frye erects and upon which he builds his elaborate taxonomies. He says that criticism must be schematic because the nature of poetic thinking itself is schematic.[70] Whether the patterns Frye observes—his five modes of fiction and five levels of symbolism, his four *mythoi* and twenty-four phases, and so on—actually exist in literature or whether they exist in the mind of their beholder is not always an easy question to answer.

Attempts at a taxonomy of literature would seem to be pointless if the aim is merely to attach labels, but the desire to know and to name literary differences and similarities is another matter. Frye's schematic taxonomy is in part a method for ordering recognized doctrines, the best example of which is the second essay of the *Anatomy*. But he also sees classification as a propaedeutic for inquiry. It is a method for isolating a subject of discussion so that inquiry may proceed. There is also in Frye's taxonomies a peculiarly inventive quality which seems to spring from a rage for order that is aesthetically rather than instrumentally motivated. The words of a scientist may help to make the point. Claude Lévi-Strauss quotes a biological taxonomist as saying that

> Scientists do tolerate uncertainty and frustration, because they must. The one thing they do not and must not tolerate is disorder. The whole aim of theoretical science is to carry to the highest possible and conscious degree the perceptual reduction of chaos that began in so lowly and (in all probability) unconscious a way with the origin of life. In specific instances it can well be questioned whether the order so achieved is an objective characteristic of the phenomena or is an artifact constructed by the scientist. That question comes up time and again in animal taxonomy. . . . Nevertheless, the most basic postulate of science is that nature itself is orderly. . . . All theoretical science is ordering and, if systematics is equated with ordering, then systematics is synonymous with theoretical science. . . . Taxonomy, which is ordering par excellence, has eminent aesthetic value.[71]

"Given this," concludes Lévi-Strauss, "it seems less surprising that the aesthetic sense can by itself open the way to taxonomy and even anticipate some of its results."[72]

There is a good deal of evidence that Frye's aesthetic sense does anticipate his own results. In fact, some of his categories seem to spring directly from an urge to construct an ordered artifact. Why are there four aspects to his central unifying myth (*agon*, *pathos*, *sparagmos*, and *anagnorisis*)? Partially, at least, because there are four *mythoi* by prior definition, and Frye's sense of order demands that they be made to correspond. Why are there six phases for each *mythos*? Because Frye says he recognizes them (*AC*, p. 177). Or why are there four forms of prose fiction? Because Frye's sense of order seems to require four: after defining three of the forms on the basis of the extroverted-introverted and the personal-intellectual dichotomies, he says "our next step is evidently to discover a fourth form of fiction which is extroverted and intellectual" (*AC*, p. 308). That this is Frye's "next step" is at least partially a result of his compulsion for symmetrically ordering his categories.

In fact, sometimes Frye seems to offer literature as an explanation for his categories rather than vice versa: literary works become exemplary explanations for the schema itself. William Righter believes that Frye's work

> turns away from the traditional Anglo-Saxon commitment to interpretation. It has been an almost unchallenged presupposition of our critical thought that criticism is some sort of second-order language which comments on, explicates, or explains something quite distinct from itself: a literary work which is assumed to be an imaginative creation of the first order. Frye violates this presupposition in two important ways. First, in spite of individual insights of the greatest interest he is hardly concerned, especially in the *Anatomy*, with particular literary works and their interpretation. He almost reverses the process. . . . The literary work acts as the "explanation" of a symbolic scheme, making the critical work the first order of language on which the example acts as the commentary. . . . Secondly, his lack of concern with particular literary works and his breadth of concern with literature as a whole have created his own intensely personal form of metacritical language, perhaps of a third order, working at a higher level of abstraction than we normally expect of critical thought. [73]

Righter is correct in underlining the impression we often have that Frye's critical order itself is an imaginative construct which needs no justification other than its own existence. Perhaps this should not be surprising, considering the fact that Frye practically equates poetry and criticism at the anagogic level. In *Fearful Symmetry* Blake as poet and Frye as critic tend to merge into one: it is often difficult to determine whether we have Blake's ideas or Blake as interpreted by Frye or simply Frye's ideas themselves. It is almost as if the critic has become artist, forging his own myths out of the uncreated conscience of his race.

In fact, because Frye sees criticism as creative, he has frequently emphasized the necessity of breaking down the barriers that separate the artist from the critic. He says that he learned from E. J. Pratt—his teacher and Canada's most important English poet—"to become more detached from the romantic mystique that opposes creative writers to critical ones" (*SM*, p. 24). The same note is sounded on both the first and last pages of the *Anatomy*.

The conception of the critic as a parasite or artist *manqué* is still very popular, especially among artists. It is sometimes reinforced by a dubious analogy between the creative and procreative functions, so that we hear about the "impotence" and "dryness" of the critic, of his hatred for genuinely creative people, and so on. The golden age of anti-critical criticism was the latter part of the nineteenth century, but some of its prejudices are still around. [*AC*, p. 3]

If I have read the last chapter of *Finnegans Wake* correctly, what happens there is that the dreamer, after spending the night in communion with a vast body of metaphorical identifications, wakens and goes about his business forgetting his dream, like Nebuchadnezzar, failing to use, or even realize that he can use, the "keys to dreamland." What he fails to do is therefore left for the reader to do, the "ideal reader suffering from an ideal insomnia," as Joyce calls him, in other words the critic. Some such activity as this of reforging the broken links between creation and knowledge, art and science, myth and concept, is what I envisage for criticism. [*AC*, p. 354]

Frye does not want us to think of criticism "as somehow sub-creative, in contrast to the 'creative' writing of poems and novels."[74] His own work illustrates the kind of creativity Wilde describes in "The Critic as Artist."

How are we to respond to this creative aspect of Frye's work, to his intricate schematic designs and his rage for order? Are we to lament the fact that it obliterates the traditional distinction between the first-order language of poetry and the second-order language of criticism and thus conclude, with William Righter, that Frye's work is a "perversity of invention," and "eccentric episode in literary history"?[75] Are we to look upon Frye with suspicion because the total form of his criticism is a source of pleasure in itself? I think not. There is no good reason why criticism cannot instruct and delight at the same time.

This is to say that Frye's criticism goes beyond a strict functionalism where practical and utilitarian values reign supreme. Readers who find a special fascination in the creative intellectual structures Frye builds must make their appeal finally to taste and sensibility. But there is no need to apologize for the aesthetic interest or to consider Frye's criticism less valid because of it. Meyer Abrams, though commenting on only a part of Frye's artistry, namely, his extraordinary ability for combining dissimilars and for discovering resemblances in apparently unlike things, makes a sound assessment.

> When we are shown that the circumstances of Pope's giddy and glittering belle have something in common with the ritual assault on a nature goddess, that Henry James's most elaborate and sophisticated social novels share attributes with barbaric folk tales, and that the ritual expulsion of the *pharmakos*, or scapegoat, is manifested alike in Plato's *Apology*, in *The Mikado*, and in the treatment of an umpire in a baseball game, we feel that shock of delighted surprise which is the effect and index of wit. Such criticism is animating; though only so, it should be added, when conducted with Frye's special *brio*, and when it manifests a mind which, like his, is deft, resourceful, and richly stored. An intuitive perception of similars in dissimilars, Aristotle noted, is a sign of genius and cannot be learned from others. Wit-criticism, like poetic wit, is dangerous, because to fall short of the highest is to fail dismally, and to succeed, it must be managed by a Truewit and not by a Witwoud. [76]

The fact that Frye is a Truewit will not provide the ultimate justification for his work. But it does provide one good reason for reading him, especially for those who believe that criticism need not exalt instruction at the expense of delight.

There is finally, however, more to be said of Frye's intricate formal structure than simply that it delights; for it contains a kind of truth which, although not literally corrigible in the way of a philosopher like (say) Popper would like, is nonetheless real. The structure itself teaches us by explaining. It tells us much about the world of literature that we did not previously know and that we could not have said in any other, more literal form. To say that the formal structure itself has explanatory power is to point back to my first claim, that Frye's criticism has instrumental value. And to say that the formal structure embodies one kind of truth is to point forward to my final claim, that Frye's critical theory is similar to metaphysics.

Two of Frye's more sensitive readers have, in fact, likened his work to metaphysics.[77] The parallel has broad and ambiguous connotations, but perhaps it can be explored briefly as a final way of suggesting the nature of Frye's achievement. If we define metaphysics as speculative (rather than empirical) inquiry, which asks questions about first principles and the nature of reality, then Frye in some respects is not unlike a metaphysician. He has his own solution to the problem of the One and the Many and to the materialist-idealist dilemma. The most crucial points of his theory depend on premises about the relation between mind and body, space and time, being and becoming. He has developed his own expansive, conceptual universe in which all forms of thought, action, and passion are assigned their appropriate places. In fact, there is a parallel between Frye's work and what Richard McKeon calls the "transcendental" form of metaphysics, a form of metaphysics which

> seeks being and intelligibility in a reality and intelligence which transcends becoming and opinion, [and which] has always had an affinity with the assimilations of dialectic and the construction of systems based on hierarchies of value. The emphasis in transcendental or systematic traditions is appropriately (since *"systems"* means "a whole," "a constitution," "a flock," "a company," "a musical scale") on organic wholes, on syntheses and systems in which wholes and parts mutually influence each other. . . . We have gained confidence in the discovery and institution of a system of communication and a system of communities by which to order what we say and do, and even what we think and know about the order of things. We hope to trans-

form partial discussions with their divisions, oppositions, and polarizations by providing an originative principle of discussion in what we like to call "dialogue," and to transform partial economic, social, and political communities by reordering them in the inclusive cultural community of mankind. The ordering of the new architectonic principle of culture will be an open-ended use and advancement of freedom and universality. . . . Systems of culture and communication are generative constructions used to open up meaning and values and to remove limitations to action and insight. Culture and communication depend on ordering principles and systems, and metaphysics has been and must continue to be, a systematic ordering of parts in wholes holoscopically and systematic constructing of wholes from parts meroscopically. [78]

There is an affinity between McKeon's description of transcendental metaphysics and the whole of Frye's work, with its transcendence of becoming, its dialectical systematizing, its opposition to partial views, its emphasis on inclusiveness and dialogue, and its holoscopic and meroscopic ordering of reality. Frye, of course, is not actually constructing a metaphysical system, but what he does construct has its roots in the grandeur of conception and the subtlety of thought that distinguishes metaphysics.

The great metaphysical systems, like Plato's or Spinoza's have a range and variety and power which makes them survive critique and "refutation." The eminence of the mind behind them has something to do with this resiliency and vitality. Another reason, as John Holloway remarks, is that "metaphysical systems are often generated by some hitherto neglected great idea of which the writer has taken possession: some radically new point of view from which life may be seen —from which the lines of force, as it were, may be seen running in new directions." [79] Although Frye is not doing metaphysics, he does invite us to consider a broad point of view from which things take on a new appearance. And behind it all we see a distinguished intellect thinking and writing. With the analogy in mind, we might say that Frye constructs a "metacritical" universe.

It is a universe in which art stands at the center, flanked by history, action, and event on one side and by philosophy, thought, and idea on the other. Art, for Frye, is the preeminent creation of man because it figures forth the imaginative world most fully and most obviously, and the imaginative world is the locus of Frye's ultimate values. But criticism, as already said, is not restricted merely to literature and the arts. It includes all verbal structures. This is the hypothesis upon which Frye builds his theory of culture and which permits him, because criticism is the unifying principle of culture, to practice his craft upon such a grand scale. One of Frye's readers, E. W. Mandel, observes that the relationship of criticism to culture is the "informing principle" of Frye's work. [80] The more Frye writes, the more accurate Mandel's observation becomes. Certainly a part of Frye's power as a critic derives from the catholicity of perspective which permits him to apply to the nonliterary aspects of culture the principles he has learned from literature. Similarly, both fictional and nonfictional discourse are subjected to his centrifugal gaze because they are both forms of imaginative projection. The keystone of Frye's metacriticism, we keep discovering, is his doctrine of the imagination.

In *The Secular Scripture* Frye remarks that "not all of us will be satisfied in calling the central part of our mythological inheritance a revelation from God, and, though each chapter in this book closes on much the same cadence, I cannot claim to have found a more acceptable formulation" (p. 60). The context of this observation is still another of Frye's many efforts to name the imagination's sense of otherness, but what is perhaps most revealing about the passage is the dependent clause, tucked away in the middle. To speak of the cadence of closure calls our attention to the close relationship between the rhythm of Frye's ideas and his sense of an ending. Like the reversible motto of Eliot's "East Coker," Frye's endings are also his beginnings. The conclusions to many of his books, even to chapters within books, frequently return to his own sense of what is fundamental—glimpses of that "third order of experience" which only the imagination can provide. The return of endings to beginnings is still another example of the continuity which, as said at the beginning of this introduction, characterizes Frye's work.

The metacritic engages in a bold enterprise, and he cannot help but be haunted by the many fallen structures which lie along the road to the eternal city of man's dreams, both intellectual and imaginative. Much is risked because much is attempted. The ambition to write on such a broad front, as Frye himself points out, makes a critic particularly vulnerable to objections. But in Frye's case the risk has been worth taking: a great mind has produced a great body of knowledge which will continue to instruct and delight so long as critics ask questions and dream dreams. The essays which follow are a part of that body of knowledge.

1

GRAMMARS OF THE IMAGINATION

I have often found myself drifting from
the research library into the under-
graduate working library, because of the
increasing affinity of my work to obvious
books.

Spiritus Mundi

MYTH AS INFORMATION

The first volume of the English translation of Ernst Cassirer's *Philosophy of Symbolic Forms* has just appeared. As the German edition of this volume was published in 1923, the translation is very belated and by now will chiefly interest students of philosophy who are not sufficiently concerned with Cassirer or acquainted with German to have consulted the original. This is a restricted range of usefulness, not enlarged by the fact that the real contemporary importance of Cassirer's thought is displayed not in this book but in the later *Essay on Man*, written in English and now available in a pocket edition. The *Essay on Man* is crisper, more concise, more conclusive in the direction of its arguments, and, as befits its American setting, more evangelical. Cassirer's work as a whole has been pretty thoroughly assimilated since his death in 1945, and the first volume of his magnum opus has now a largely historical importance for anyone who, like the present writer, cannot claim to be a technically competent philosopher.

That historical importance is, of course, very considerable. It is hardly too much to say that the bulk of what is distinctive in twentieth-century thought, in the nonmathetical division, has been constructed around the word *myth*. The major political philosophies of today, whether democratic, communist, or fascist, are still firmly rooted in their nineteenth-century formulations. But when the century opened, the study of myth in psychology by Freud, and in anthropology by Frazer and others, had started a radically new departure in

Review of Ernst Cassirer, *Philosophy of Symbolic Forms*, vol. 1, trans. Ralph Manheim. Preface and Introduction by Charles W. Hendel (New Haven: Yale University Press, 1953). Reprinted by permission from *The Hudson Review*, vol. 7, no. 2 (Summer 1954). © 1954 by The Hudson Review, Inc.

social thinking, and in 1922, the year that Proust died with his great mythical *Recherche* complete, the appearance of *The Waste Land*, *Ulysses*, and the more ectoplasmic *Fantasia of the Unconscious* startled the literary public also into realizing the importance of myth. It was the next year that Cassirer began to bring the problem into systematic philosophy, and in the thirty years since then the word *myth* has continued to produce that uninterrupted flow of talk which is generally called, and sometimes accompanies, a steady advance in thinking.

Cassirer appears to have done a good deal to break down the provincialism of the discursive reason in philosophy. Logic is based on language and is a specialized development of language, but it is by no means the final cause of language. Not only is language itself prelogical, but there is no evidence whatever that man learned to speak primarily because he wanted to speak rationally. The simultaneous and parallel development of the languages of myth and literature shows that there are other kinds of structures to be made out of words. Thinking is one of many things that man does; hence it is part of a whole, the whole being the "functional unity" of human work in the world. To put logical thought in its place as one of a number of human operations is more realistic than to consult it as an oracle which reveals to man the existence of a systematic and rational order in the objective world. For when reason in the mind discovers rational order in the universe outside it, this discovery is largely a matter of falling in love with its own reflection, like Narcissus.

The "philosophy of symbolic forms," then, is a philosophy which starts by looking at the variety of mental constructions in human life. These include science, mathematics, philosophy, language, myth, and the arts, which in the aggregate are called culture. Each of these constructions is built out of units called symbols, which are usually words or numbers, and which, approximately, owe their content to the objective world and their form to the categories of human consciousness. For further details see Professor Hendel's lucid introduction, which traces Cassirer's conception back to the "schema" of

Kant. We may also divide these constructions into a logical group and another group which is either pre- or extra-logical, and which consists mainly of language, myth, and the arts. Folke Leander, writing in the volume of the Library of Living Philosophers devoted to Cassirer, remarks that Cassirer has not established the relation among these three, any more than he has established that there are in fact three of them, because there is no adequate treatment of aesthetics in his work. (The chapter on art in the *Essay on Man* is largely amiable burble.) It is perhaps worthwhile trying to follow up this suggestion and to see if we can discover what, on the basis of Cassirer's general conception of symbolic form, the relation of myth actually is to language on the one hand and to literature (the only one of the arts which seems to have a *direct* connection with myth) on the other.

The relation of grammar to logic may provide us with a useful analogy. Logic grows out of grammar, the unconscious or potential logic inherent in language, and we often find that the containing forms of conceptual thought are of grammatical origin, the stock example being the subject and predicate of Aristotelian logic. It would be interesting to develop John Stuart Mill's suggestions about the relations of grammar and logic, which are referred to by Cassirer and are perhaps not as indefensible as he thinks, though they may need restating. One wonders, for instance, about the parallelism between the parts of speech and the elements of thought in our Classical-Western tradition, where nearly all the important languages belong to the Aryan group. There is surely some connection between the noun and the conception of a material world; the verb and the conceptions of spirit, energy, and will; the adjective and universals; the adverb and value; the conjunction and relation; and so forth, that would bear investigating.

It is disappointing to find that not even in the *Essay on Man* is there any reference to the *contemporary* problems involved in the relation of grammar and logic. Cassirer shows how language begins in spatial mythopoeia and the projection into the outer world of images derived from the human body. He does not show how these metaphors organize our writing and thinking as much as ever today: nearly every time we use a preposition we are using a spatial myth or an unconscious diagram. If a writer says: "But on the other hand there is an additional consideration to be brought forward in support of the opposing argument," he may be writing normal (if wordy) English, but he is also drawing elaborate geometrical doodles, like an armchair strategist scrawling plans of battle on a table cloth. Again, the fluid primitive conceptions dealt with by Cassirer, the Polynesian *mana*, the Iroquois *orenda*, and the like, are participial or gerundive conceptions: they belong in a world where energy and matter have not been clearly separated, either in thought or into the verbs and nouns of our own less flexible language structures. As energy and matter are not clearly separated in nuclear physics either, we might do well to return to such "primitive" words ourselves. The words *atom* and *light*, for example, being nouns, are too material and static to be adequate symbols for what they now mean, and when they pass from the equations of the physicist into the linguistic apparatus of contemporary social consciousness, the grammatical difficulties in the translation show up clearly.

Of course one would have to avoid the scholar's mate in this kind of argument: the fallacy of thinking that we have explained the nature of something by accounting for its origin in something else. Logic may have grown out of grammar, but to grow out of something is in part to outgrow it, and to try to reduce logic to grammar would be as futile as a good many earlier attempts to reduce grammar to logic. For grammar may also be a hampering force in the development of logic and a major source of logical confusions and pseudoproblems. These confusions extend much further than even the enormous brood of fallacies spawned by paronomasia, or the use of words in a double or manifold sense, which make up the greatest number of such booby traps. Even Cassirer's major effort in thought illustrates a grammatical problem: he abandoned the search for a systematic or rational unity in human consciousness in favor of recognizing a "functional unity" of a number of various activities that obviously do exist. This had the effect of transferring his conception of reason from the definite to the indefinite article, of saying that reason is *a* phenomenon of human consciousness, which is indisputably true, instead of saying that human consciousness is rational (or *the* reason), which involves one in a wholly unnecessary struggle for the exclusive possession of an essence. The other day two students came to me and one said: "I say art is expression; Jim here says it's communication: which is it?" I said that if he would admit that art may communicate, Jim would probably admit that it may also express, and they could divide the essence peaceably between them. It was the same grammatical *pons asinorum* on a small scale. It is no wonder, then, that many logicians tend to think of grammar as something of a logical disease. Some of them have maintained that mathematics is the real source of coherence in logic. I have no opinion on this, but as a literary critic I know that as long as logic continues to make a functional use of words, it will continue to be involved in all the problems of words, including grammar and rhetoric.

When people speaking different languages come into contact, an *ideogrammatic* structure is built up out of efforts at communication. The figure 5 is an *ideogram* because it means the same number to people who call it *five*, *cinq*, *cinque*, *fünf*, and a dozen other things. Similarly, the purely linguistic associations of English *time* and French *temps* are perceptibly different, as a comparison of the phrases *good time* and *beau temps* shows. But it is quite practicable to translate Proust or Bergson on time into English without serious risk of misunderstanding the meaning. When two languages are in different cultural orbits, like English and Zulu, the ideogrammatic structure is more difficult to build up, but it always seems to be more or less possible. The problems of communication between two people speaking the same language may be at least equally great, because more difficult to become aware of, but even they can be surmounted.

This ideogrammatic middle ground between two languages must itself be a symbolic structure, not simply a bilingual dictionary. When we learn a closely related language like French we discover French equivalents for all English words and constructions. But obviously one cannot walk into a Polynesian or Iroquois society and ask: "What are *your* words for *God, soul, reality, knowledge?*" They may have no such words or concepts, nor can we give them our equivalents for *mana* and *orenda*. Yet it is equally obvious, after examining the evidence in Cassirer's book, that it is possible, with patient and sympathetic study, to find out what is going on in a Polynesian or Iroquois mind, and thereby do something to disentangle one's own mental processes from the swaddling clothes of their native syntax. But we can only do so by trying to get the "feel," the sense of a comprehensible and communicable inner structure, in the other language, which can be identified with another inner structure growing out of our own language, even if its syntactic setup is entirely different. It is out of such ideogrammatic inner structures, whether produced linguistically between two languages or psychologically between two people speaking the same language, that the capacity to assimilate language to rational thought develops. The humanistic theory of education has always, and rightly, stressed the importance of the conflict of different habits of linguistic expression, specifically of the modern and Classical languages, in the training of the mind. In his *Essay on Man* Cassirer suggests that the historical origin of scientific and mathematical thought may have been a similar linguistic conflict in Mesopotamia between the Sumerian and the Semitic Akkadian languages.

It is not so often realized that the relation between grammar and literature is closely parallel to the relation between grammar and logic. Poetry seems to be much more deeply involved in verbalism because so much of it is untranslatable and because ambiguity and paronomasia are as much virtues in poetry as they are vices in discursive thought. Yet in reading a poem we make an effort to comprehend the meanings of the words employed in it, which is quite separate from the understanding of their dictionary meanings. The question of what a word conventionally means is always qualified, sometimes contradicted, by the other question of what it means in the poem; and the poet, like the philosopher, may protest against a merely conventional understanding of his more precise meaning, his "sens plus pur," in Mallarmé's phrase. Poetry, as much as discursive or rational writing, grows out of language, yet remains in a state of tension against language. Hence, the development of an understanding of literature, as of rational thought, involves the building up of ideogrammatic inner structures like those above mentioned, though the inner structures in this case would not be structures of ideas but of something else.

The content or sense of poetry, its aspect as an imitation of nature, is always more or less translatable into another language or another aspect of the same language. But to render the sense of a poem only is not full communication. What cannot be translated is a complex of elements, of which one is a quality that we may vaguely call word-magic, and which seems to depend on the characteristics of the language employed. Yet one feels that poetry is more communicable than this. Surely the languages of Europe have cooperated to produce a great literary culture in a way that goes far beyond such a mixture of exchangeable sense and competing tintinnabulations. We seem to have missed something. The content of a poem, we say, is translatable. What about the form, which is usually the complementary term to content? Nobody would call word-magic or anything dependent on linguistic factors the form.

Cassirer's "symbolic form" is neither subjective nor objective: it is intermediate, taking its structure from the mind and its content from the phenomenal world. In the symbolic forms of all the arts this inseparable unity of a mental constructive principle and a reproductive natural content reappears. Painting, for instance, has the imitation of nature as one of its elements, and design, the symmetry and balancing of outlines and masses, as the other. Abstract, or, more strictly, nonrepresentational painting (which is still imitating nature in the Aristotelian sense) is about as close to the formal pole as we can get; *trompe l'oeil* puzzles are nearest to the imitative pole. For some reason the main emphasis has been well over toward the imitative end in nearly all the theory and most of the practice of Western painting. Music, on the contrary, has always been primarily formal in our tradition, and imitative or "programme" music kept within strict bounds. Literature, like painting, has, at least in its criticism, tended to give more attention to its extroverted, nature-imitating aspect. Its formal or constructive principles are still so little understood that there is no adequate terminology to describe them.

The word *myth* means different things in different fields: in literary criticism it is gradually settling down to mean the formal or constructive principle of literature. Where there is a fiction, the shaping form, to which every detail in the writing has to be assimilated, is the story or plot, which Aristotle called *mythos* and declared to be the "soul" of the fiction. In primitive periods such fictions are myths in the sense of anonymous stories about gods; in later ages they become legends and folk tales; then they gradually become more "realistic," that is, adapted to a popular demand for plausibility, though they retain the same structural outlines. Profound or "classic" works of art are frequently, almost regularly, marked by a tendency to revert or allude to the archaic and explicit form of the myth in the god-story. When there is no story, or when a theme (Aristotle's *dianoia*) is the center of the action instead of a mythos, the formal principle is a conceptual myth, a structure of ambiguous and emotionally charged ideas or sense data. Myths in this sense are readily translatable: they are, in fact, the communicable ideogrammatic structures of literature.

Literature resembles mathematics and differs from other structures in words in that its data are hypothetical: mathematician and poet alike say, not "this is so," but "let this be." Mathematics appears to be a kind of informing or constructive principle in the natural sciences: it continually gives shape and coherence to them without being itself involved in any kind of external proof or evidence. One wonders whether, in the future, when we shall know so much more about what literature says and how it hangs together than we now do, we shall come to see literary myth as similarly a constructive principle in the social or qualitative sciences, giving shape and coherence to psychology, anthropology, theology, history, and political theory without losing in any one of them its own autonomy of hypothesis. Thus, it looks now as though Freud's doctrine of an Oedipus complex were an explanation for the dramatic effectiveness of *Oedipus Tyrannos*. Perhaps in another few years we shall decide that we have got it the wrong way round: that the dramatic myth of Oedipus informed and gave coherence to Freud's psychology at this point. Such a reversal of perspective would bring us close to Plato, for whom the purest formulation of dialectic was either mathematical or mythical. The basic structure of myth is the metaphor, which is very similar in form to the equation, being a statement of identity of the "A is B" type. I imagine that the third quarter of the century will see Cassirer's principles developed in some such direction as this.

THE SHAPES OF HISTORY

The synthesis of modern thought is the philosopher's stone of our age, and any such synthesis would have to contain, if it did not actually consist of, a philosophy of history. The two greatest modern achievements in this field are represented by Marx and Spengler, one a Communist and the other more or less a Nazi. What we want, clearly, is an equally impressive structure which will make room for humane values and established religion and not scare the pants off the middle-class reader. So when the first six volumes of Toynbee's *A Study of History* came out in a one-volume abridgment, it scored a smashing popular success. This success was due mainly to *Time*, which has a deep interest in all books that promise to draw a cultural *cordon sanitaire* around Marxism.

A Study of History presents an enormous mass of historical material strung along a thin line of argument often represented only by a single word, generally Greek. In the original, one can snuggle down to read endlessly about hundreds of fascinating subjects, with a comfortable feeling that all the time all this is proving something, though we may have to look back at the table of contents to see just what it is. The abridgment, by exposing the lines of communication more clearly, indicates that Toynbee is not writing a philosophy of history so much as unrolling a vast historical panorama. His material does not really "prove" anything: it provides the detail of his vision, and he leads us toward an imaginative total apprehension which can skip over the logical, and sometimes even the factual, stage. I have read many critiques of Toyn-

Review of Arnold J. Toynbee, *A Study of History*. Abridgment of vols. 1–4 by D. C. Somervell (New York: Oxford University Press, 1947). Reprinted from *The Canadian Forum*, vol. 27 (March 1947).

bee, ranging from eulogy to invective, and have been struck
with the fact that if one is in broad sympathy with what he is
trying to do, his errors, however numerous, appear as blem-
ishes in a picture rather than as wrong turns in a chain of
reasoning. But if one is not in sympathy with him, everything
seems equally pointless, and the whole pattern dissolves in
chaos.

Toynbee worked out his plan independently of Spengler,
and when Spengler's *Decline of the West* appeared after the
last war he thought at first that his work had been done for
him. Spengler says that the essential shape of history is neither
a chaos of accidents nor a steady linear advance, but a series of
social developments which he calls "cultures." These cultures
behave exactly like organisms: they grow, mature, decline,
and die; and they all last about the same length of time. Each
begins in a "spring" of an agrarian economy, a feudal and
aristocratic society, and a mystical iconic religion; and
matures into a "summer" of city-states and individualized art;
thence into an "autumn" of urbane sophistication in art and
economic expansion. At that point the "culture" changes to a
"civilization" and plunges into a "winter" of huge cities,
impoverished agriculture, dictatorships, and annihilation
wars. The possibilities of its arts are exhausted, and its great
achievements are technical feats of engineering and civil and
military administration. The culture to which we belong is a
"Western" one, which had its spring in the Middle Ages, its
summer in the Renaissance, its autumn in the eighteenth
century, and began its winter with the French Revolution.
Previously there had been a classical culture which went
through the same stages. The heroes of Homer correspond to
those of our own age of chivalry; the era of Greek city-states to
our Renaissance, and the last glories of Athens to our age of
Bach and Mozart. With Alexander the "civilization" phase of
world empires begins, for Alexander corresponds to our
Napoleon. The "decline of the West" has thus reached about
the stage of the Punic Wars in classical times, and the Roman
empire and the reign of the Caesars indicate what is ahead of
us. In addition to these two great cultures, Spengler deals with

an Egyptian, a Chinese, and an Indian one, an Arabian or Syrian one (he calls it "Magian") which began around the time of Jesus and aged into Mohammedanism, and a new Russian one which is just beginning. Apart from these culture growths, human life presents a mere continuity of existence without shape or significance. Primitive societies and exhausted ones alike "have no history."

When one culture follows another in time, Spengler says, it does not really learn from its predecessor, and thus there is no general progress in history. When two cultures conflict, the more aggressive one may stunt and dwarf the other, producing what Spengler calls a "pseudomorphosis." Classical civilization did this to Magian culture, and Western civilization is doing it now to Russia. But no Westerner can ever understand what goes on in a classical or Indian mind: he can only guess at it by seeing how all the products of the other culture fit into a consistent mental pattern which is not his. This overall pattern can be grasped, not, of course, through abstract propositions, but through symbols. Classical culture lives in a "pure present": it has nothing of our sense of time and history: it thinks of architecture as a columnar mass, of tragedy as stylized attitude, of sculpture as bodily form, of mathematics as integral numbers and enclosed spaces, of music as a relation of single notes, of diplomacy as personal contact. Western culture is characterized by a feeling for the infinite: it thinks of architecture as a soaring structural energy, of tragedy as an analysis of character, of sculpture as a struggle with material, of mathematics as variable function, of music as counterpoint, of diplomacy as cabinet decisions used as long-range weapons. Magian culture is full of domes, caverns, sacred books, and esoteric traditions; Russian culture expresses a "denial of height" both in its squat architecture and in its social communism, and so on.

A good deal even of this is German romanticism at its corniest, and some more sinister features are involved. We should, Spengler thinks, accept the character of our age and not sigh for a vanished past or a Utopian future which (Toynbee agrees) is the shadow of a tired mind. We can think up new variations of the arts, but new organic developments are no longer possible, and we should leave them to misfits and get on with our big wars and dictatorships . . . Was the Rome of the Caesars, the Rome of Virgil and Horace and Ovid and Catullus, really interested solely in aqueducts and brass hats? Don't interrupt the professor. The author of Spengler's next book, *The Hour of Decision*, is just another Nazi stumblebum. But his thesis has bitten deeply into us: we are all Spenglerians to some extent, and if the enemy has any ammunition that we can capture, we should fire it back at the enemy.

Much of Toynbee's book, especially the first three volumes, reads like an improved version of Spengler backed up by a far greater knowledge of history. He also isolates the "civilization" or "society" as the unit of historical study. The first three volumes trace the "genesis" and "growth" of these societies, and the next three, "decline" and "disintegration," though in volume four he avoids the "decline" (*Untergang*) of Spengler's title and adopts "breakdown" instead. Spengler's six or eight civilizations are all included in a much fuller survey of twenty-one. The main improvement on Spengler comes in the role assigned the proletariat in the last stage. To Spengler, the proletariat is nothing but a rabble: Toynbee sees that an internal proletariat (the exploited members of the society) and an external one (the barbarian nomads outside) combine to form a "universal Church," which becomes at once the coffin of the old society and the womb of a new one, so that a real spiritual progress from one society to another can occur. For reasons too complicated to examine here, this gives Christianity a far more satisfactory historical explanation than Spengler gives it.

At the beginning of volume four there comes a crisis in Toynbee's argument, the question of the cause of decline, which involves a direct examination of Spengler. But he fails to pass this crisis, and all the rest of his book has the air of a dodged issue. He fires off two very damp squibs at Spengler. First he calls him a "fatalist," which is irrelevant: to predict the death of every living organism may be tactlessness, but it is not fatalism. Then he complains that Spengler uses a metaphor as though it were a fact. But *A Study of History*, organized throughout on such figures as "nemesis of creativity," "withdrawal and return," "schism and palingenesia," is a rather glassy house from which to throw this stone. As we have seen, an intuitive response based on an imaginative grasp of the symbolic significance of certain data is demanded by Toynbee as well as Spengler. Toynbee's real answer is that civilization is not an organism. An organism has a life span predetermined from the start; a civilization is a way of social life initiated by an environmental challenge and dependent for its continuity on maintaining a social will and judgment sufficient to meet further challenges. If it collapses, there is always a definable and at one time avoidable cause.

Spengler's evidence for the organic nature of culture is of a kind which Toynbee shows himself much less skillful in handling. If, says Spengler, we study the growth of painting from Giotto to Rembrandt, we can see, in its development of interest in landscape, realistic portraiture, and the handling of light, a steady advance in self-consciousness and in the exploring of a certain range of possibilities. It is not getting better or worse: it is simply growing older. If we compare modern America with classical Rome, we shall see parallels of a kind that do not appear when we compare it with the age of Charlemagne, and these parallels can be accounted for only by a conception of cultural age. Spengler does not say, any more than Toynbee does, that "breakdown" is inevitable: he says growing older is inevitable, and he is quite as insistent as Toynbee on the importance of "self-determination" to prevent breakdown at a late stage. And his powerful argument proving that Western culture is a relatively old one still stands completely unrefuted. It will not do to suggest, like a lazy book reviewer, that it may, after all, rest on nothing but a false analogy. It doesn't.

Toynbee's conception of history is so closely related to Spengler's that when he throws out Spengler's thesis, most of his own would go with it if he did not continually accept in practice what he denies in theory. He is stuck with many organic metaphors which he does not know how to avoid

using. The death-and-rebirth rhythm of *The Golden Bough* is
an essential part of his structure: he is quite right, and
Spengler quite wrong in ignoring it; but it happens to be an
organic rhythm. Civilizations still "grow," even if they suddenly turn into machines and "break down," and then into
inorganic substances and "disintegrate." He quarrels with
Gibbon's ghost for regarding the Antonine age as a real
summer instead of an Indian one. He has no class of things
with which to associate his conception of civilization and has
to define it in circular terms like "entity." Of his twenty-one
civilizations, every one except ours has gone through what look
suspiciously like organic stages of a "time of troubles," a
universal state and a universal church; and the constant
assertions that ours is an exception are not very convincing
even to Toynbee himself, as the troubled cadences of his sixth
volume, with its many uneasy glances at the parallels to
"disintegration" in our own time, abundantly show. One has
the feeling that he is afraid that the logical consequence of his
own argument will land him in Spengler's "pessimism." But
whatever one thinks of Spengler's pessimism, the optimism of a
man who can write in 1939 that it is too early yet to say
whether we have come to our time of troubles seems rather
woebegone.

Unlike Spengler, primarily a philosopher who picked up his
history as he went along, Toynbee is primarily a historian, and
his philosophical basis consists largely of his own hunches,
some of Bergsonian origin. There are many places where he
does not even see that a prior philosophical problem is
involved. Thus, his survey of the causes of breakdown itself
breaks down through ignoring the question of what constitutes
a historical cause. Pascal says that if Cleopatra's nose had been
an inch longer it would have changed the world's history.
Spengler says that different characters might have replaced
Antony and Cleopatra, different battles might have been
fought, and the course of historical events might have been
superficially quite different, but the fundamental relationship
of a moribund Egyptian culture, an aging classical one, and a
nascent Syrian one would have still been there. This distinc-

tion between history and chronicle is one of the profoundest of Spengler's insights. The distinction disappears in Toynbee, and in consequence he takes us back to the old "practical" view of history as a chaotic sequence of lucky and unlucky accidents, a roulette game in which a gambler's luck may hold if he figures out a system to beat the laws of chance.

Both Spengler and Toynbee talk about Marx as though he were a second-rate thinker: the Nazi calls him a Jew and the English liberal a German Jew. But I suspect that Marx is holding the nutcracker that the reader of both Toynbee and Spengler wants. New instruments of production change the whole character of a society; and the technique for producing new instruments of production at will brought in by the Industrial Revolution has changed the whole character of history. There is now a completely new factor in the situation which cannot be wholly absorbed into a dialectic of separate "civilizations," important as that is. The question whether Western civilization will survive or collapse is out of date, like the same question about the British Empire, for the world is trying to outgrow the whole conception of "a" civilization and has reached a different kind of problem altogether. Because the Industrial Revolution started in the West, its transformation of the world has looked like the expansion of Western society, and in fact has partly been that, but something else is also happening. The factors which are the same all over the world, such as the exploitation of labor, have always been, if not less important, at any rate less powerful in history than conflicts of civilizations. Now they are more important, and growing in power. Toynbee feels that world peace now is essentially a question of getting the five surviving civilizations to live together in spite of their traditional differences in outlook. But this is the old league of sovereign nations again, the balance-of-power fallacies revised to rationalize the new setup of national "blocs." The conception of United Civilizations, like the conception of United Nations, is pretty, but it isn't the real thing.

A Study of History is already something of a museum piece. Volumes four to six were the product of the thirties, that horrible period of impotent democracy and rampant fascism, and their general tone of hoping against hope that as much as possible of the status quo will "survive" reflects what we all felt then. Now we have the atom bomb and Russo-American imperialism before us, but some years have elapsed in war work since the completion of volume six, and perhaps a fresh start will bring a fresh energy. The great synthesis of Marx and Spengler has yet to be written, but so has half of Toynbee's book.

If you spend much time in libraries, you will probably have seen long rows of dark green books with gold lettering, published by Macmillan and bearing the name of Frazer. Fifteen of them have the running title of *The Golden Bough*. Then there's *Folklore in the Old Testament*, three volumes. *Totemism and Exogamy*, four volumes. An edition of Pausanias, the traveler who wrote a description of Greece about A.D. 200, six volumes. *The Worship of Nature*, two volumes. *The Fear of the Dead in Primitive Religion*, three volumes. *The Belief in Immortality*, three volumes. These are the biggest lots, but there are many more: editions of Addison's essays and Cowper's letters, two volumes each; editions of several other classical authors; a book of extracts from the Bible; lectures, essays, fugitive pieces. It would take a good many months of hard work, without distractions, to read completely through Frazer.

The man who produced all this was the son of a Scottish Presbyterian minister, born in Glasgow in 1854. He was two years older than Bernard Shaw and not unlike Shaw in physical type: lean and wiry, with a pointed beard and glittering blue eyes. His father wanted him to study law, and in England that's a good profession to choose if you want to do other things. He did qualify as a barrister, but he spent his whole working life in universities, mainly as a fellow of Trinity College, Cambridge, emerging at intervals to collect honorary degrees and decorations. He got a knighthood, the Order of Merit, the Legion of Honor, and a shower of doctorates. He was naturally shy and retiring, said to have been a poor

Reprinted from *Architects of Modern Thought*, 3d and 4th series (Toronto: Canadian Broadcasting Corp., 1959).

speaker unless he had a script, and, like many shy people, bristly and somewhat intolerant in conversation. Apparently it was Lady Frazer who managed him and helped get him his degrees. She wrote books too, mostly translations from the French. Frazer died in 1941, at eighty-seven, the victim of a Nazi bomb, and Lady Frazer with him.

He was a fine classical scholar who grew up in the later Victorian period, after Darwin had changed the whole direction of science. Anthropology was a new and exciting subject, and for Frazer it threw a flood of light on his classical studies. The Greeks and Romans had been primitives once too, and many things had survived in their religion that were very like the things being reported from the African jungles and the Australian bush. The biblical scholar Robertson Smith had studied primitive Arabian tribes to discover the sort of religion that's concealed in the earliest layers of the Old Testament. He had also worked on a theory that had a great influence on Frazer: that in primitive societies ritual precedes myth: people act out their beliefs first and think up reasons for them afterward. Then again, German scholars following the Grimm brothers, especially a scholar named Mannhardt, were turning up curious customs in the German countryside that seemed to be filling in the outlines of a nature cult centuries older than Christianity. Scholars were taking much the same view of primitive man that primitive man was supposed to have taken of his own life, as a kind of dream in which everything was charged with a mysterious fascination, and they pounced eagerly on anything that had to do with "folk."

Frazer was a professor of social anthropology, yet he never to my knowledge did any real fieldwork and never came much closer than the Cambridge library to primitive societies. He certainly doesn't sound like a man who had any firsthand knowledge of primitive life, or ever wanted to have any. He speaks, for instance, of something being familiar "to the crude intelligence not only of the savage, but of ignorant and dull-witted people everywhere." *The Golden Bough* is really a work of classical scholarship that uses a very large amount of illustrative material from anthropology and folklore. In the

course of his classical reading, Frazer came across a custom in
Roman life that puzzled him, and as he pondered it, the work
of Robertson Smith on the Bible and of Mannhardt in Germany began to suggest hundreds of parallels to it; and finally
the puzzling Roman custom became the key to a vast amount
of ritual, myth, folklore, superstition, and religious belief all
over the world. So it was that his essay on *The Golden Bough*,
which first appeared in 1890, had expanded to three volumes
by 1900, and into twelve, in the usual format, by 1915—a
book of about 4000 pages. The length of the book is the result
of the enormous mass of material collected as evidence: if you
know only the one-volume abridgment he made in 1922, you
haven't really missed much of the main argument. He was a
disciple of Darwin in believing that if you were going to be
properly scientific, for every statement you had to choke your
reader with examples and illustrations, and his text walks over
a thick pile carpet of footnotes from Greek and Latin literature, from the Old Testament, which Frazer read in Hebrew,
from monographs and periodicals in English, French, German, Italian, and Dutch.

Near Rome, in the time of the Caesars, there was a grove
sacred to the goddess Diana, in which there was a runaway
slave who was called the priest of the grove and the King of the
Wood. When he got there he found his predecessor in charge,
and what he had to do was to break a branch off a certain tree,
then attack and kill his predecessor. Then he was King of the
Wood until some other runaway slave did the same thing to
him. Why was there such a custom? That was the question
that started Frazer off on the twelve-volume journey that
another anthropologist, Malinowski, has called "the greatest
scientific Odyssey in modern humanism."

Frazer begins by explaining that magic is the belief that you
can affect things either by imitating them or by getting hold of
part of them. If you have an enemy, magic suggests that you
imitate killing him, say by sticking pins in a wax image of him,
or that you get something belonging to him, like a lock of his
hair, and then injure that. Primitive tribes take a magical view
of their leader or king. As long as he's strong and virile, the

tribe will hold together and their food supply will be steady: if he gets old and feeble, so will the crops. So magic reasons that a king ought to be killed when his strength fails. It sounds like a funny way of preserving his strength, but the idea is to transfer it to his successor and distribute what's left over to the tribe. Magic assumes that you can get the qualities of something by eating it; so if you want the magic strength of the king, you eat his body and drink his blood.

Out of this pattern of ritual a great number of religions have developed, mostly around the Mediterranean Sea. The central figure is a god conceived in the form of a young man, who represents the fertility of the seasons in general and of the crops in particular. Hence, his body and blood become identified with the two chief products of the crops, bread and wine. At the center of this religion is a ritual representing the death and rebirth of the god, usually lasting three days. The god was called Adonis in Syria, Attis in Asia Minor, Osiris in Egypt, Dionysus in Greece, Balder in the North. There are also a great number of folk customs surviving among the European peasantry that feature similar figures, like the King and Queen of the May. Originally, Frazer thinks, these gods or mythical figures were represented by human beings who were sacrificed, and in peasant customs, even in children's games, there are many mock executions that at one time weren't mock at all.

An immense number of side issues are explored and problems solved, or at any rate fascinating guesses made, in every field of mythology and folklore. There is the "scapegoat" ritual, for instance, where an old man or woman who represents death and sterility is killed or driven away. There is the symbolism springing from the use of a temporary or mock king to serve as a substitute for the real one: he has a brief reign and is then executed, and this figure survives in all the lords of misrule and kings of the carnival in medieval Europe, besides being involved in the mockery of Jesus in the Passion. There is the connection which gives Frazer his title between the branch broken off by the King of the Wood and the golden bough Aeneas broke off before he could visit hell in Virgil's

Aeneid. Virgil compares the golden bough to the mistletoe, and Frazer thinks it was the mistletoe, regarded as sacred in the ancient *cultus* of Europe.

Some of the side issues spill over into other books. The most important of them is the question of totemism, the identifying of a tribe with a certain animal or plant which is ceremonially eaten at stated times, and which for complicated reasons has been of great importance in developing the structure of primitive societies. Frazer's four volumes on *Totemism and Exogamy* (which means the rule that a man must marry outside his totem clan) are still an important source book for this subject. His other books are mostly in the form of compilations. As a teacher who made hosts of readers familiar with the conceptions of anthropology, Frazer is very important; as a scholar who could apply literary and scientific knowledge to the same problem, he is equally so. But as an architect of modern thought, he has to stand or fall by *The Golden Bough*.

I am not competent to discuss *The Golden Bough* as anthropology because I'm a literary critic, and I don't know any more about anthropology than the next man. Before you ask whatever possessed the CBC to get me to talk about Frazer, I should say that *The Golden Bough* seems to be at present more a book for literary critics than for anthropologists. It is, after all, a study of comparative symbolism, and one would expect that to appeal most to artists, poets, critics, and students of certain aspects of religion. When it first appeared, *The Golden Bough* was called an example of the Covent Garden school of anthropology, meaning that it was full of vegetation, Covent Garden being a market. There doesn't seem to be much of a Covent Garden school of anthropology left. I've just checked through several textbooks on anthropology to see what they said about Frazer. They were respectful enough about him as a pioneer, but it would have taken a Geiger counter to find much influence of *The Golden Bough* in them. Of course, there's a lot of fashion in such matters, but there's also a real problem involved.

Frazer often refers to what he calls the "comparative

method." In his early years, tremendous strides had been made
in biology through comparative anatomy. Those were the days
when there were stories about scientists who could reconstruct
a whole skeleton of an unknown animal from one piece of
tailbone. In the comparative study of languages, too, a
fascinating new world had opened up. But to make valid
comparisons you have to know what your primary categories
are. If you are studying natural history, no matter how
fascinated you may be by anything that has eight legs, you
can't just lump together an octopus and a spider and a string
quartet. Now it is the anthropologist's business, as I understand it, to study individual cultures: those are his primary
categories. So when Frazer compares rituals all over the world
without telling us anything about the societies they fit into, he
is not doing what many anthropologists, at least at present,
have much interest in doing. At the same time, he is doing
precisely what the student of symbolism, looking for the
recurrence of a certain symbolic theme through all the world's
cultures, wants to see done.

To appreciate *The Golden Bough* for what it is we have to
see it as a kind of grammar of the human imagination. Its
value is in its central idea: every fact in it could be questioned
or reassessed without affecting that value. We don't have to
assume that once upon a time everybody everywhere used to
eat their kings and then gradually evolved slightly less repulsive customs. Frazer's ritual is to be thought of as something
latent in the human imagination: it may have been acted out
literally sometimes, but it is fundamentally a hypothesis that
explains features in rituals, not necessarily the original ritual
from which all others have derived. *The Golden Bough* isn't
really about what people did in a remote and savage past; it is
about· what the human imagination does when it tries to
express itself about the greatest mysteries, the mysteries of life
and death and afterlife. It is a study, in other words, of
unconscious symbolism on its social side, and it corresponds to
and complements the work that Freud and Jung and others
have done in psychology on unconscious symbolism on its
individual side, in dreams and the like. It is extraordinary how

closely Frazer's patterns fit the psychological ones. Frazer's dying gods are very like the libido figures of Freudian dreams; the old men and women of Frazer's scapegoat rituals correspond to Freud's parental imagos; the temporary kings of the carnival are the social forms of what Freud has studied in the mind as the mechanism of wit.

A ritual, in magic, is done for practical purposes, to make the crops grow, to baffle enemies, to bring rain or sunshine or children. In religion, a ritual expresses certain beliefs and hopes and theories about supernatural beings. The practical results of magic don't work out; religious beliefs disappear or change in the twilight of the gods. But when deprived of both faith and works, the ritual becomes what it really is, something made by the imagination, and a potential work of art. As that, it can grow into drama or romance or fiction or symbolic poetry. Poetry, said Aristotle, is an imitation of nature, and the structures of literature grow out of the patterns that the human mind sees in or imposes on nature, of which the most important are the rhythms of recurrence, the day, the month, the four seasons of the year. Poets can get from Frazer a new sense of what their own images mean, and critics can learn more from him about how the human imagination has responded to nature than from any other modern writer.

For the student of religion, *The Golden Bough* is of immense value in showing the positive importance of myth. Up to Frazer's time, interest in religion was confined mainly to theology or to history, and myth was felt to be just something that wasn't true—something all the *other* religions had. But now we can see more clearly how religion can appeal to the imagination as well as to faith or reason. Frazer's god-eating ritual is a kind of primitive parody of Christianity and shows us how magic and superstition, even in their weirdest forms, can be seen as gropings toward a genuine religious understanding.

In Oxford, Frazer used to be referred to as "the Cambridge fellow who can write," and it is certainly true that he can write. He can take a great inert mass of evidence and with a few selective touches make it into a lively narrative that keeps you turning the pages into the small hours. Of course, people who can't write are not only apt to be jealous of people who can, but often believe quite sincerely that anybody who is readable must be superficial. That is why you get so many sniffy remarks about Frazer's "highly imaginative" or "picturesque" style in books that are a lot harder to get through than his are. But no matter what happens to the subjects he dealt with, Frazer will always be read, because he can be. There are other aspects of his style I don't care so much for. He's fond of relapsing into fine writing, and when he does, he goes in for a kind of languid elegance that reminds one of a heroine of a Victorian novel about to expire with refinement and tight corsets. But for sheer power to organize material he ranks in the first class, with Gibbon or Macaulay, and a more recent encyclopedic writer, Toynbee, has learned a lot from him.

I would not say that Frazer was a great thinker. Like Darwin, he got hold of one tremendous intuition and spent his life documenting it, but apart from that he had a rather commonplace mind. People often believe that if a man spends his time among books he will lose contact with life: actually this very seldom happens, but it is true that Frazer looks at the world through a study window. In all his work I have found only one specific expression of interest in the events of his own day, a letter urging the union of England and France, and even that was published twenty years after it was written. He gives the impression of a Victorian liberal of a somewhat vague and sentimental kind. The theory of evolution popularized the idea that man had developed from lower forms of life, and it was easy to extend that to a theory of progress, to seeing man as still developing out of savagery into higher and higher civilization. A lot of people still think that biological evolution and historical progress are the same thing, and that one is the scientific proof of the other. Frazer thought so too, and he never doubted that man had gone steadily up an escalator from ape-man through savagery to twentieth-century Cambridge.

Now Frazer's "comparative method" is one that puts together myths from the ancient world, customs from contemporary primitive societies, and survivals of ancient beliefs in our own day. Such a method obviously hasn't anything historical about it and can hardly justify him in making any historical statements. But still, there is a historical framework to his book that is provided by his Darwinian escalator. All human societies, he believes, belong at certain points on this escalator, from the lowest, like the African bushmen, to the highest, like us. Societies that are on the same level will behave in pretty much the same way, no matter how far apart they are. This is the principle he relies on when he compares rituals that are vastly remote in time and space. In the final pages of *The Golden Bough*, Frazer ties this theory up. He suggests that there have been three ages of man: an age of magic, an age of religion, and an age of science, the last one just beginning.

Magic, Frazer says, is psychologically much the same thing as science. The magician's aim, like the scientist's, is a practical and secular aim: he believes that nature obeys fixed laws, and he tries to turn those laws to his own advantage. The difference between magic and science is not in attitude, but in the fact that magic is wrong about natural law and science right. Because the magician's notions of nature are crude, magic doesn't work, and so man turns from magic to religion, which for Frazer is a belief in mysterious external powers that man thinks he can either placate or get on his side. It is our job now to outgrow religion—Frazer isn't very explicit about this, but that is clearly what he means—and enter on an age of science, or true magic. In a series of lectures called *Psyche's Task*, he says that many of the fundamentals of civilization today, respect for government, for private property, for marriage, and for human life, grew out of primitive superstition, and all we have to do is separate the superstition in them from their rational sense.

One thinks of G. K. Chesterton's remark about the Victorians who saw the whole of human history in the form of one of their own three-volume novels, sure that they were the third volume and that history was turning out well because it was turning out with them. I imagine that not many scholars today would endorse Frazer's view that magic has always and everywhere preceded religion: it seems clear that magic and religion start off together. If there is any intermediate stage between magic and science, it isn't religion, which is quite distinct from both, but such things as alchemy and astrology. Also, there is a lot in magic—its dependence on tradition and authority, its secrecy, its emotional and dramatic elements—that make it something very different from any kind of rationalism, however crude. And if magic is just wrong science, surely primitive societies have and apply a lot of very sound knowledge of nature, which is scientific according to Frazer's definition—if they didn't they would starve to death.

As for the happy ending of his three-volume novel, outgrowing religion and becoming reasonable and scientific about everything doesn't sound like much of a program for the world in 1958. One person that Frazer seems to have had absolutely no use for was Freud, in spite of the fact that Freud based one of his books, *Totem and Taboo*, on Frazer's work. Maybe this was just prudery, but why should a man handling Frazer's kind of material be prudish? The answer seems clearly to be that Freud's discoveries about what is going on inside civilized man today makes one feel a lot more doubtful about this being an age of reason. For Frazer, it was fine for savages to be brutal and incestuous, but for well-dressed people in the nineteenth century to be full of brutal and incestuous impulses was a reflection on progress. True, Frazer often warns us that our civilization is a very thin veneer on top of what is really savagery and superstition still. But by this he appears to mean that outside the cities and universities there is a countryside full of people who want to sow their fields at the new moon and sacrifice a cat to make the crops grow. It never seems to occur to him that there might be things just as silly and more dangerous in civilization and progress themselves.

It seems a curious trick of fate that made Frazer the influence he is today. He was an old-fashioned agnostic who revolutionized our understanding of religion. He was a devotee of what he thought was a rigorous scientific method who profoundly affected the imagery of modern poetry. He was a believer in progress through reason who has told us more than any other man, except perhaps the Freud he disapproved of, about the symbolism of the unconscious. In a way he's not so much an architect of modern thought as of modern feeling and imagination. But one of the great discoveries of modern thought is that feeling and imagination are inseparably a part of thought, that logic is only one of many forms of symbolism. And that is a discovery Frazer helped to make.

WORLD ENOUGH WITHOUT TIME

For some twenty-five years, a group of scholars have met each summer on the shores of Lake Maggiore in Italy to hold a conference in a field that might loosely be described as comparative religion, though what gets compared is, more precisely, the morphology of symbolism. This annual conference has been given the name Eranos: its papers are published in Eranos *Jahrbucher*, and three selections of them have appeared in English. The third, *Man and Time*, is assembled mainly from the 1951 session. The general direction of Eranos is Jungian, and structures of symbolism are seen as emanating from a collective unconscious through a consciousness which has accepted the Jungian shift from a rational ego, opposed to the unconscious, to an individuality in rapport with it. The latter is able to manifest the unconscious in the form of the archetypes, or psychological symbols, which it uses to express itself, in contrast to the logical and discursive structures of rational consciousness.

It must be great fun to attend these Eranos conferences; the published papers have much of value in them, and no one can reasonably deny that Jung is one of the seminal thinkers of our time. This is, however, an age of charismatic leaders in culture

Review of *Man and Time: Papers from the Eranos Yearbooks*, ed. Joseph Campbell, trans. Ralph Manheim and R. F. C. Hull (New York: Pantheon, 1957); and of five books by Mircea Eliade: *Cosmos and History: The Myth of the Eternal Return*, trans. Willard Trask (New York: Harper, 1959); *Birth and Rebirth* (New York: Harper, 1958); *Patterns in Comparative Religion*, trans. Rosemary Sheed (New York: Sheed and Ward, 1958); *The Sacred and the Profane: The Nature of Religion*, trans. Willard Trask (New York: Harcourt, Brace, 1959); *Yoga: Immortality and Freedom*, trans. Willard Trask (New York: Pantheon, 1958). Reprinted by permission from *The Hudson Review*, vol. 12, no. 3 (Autumn 1959). © 1959 by The Hudson Review, Inc.

and thought as well as in action, and such a leader has two types of followers: the centrifugal ones who find his ideas useful and apply them in their own work, and the centripetal ones who keep revolving around the Master expounding his message for our times. The disastrous effects of making Marx into an intellectual charismatic leader are now patent to the free world; and in Marxism today one finds a good deal of straightforward science mixed up with inspirational harangues on the relation of dialectic materialism to the theory of atomic structure or the consistency of neo-Lamarckian genetics with Marxism-Leninism. (You argue that both are in accord with modern science, and things equal to the same thing, etc.) And in *Man and Time*, too, there is a good deal of the same type of thing produced by what might be called Jungian commissars. Thus, the opening paper, on "Art and Time," by Eric Neumann, hardly contains a genuine statement about either art or time: it is an elegy on the dilemma of modern man and the crisis of the human spirit and the collapse of the aggressive consciousness in the modern psyche and the rise of the Terrible Mother and all the rest of the Jungian *topoi*, with an occasional gesture in the direction of modern artists asserting that their work illustrates and proves all this. The difference between such homiletic and that of, say, Max Nordau's *Degeneration* in the last century is that the rhetorical tone has shifted from the paternal and indignant to the maternal and solicitous, and that the references are less concrete, if less wrongheaded. Of any positive problem about art and time, such as the treatment of time in Proust or *Finnegans Wake* or the Eliot *Quartets* or Auden's *For the Time Being* or their counterparts in Continental literature (Rilke gets quoted, but not for anything he said about time), we hear nothing. It is an occupational disease of preachers, whether of the pulpit, the soapbox, or the lectern, to proclaim the superiority of their anxieties to all phases of human culture that are not equally obsessed by them, and there is a failure in urbanity here which seems to me more significant than it looks: we shall keep it in mind as we proceed.

Two other lay sermons, Helmuth Plessner's "On the Relation

of Time to Death" and G. van der Leeuw's "Primordial Time and Final Time," are sufficiently described by their titles. There are also two papers on time in science. One, Adolf Portmann's "Time in the Life of the Organism," talks mainly about what we used to call instinct in the birds and the bees and about the "hallowed character of lunar animals," including women, who respond organically to a lunar cycle. A more elaborate paper, Max Knoll's "Transformations of Science in Our Age," lines up parallels between Jungian psychology and modern science. There is, for example, a principle of indeterminacy in Heisenberg's version of the quantum theory and a "relation of uncertainty" between conscious and unconscious in Jungian psychology, because even Jungians don't claim to know *all* about the unconscious. There are more interesting things in this paper, but some of the analogies are unnerving.

It is characteristic of disciples that they are never quite up to date: it takes all the running *they* can do to keep in the same place. Actually the Master has announced a new theme for his discussion, the theme of "synchronicity," or coincidence. A really staggering coincidence has about it, Jung says, a strong quality of the numinous. We feel simultaneously that there must be some explanation and that any explanation would be useless to us because it couldn't fit into our customary thinking apparatus. In fact, we may almost define a coincidence as a piece of design that we can't use. However, many structures of thought, from astrology and other forms of divination to certain types of mysticism, have been based on the conception of synchronicity. The conception is one way of trying to impose pattern on the pure flux of our ordinary experience of time, the Heraclitean river into which no one steps twice. Its postulate is that of a preestablished harmony, in contrast to the postulate of causality which underlies science, which is based on our ordinary experience of sequential time, and which we struggle vainly to apply to coincidence when we try to "explain" it. Jung's treatment of this theme is brief and somewhat inconclusive: for example, he considers no type of causation except the efficient cause of ordinary scientific method which always precedes its effect. A formal cause or Aristotelian *telos* might have more relevance to the idea. Still, it's a good speculative rubber bone to chew on and forms a basis for the really significant part of *Man and Time*: a series of scholarly essays on the conceptions of time found in various religions and cultures.

Among them is a paper on "Time and Eternity in Indian Thought" by Mircea Eliade, a scholar of Rumanian origin now in Chicago, whose books are rapidly appearing in English translation. Five of them, listed at the beginning of this review, are on my desk. They might be described as essays toward a grammar of the symbolism of religion. By "religion" I mean religion considered as a universal human cultural phenomenon, as distinct from "a" religion, which is a specific and exclusive institution, almost always claiming to result from a specific and exclusive revelation. "Religion" in this sense might be called a way of life that expresses a search for identification. As such, it does not need a personal God, for it may identify man simply with his own society through a symbol of solidarity, as in totemism or Communism. The religious tendency seeks the existential, usually some functioning institution that responds to faith and commands loyalty. In any period of crisis or uncertainty, the need for some sort of identification becomes very strong, and a great variety of objects of it are proposed, all of them advertised with much the same formula: "we're in a bad state; this is what will help." But while the pitch, so to speak, is usually thrown into discursive language, the effective appeal is through symbolism and myth; hence, all studies of "comparative religion" tend to become comparisons of mythology rather than doctrine.

The conception of a grammar of religious symbolism has haunted scholars for centuries and has had an even greater fascination for poets. Poets, in fact, are so keen about it that they will use the most fantastic books purporting to provide one, as a glance into the background of Goethe, Victor Hugo, and Yeats, to name three at random, will soon show. There are many reasons for this interest: the central one is that poetry, as

distinct from discursive language, uses the language of identification, based as it is on the metaphor, which is a relation of
identity. In Christianity, many important doctrines, such as
the divinity of Christ or the real presence or the Trinity, can
only be expressed grammatically by metaphor. There is thus a
strong natural alliance between the language of poetry (and
the imaginative language of works of culture generally) and
the aim of the religious impulse, which in the long run can find
no other speech than that of the poetic symbol. Renaissance
poets used classical mythology as a counterpoint to Christianity, making use of mythological handbooks which tried to
relate the two. Romantic poets used similar handbooks, and
poets who came of age around 1900 used everything from
elementary anthropology to Blavatskian theosophy. But of
course the great landmark in such studies was *The Golden
Bough*, ostensibly a work of anthropology, but actually a piece
of classical scholarship with anthropological illustrations. It
was promptly seized on as a work of literary criticism, which it
was: its influence on modern literature is familiar, but the
reasons for it may be less so.

The Golden Bough suggested what Christian apologists back
to the first century had been suggesting: that at the core of
primitive religion, the world over, was a parody of the
Christian sacrament. A divine king, regarded either as a god or
as the chosen son of the tribe's god, is killed at the height of his
vigor; his flesh is eaten, his blood drunk, and so his divinity
passes into the tribe and unites them in one body. In an
agricultural tribe, his flesh and blood would be identified with
the harvest and the vintage, the bread and the wine. It was not
really necessary to Frazer's argument to assume that his grisly
rite ever had anything more than a sporadic historical existence. Its real existence is as a symbolic key to a great number
of actual rituals which express some aspect of it, ranging from
cults of human sacrifice to May Day games. In a way it was
unfortunate that it should have been Frazer, with his naive
Victorian evolutionism and his top-lofty attitude toward
primitive thinking, who got the tremendous intuition of this
book. His escalator philosophy of progress, from magic

through religion to science, made him think of his symbolic pattern as immemorially archaic, instead of something constantly latent in the human mind. For *The Golden Bough* is really a study of unconscious social symbolism as expressed in ritual, and hence it is closely linked, as Freud immediately recognized, to Freudian psychology, which studies unconscious individual symbolism as expressed in dream. On this point the differences between Freud and Jung are not particularly significant, and the Jungian interest in similar patterns is reflected in the Eranos papers. Mr. Eliade's books take this interest a step farther.

Frazer's book made great use of what Frazer called, using capitals, the Comparative Method. For many anthropologists, his use of it was overenthusiastic and premature, because they were trying to relate such phenomena as vegetation myths to the cultures which produced them, instead of comparing them with each other. That was another reason why *The Golden Bough's* main influence was in literature and comparative religion rather than anthropology. Mr. Eliade clearly feels that, his own interest being in comparative religion, it is possible to revert to nineteenth-century comparative methods now that anthropology and psychology have developed their own structures and are less in danger of being twisted out of shape by an alien interest. He says in his introduction to *The Sacred and the Profane*: "There is always the risk of falling back into the errors of the nineteenth century, believing with Tylor or Frazer that the reaction of the human mind to natural phenomena is uniform. . . . But the important thing for our purpose is to bring out the specific characteristics of the religious experience, rather than to show its numerous variations and the differences caused by history." In other words, he is going back to the method of Tylor and Frazer with slightly more cautiousness and with the object of showing a uniformity in general religious symbolism which reappears as a unity in the symbolic structures of the higher religions, particularly Christianity.

Patterns in Comparative Religion is a remarkable introduction to the grammar of comparative symbolism. It suggests that in fact there is such a thing as a universal natural theology, of the type that Tylor called animism. Eliade thinks of this animism, however, not as chronologically prior to all other religions, as Tylor did, but as latent in all religious structures and the key to most of their imagery. He begins with the sky-god, which, following Father Schmidt and Dumézil, he regards as a practically universal conception. The sky-god is regularly the supreme or original god, though in the course of time intermediate figures begin to occupy the foreground of mythology, and he becomes a *dieu fainéant* without a cult, only appealed to as a last and desperate resort. We then move on to the imaginative conceptions that have been constructed out of the different aspects of nature: solar and vegetation cycles, where Frazer's work is incorporated; symbolism of trees, stones, and water; sacred places and sacred time. There is a particularly interesting chapter on "The Moon and Its Mystique," which derives an extraordinary number of imaginative patterns from the moon, notably the three-day rhythm of death, disappearance, and rebirth that turns up so often in religion.

At the heart of this animistic symbolism is the theme of death and rebirth, the theme that is studied in *The Golden Bough* in terms of social ritual and in Jung's *Symbols of Transformation* and elsewhere in terms of individual dream. The divine king is magically identified with the powers of nature, hence his death and revival is identified with the passing of the natural cycle through darkness, cold, and sterility to a new life. The king revives in two ways: within the tribe, making one body out of them, and by having his divinity transferred to a successor: the successor is thus not thought of as a different person, but as a continuation of the same power in a revitalized form. The Jungian quest is similar; the ego descends into the underworld of the unconscious, struggles with the powers of darkness and chaos it finds there, and returns as an "individual," with the same life revitalized. Eliade's other books deal chiefly with this central pattern of symbolism, and their central conception is that a renewal in time is normally thought of as a renewal of time.

In *Cosmos and History*, Eliade works out a pattern often referred to in *Man and Time*, which I assume develops out of Gunkel's classic *Schöpfung und Chaos*, with some influence from Otto's *Idea of the Holy* and perhaps some from Kierkegaard's *Repetition*. According to this book, religion is normally characterized by a revolt against living in time. Life in time, with all its failures and errors, its frustrations and sins, its loose ends, unfulfilled purposes, and postponed decisions, with the inevitability of death and the hopelessness of salvaging much, if anything, from the temporal flux, is intolerable even to the secular imagination, to say nothing of the religious one, once the anaesthetic of youth wears off. Hence the frequency of the feeling "from now on things are going to be different," the spasmodic resolutions, often made at the new year, to impose a consistent pattern of action on time. Religion meets this feeling by postulating a mythical period, usually before time began, when the essential patterns of significant action known as rituals were laid down by divine command. Hence, overriding one's confused existence in time is a sacramental pattern of regularly repeated rituals or significant acts, carried out exactly in accordance with instructions issued "once upon a time," or *in illo tempore* as Eliade says. These rituals follow the cycle of nature and incorporate its symbolism, at the center of which is the scapegoat, the symbol of the old life now to be banished forever. As religion develops, primordial time often develops a corresponding final time, an apocalypse or Last Judgment when time regains its original timelessness. In the higher religions this sacramental pattern tends to absorb increasingly the secular life. Of the higher religions, Judaism and Christianity at least have an intermediate revelation placed squarely in the middle of time itself. In Christianity the historical revolt against time was made by the Incarnation and is continued in the sacramental life of the Church. In the latter, the sense of history as a nightmare from which one keeps trying to awake, as Stephen says in *Ulysses*, is finally annihilated. The great contemporary rival of Christianity, Communism, bases most of its imaginative appeal on its promise to abolish history, or the record of class struggles, and lead mankind into a superhistorical era. In our ordinary experience of time we are dragged from a past that no longer exists toward a future that does not yet exist through a present that never quite exists. The hope of the religious impulse, whether it is committed to a God or not, is to live in a real present, a pure duration that is difficult to characterize except through some kind of paradox.

Birth and Rebirth studies the symbolism of the *rite de passage* as we find it in various rituals and religious doctrines, with particular emphasis on the aboriginal Australian variety. The ritual of initiation usually takes the form of a mimic death and resurrection, and the death is usually symbolized as being swallowed by a monster, or, less concretely, as being taken down into a dark and labyrinthine world, exposed to threatening beings, and the like. From this the initiate returns as newly born, an infant in relation to another stage of being. The ritual death has about it the symbolism of a reduction to a world of chaos, where ordinary social life disappears into what often takes the form of a carnival or period of sexual license. In the higher religions, the same pattern reappears as baptism (descent to the world of water) or as a death to the world which brings a renewed life in a pure present, where we no longer take thought for the morrow.

Yoga: Immortality and Freedom, a work of formidable scholarship, pursues the same symbolism into one of the higher religions, the Indian experimental mysticism known as yoga. In yoga, and in Hindu thought generally, the anxiety engendered by living in time is called karma, thought of as a process of causality that follows one through death to endless rebirths. The discipline of yoga requires, first, that the physical world should be reduced to chaos (maya or illusion) and that the initiate should die to the world by regarding not only his body but his ordinary consciousness as part of that chaos. The process of dying to the world is carried to extraordinary lengths and includes suspension of breath and immobilization of both body and mind. Then, through an equally thoroughgoing discipline of meditation, a new and timeless consciousness is established which is a pure present (*jivan-mukta*) and

unites one to reality or nirvana. The word *freedom* in Mr.
Eliade's title reflects the yoga doctrine that freedom and
immortality are really the same conception and can be found
only in surmounting the world of time.

It is obvious that such studies as Eliade's have an immediate
relevance to literary criticism—so immediate that a critic who
ignores this kind of work altogether is risking his competence
in his own field. It is impossible to deal adequately with
contemporary literature without some understanding of cyclical and initiatory symbolism. The sense that life in time is
imaginatively intolerable is the basis of literary existentialism,
and the free act, especially the act that asserts its freedom in
the face of death, has the same quality of triumph over time in
existentialist literature that the initiatory rite has in the
Australian bush. The initiatory rite and its symbolism recur in
every work of fiction that leaves the hero wiser than it finds
him, or endeavors to leave the reader so. We soon realize, too,
that on this point there is no difference between contemporary
and traditional literature, as such symbolic patterns have been
organizing literature from the beginning. The symbolism of
descent into chaos is as prominent in *King Lear* as in *The
Waste Land*, and sea monsters were swallowing maidens for
thousands of years before Dylan Thomas's long-legged bait.

The study of yoga recalls the growth in popularity of
Oriental themes in modern literature. This growth, unlike the
development of classical mythology centuries earlier, seems
less a matter of supplementing Christian symbolism with
another line of imagery than of replacing it with analogous
patterns. The reason for the replacement is apparently to
avoid misleading associations. The statement "the practice of
the dharma releases one from the law of karma and leads to
nirvana" does not differ greatly in substance from the statement "if you're good you'll stop being bad and will get into a
better state of mind," but it gives less of a feeling of being sent
back to Sunday school. Still, there are some genuine affinities
between the sense of spiritual autonomy in Hinduism and
Buddhism and certain types of Western individualism: one
feels the appropriateness of Thoreau's reading the Bhagavad-

gita on the Merrimac River. The techniques of Zen Buddhism, aimed at immobilizing the mind through paradox, have much in common with yoga (one would like to see Mr. Eliade do a parallel study of Zen), and again one feels that the use made of Zen in Kerouac and others has a real point, often ignored or misunderstood. The "beat" writers are trying to identify the genuine proletariat, the body of those who are excluded from the benefits of society and have sense enough to realize it. For such a proletariat, the road to freedom is not through organizing a revolution to seize power from the squares and become squares in their turn, but through breaking the current of social energy by drifting, bumming, playing jazz, taking dope, or what not, and entering the world of the pure present through the break. The beat philosophy may be wrong—that is, it may be crazy itself instead of merely making use of craziness—but its symbolism is a contemporary cultural force to be reckoned with.

Mr. Eliade has little interest in literature, and it is perhaps unreasonable to expect him to extend his already enormous erudition to include it. We are merely told in *Cosmos and History* that Eliot and Joyce used the myth of repetition, and in *Birth and Rebirth* that Eliot and Joyce use initiatory patterns of symbolism. But in *The Sacred and the Profane* it seems clear that the absence of literary parallels is not a simple omission but a deliberate exclusion. Here Mr. Eliade reverts to his theme of the sacred universe, as expressed by the primitive mind, and applied to the sacred object, the tree or stone surrounded with a sense of the numinous; the sacred place, whether an enclosed "holy ground" or a temple or city situated at the center of the world midway between heaven and hell; sacred or mythical time, of the sacramental kind already discussed, and the sanctification of life that results from all this. The sacred mind is contrasted with the profane mind of enlightened, conscious, history-absorbed modern man, who simply doesn't see any sacred significance in anything anywhere, who feels "he will not be truly free until he has killed the last god," and whose literature is full of "camouflaged" myths designed only to "kill time."

The Sacred and the Profane is not exactly a preachy book, but it comes the nearest of the five to setting out the author's own views, and it displays the same kind of almost frightening insensitivity to culture that we noted at the beginning as characteristic of preachers of anxiety. For surely the contrast is not simply between the sacred and the profane, but also between the projected and the contained. Sacred trees and stones, cities at the navel of the earth, a primordial time of the gods, are all projections, and it would be the silliest kind of self-hypnosis to try to talk ourselves into accepting such projections again. The difference between superstition and religion, which seems to disappear from Mr. Eliade's argument, is that in religion such feelings are transferred from the physical to the spiritual world, from outer time and space to inner experience. The development of culture, especially literature, which cuts off the projecting of the imagination by appealing directly to the sense of imaginative coherence itself, is of immense help in the development of a higher religion and is probably essential to it. It is not merely that science has destroyed the sense of sacredness in time and space, but that poetry has recovered it for the world to which it really belongs. As for killing the last god, any god who can die is better dead, and I see no reason for thinking that myths are more camouflaged in modern movies than they are in Old Testament history. Mr. Eliade is very far from being a Jungian disciple, but he shows a similar desire to oversimplify our present situation into a dilemma, and a similar impatience with the effort of literature to turn away from crisis and commitment and devote itself to purifying the imaginative dialect of the tribe. It is a curious irony, revealing much about the general dither of our time, that such work as his should be primarily of literary importance.

TOTAL IDENTIFICATION

Professor Northrop's ambitious attempt to provide a philosophical basis for the union of Eastern and Western thought has attracted a good deal of attention. It is the work of an average but active intelligence, well informed on its own subject, which is philosophy; and though his grasp of history and art is less sure, it would be a very unusual erudition indeed which could derive no profit from all the information he provides about causation in Aristotle, the person in St. Thomas, the metaphysical assumptions underlying Renaissance science and the way that nuclear physics has affected them, the relation between Oriental philosophy and art, and the place of Mexico in the contemporary scene. The real value of the book is, I think, as a quarry of such information, and the fact that I find its thesis inconclusive does not, for me, affect that value. The style is a lecturer's style, ranging from lucid exposition to a habit of wordy repetitiveness doubtless acquired from watching difficult ideas bounce off faces of sleepy undergraduates.

The author quotes a Mexican writer as saying that American civilization is Utopian in shape. The postulates of American democracy are, on a social and moral plane, both admirable in their idealism and practicable in their application; but above that plane certain limitations begin to appear. The principles of the American constitution do not provide a cultural synthesis comprehensive enough to make an integral place for, in particular, the arts, philosophy, and religion. There is unity in American civilization; there is not enough in its culture. In

Review of F. S. C. Northrop, *The Meeting of East and West* (New York: Macmillan, 1946). Reprinted from *The Canadian Forum*, vol. 26 (March 1947).

American education, the various subjects of study are autonomous and separate, the central principles common to them
being lost; American taste in the arts inclines either to the
highbrow and insulated, or the lowbrow and barbarous; and
the God in whom American coins trust is a vague haze of
benignant morality.

Hence, for many American thinkers today the gigantic
synthesis of religion, philosophy, science, and politics achieved
in the Middle Ages looms up in front of them like an
intellectual Utopia which complements that of their own
moral idealism. American magazines and books are thickly
strewn with admiring references to Aristotle, St. Thomas, the
seven liberal arts, and the medieval preservation of personal
values; and of deprecatory ones to the cult of self-analysis, the
dehumanizing of the individual, and the centrifugal movements in politics and science which came with the Renaissance
and sent us all skittering down the butterslide of introversion
into our present Iron Age. It is an idea which should be left to
Catholics, who know what they want to do with it; writers
who have got a phallic father or something identified with
what they call the "Puritan tradition" are apt to develop a
sloppy habit of comparing the theory of Catholicism with the
practice of Protestantism.

Professor Northrop takes over from there. He feels that the
Thomist synthesis is too full of fictions to serve for what he feels
is required today, in a world which contains Russian Communism and the cultural traditions of China and India in
addition to the great variety nearer home. To provide a basis
for global understanding, we need a supersynthesis in which
the two major elements will be a Western-democratic-scien-
tific complex on the one hand, and an Eastern-contemplative-
aesthetic complex on the other. (Russia will not be meat in this
sandwich: the author has written an article called "Impos-
sibility of a Theoretical Science of Economic Dynamics," and
has the usual academic-liberal view of Marxism.) He says that
there is a unity in Eastern thought and in Western thought;
that these differ from one another but are reconcilable. The
fundamental datum of Eastern thought is an immediate

apprehension of experience as a totality; that of the West, a theoretical construction made from experience which represents and makes intelligible its reality. The author calls the former (I think inadvisedly) an "aesthetic" and the latter a "theoretic" approach. He feels that we can reconcile them by realizing that both actually exist simultaneously in all experience, whether Western or Eastern, as a direct two-term relationship, as, for instance, "blue" exists both as a pretty color and as a light wave with a certain rate of vibration. This gets rid of the common Western fallacy of regarding the pretty color as a subjective illusion thrown up by the theoretic word, a "secondary quality" at one remove from reality.

Philosophers will have to decide on the value of this suggestion; its social and political importance, which the author is very keen on, seems to me rather doubtful. I am not sure that "mutual understanding" necessarily makes for better relations. Ten years ago, the people who best understood Nazism were those who most wanted to fight it. Today, Russians can see the drift of American imperialism far more clearly then Americans themselves, and vice versa. Tomorrow, it may well be better for Christians to believe that Mohammedans worship an idol called Mahound than to send them educated missionaries to explain that their theism should be "softened down" and "take on more of the openmindedness of Hinduism," as our author urges. Besides, achieving "one world" involves first economic unity; second, the pooling of scientific techniques; and third, political unity. When this is done it will be found that wars are no more caused by conflicts in cultural traditions than thunderstorms are caused by clouds bumping together. It is a false analogy to say that because we should surrender national sovereignty we should also give up our language and all its literary possibilities for some dismal, idiomless Esperanto; and I think that religion, philosophy, and the arts, which latter are as dependent on locale as a fine wine, are involved in that false analogy. There is no earthly reason why the world should be culturally federalized; in the USSR economic and political federation is counterbalanced by regional developments of culture, which seems to me to make

sense. Chinese painting, for example, will influence Western
painting purely through its merits as painting, not through any
Western attempt to understand Chinese cultural traditions for
political reasons.

An Easterner might say that reconciling an aesthetic with a
theoretic component of thought is itself a theoretic project, so
that to reconcile them on these terms is really to annihilate the
Eastern direct apprehension by absorbing it into a Western
theory about its "place" in a still larger apprehension. The
author says: "the specific relation between the aesthetic and
theoretic components must be determined, thereby permitting
the newly formulated world philosophy to specify the theoretical criterion by means of which the two differing cultures
. . . can be combined." The word *theoretical* in this sentence
suggests Western. The author quotes Laotze as saying "the
sage embraces oneness," but surely Laotze does not mean by
"oneness" something to be "reconciled" to what by hypothesis
is something else. He is not talking about a mode of apprehension but about total identification; he is not simply throwing
an epigram on a philosophical ammunition dump, but hinting
at a vision as far beyond the merely aesthetic or emotional (the
author rather recklessly associates these words) as it is beyond
the merely intellectual. I imagine that whenever an Oriental
philosopher tries to tell us about his Tao, his Citta, his
Nirvana, or his Brahman, he is also telling us, in Eastern
language, that an intellectual and cultural synthesis which gets
everything in and reconciles everyone with everyone else is an
attempt to build the Tower of Babel, and will lead to
confusion of utterance. He may be wrong, but Professor
Northrop will never catch him in him in his made-in-U.S.A.
net, however skillfully he throws it.

ART IN A NEW MODULATION

This book is described on the title page as "A Theory of Art Developed from *Philosophy in a New Key*." It will doubtless become, like its predecessor, something of a general favorite, as it continues to show that Mrs. Langer is a highly readable popularizer of philosophical ideas, especially the ideas of Cassirer, to whose memory the book is dedicated. The style assumes the privileges of a public character: it is breezy, good-humored, colloquial, and occasionally swashbuckling. It is a refreshing change from the sort of aesthetics that either begins, like old-fashioned ethics, with some highly provincial legislation about what art ought to do, and then goes on to smear the art that doesn't do it, or else, in struggling to reach some vast generalization about what art as a whole *does* do, passes over its infinite variety of moods and experiences.

There are two opposed but equally indefensible views about the relation of art to reality. One is the vulgar conception of "imitation" as directly reproducing the outer world or an inner experience. According to this view, painting is essentially representation, dancing the direct expression of what the dancer really feels, and so on. The other is the conception of art as make-believe or magic which produces a trancelike state by a deliberately raised hallucination. The golden mean of Mrs. Langer's argument is a conception that she calls semblance or illusion, and identifies both with the German term *Schein* and with Aristotle's *mimesis*. She avoids the latter word because, she says, it is too close to the representational fallacy. One would think that *illusion* was at least as close to the

Review of Susanne K. Langer, *Feeling and Form* (New York: Scribner's, 1953). Reprinted by permission from *The Hudson Review*, vol. 6, no. 2 (Summer 1953). © 1953 by The Hudson Review, Inc.

trance-fallacy, but Mrs. Langer seems content with it, and distinguishes the trance-fallacy as *de*lusion. Thus, painting is a spatial art, but it is neither a representation of real space, which is not pictorial, nor does it belong in a separate spatial world which is not real. It is the illusion or semblance of space, or what Mrs. Langer calls virtual space.

Mrs. Langer goes on to show that the major arts can be classified according to the virtual fields that they occupy. As painting presents virtual space, so music presents virtual time, which, like Wyndham Lewis before her, she links with Bergson's *durée réelle*. Verbal art, or what she calls poesis, she divides into literature proper and drama. The former is a semblance of the past, or virtual memory, the latter a semblance of the future, virtual act or destiny. Sculpture is the semblance of organic form; architecture gives her more trouble, but is finally called an "ethnic domain." Dance—this is perhaps the sharpest of her insights—is a field of virtual power: it presents the illusion of human life as force or physical energy, which explains why it is so dominant an art in primitive society, where the mysterious powers of gods or of magic are central data of imaginative experience. The film Mrs. Langer believes to be a new art—she mentions the shadow plays of Turkey and Java, but evidently does not regard them as affiliated—and what it presents is virtual dream, the semblance of apparition. Because of the difference in virtual fields, two arts are never, in work of major importance, united on equal terms: one art absorbs the other, as music in Wagner absorbs poetry. She calls this the "principle of assimilation."

The function of art is to objectify feeling by creating symbols for it. By a symbol, Mrs. Langer does not mean something that directly represents a feeling, in the way that a frown represents displeasure, which she calls a symptom. Recognizing a symptom is well within the orbit of the conditioned reflex, as a dog may recognize the symptoms of anger or affection in his master's voice. The work of art is its own object, standing for itself, and unattached. Just as a name like James or John can be understood as a name apart from the people it may belong to, so a work of art can articulate or express a feeling which is a part of our total experience, whether it happens to be exactly the feeling that the artist or his audience has recently been preoccupied with or not. Understanding symbolism on this level is the prerogative of human consciousness, and the work of art is the emotional counterpart of the discursive or logical symbol on which reasoning is based. Art has, therefore, an educational importance parallel to science: it delivers us from the tyranny of inarticulate feeling, and it disciplines our sensibilities just as logic disciplines our thinking.

I see no fallacy or inconsistency in the theory itself, which may be more familiar, at least to literary critics, than Mrs. Langer realizes. The development of it, and the resulting shape of the book, have some disappointing features. The main idea is used more as a touchstone than as a central assimilating form: it is brought into the discussion of each art in turn and used to refute much the same fallacies in its criticism. One misses specific discussion of great works of art and gets too much general discussion of other critics' ideas. Sometimes this is effectively done: writers on the dance, for instance, at least the ones she quotes, seem to be a pretty inarticulate lot, and Mrs. Langer shows great tact and sympathy in translating their mooings into something more intelligible. But on the whole she is at her best when she throws the other critics away and works out an idea of her own. For instance, she interprets comedy and tragedy as expressing, respectively, the sense of the unquenchable exuberance of life and the sense of life as a contained pattern enclosed by death. These she calls the rhythms of fortune and of fate. She then seizes on the figure of the buffoon or fool as the central symbol of aggressive vitality in comedy, and the writing immediately takes on a concreteness which is often wanting elsewhere.

The least satisfactory part of the book, to me, is the section on literature. Here again she quotes critics, and the reasons for selecting these critics are not easy to follow. Her theory of literature is one that would give a good deal of importance to Proust, but instead of quoting Proust, who is always very precise when he explains what he is trying to do, she quotes some phrases from Clive Bell's book on Proust that slither around in the mind like greased weasels. She gives a curious picture of contemporary critical problems. Not all literary critics today are as confused about their subject as George Moore and Brander Matthews, and many of the matters discussed—pure poetry, significant form, the communal composition of ballads, the poetic validity of T. S. Eliot's allusiveness—are pretty dead issues by now: dead because they were never central. There is a chapter called "The Great Literary Forms," but no serious attempt is made in it to discuss the problems of literary genre. She seems ill at ease with the subject, and we find that different questions are apt to get the same answer, and that a rather circular one. Why is direct narration often useful in describing the events of prose fiction? "Because it projects them at once into the experiential mode, and assures their essentially literary form." Why may a work of nonfiction, such as an essay, be called literary? Because, "whenever it is well done, it meets a standard which is essentially literary, i.e., an artistic standard."

Mrs. Langer has deliberately adopted "the practical rule of treating a problem that belongs to several arts only in connection with the one which exhibits it most perfectly." That is, she believes in the unity of art, but discusses one art after another, and so what are really unifying principles emerge in different contexts. This puts a considerable strain on the reader: it is all very well to be promised another book in which such principles will be systematically treated, but one would like a few more cross-references in this one. The "magic circle" of the round dance is the same motif as the *temenos* or marked-off holy ground in architecture, but this point is only casually suggested through a quotation. The principle of the informing cause or "commanding form," as she calls it, is a major issue in literary criticism today, but here it is discussed only in connection with music. Again, the principle that music deals with virtual time and literature with virtual memory could be used to explain how repetition, of a kind that would be intolerable in poetry itself, can be a structural principle of music. Some reference to this would, I think, have made her discussion of song and opera considerably clearer. She raises the question of the motif in painting, giving the rosette as her example, but passes over the question of literary motif in legend and myth, saying merely that these are "not art at all, but fantasies." She speaks of "the gratuitous and silly problem of the spectator's credulity" in the criticism of drama, but discusses the same problem at some length in connection with prose fiction.

As every poet knows, one cannot use a word without being affected by its traditional associations, and as long as *illusion* is used as a central idea about art, it will have the overtones of something opposed to *reality*, and will not cut itself loose from delusion or the acceptance of the unreal. Mrs. Langer says, for instance, "All forces that cannot be scientifically established and measured must be regarded, from the philosophical standpoint, as illusory." The question involved here is not her taste in using the word, but her conception of "art," which seems to me to have something of what is called misplaced concreteness about it. Conceived as objectified feeling alone, art is seen only as something that interrupts or displaces reality, not as a permanent part of a world constructed by humanity out of reality. The argument is weakened by a persistent attempt to separate art from its own social functions. True, Mrs. Langer says, not only that art is a unity, but "that there are no higher and lower, partial and supplementary arts," which means that the difference between pure and applied art cannot be established either. And though, speaking of the relation of poetry to discursive writing, she says, "I maintain that the difference is radical," when she stops maintaining things and looks at her data, she is willing enough to admit that prose fiction belongs to literature, that it may use "just the same discursive language we use for conversation," that it is inseparable from the "great literary order" of nonfiction, and that the transition from fiction to true exposition "may at times be a fluid transition"—in other words, there are no boundary lines and, consequently, no radical differences. But the main tendency of her argument is to insulate art as a thing by itself.

It is in architecture that this is most difficult to do. Mrs. Langer says that utilitarian factors in building, such as heating, are not architectural elements, but prudently adds a footnote saying that the architect ought not to ignore them. However that may be, it seems wrong to speak of the Empire State Building as in any sense an "illusion," and I do not understand the distinction, if she is making one, between a virtual and a real ethnic domain. In short, all the arts show us, architecture most vividly, that there are two orders of reality: the world that nature presents to us, and the world that human society constructs out of it, the world of art, science, religion, culture, and civilization. Architecture is bound up with the idea, not simply of buildings, but of the city. Mrs. Langer says "a world created as an artistic image is given us to look at, not to live in, and in this respect it is radically unlike the neurotic's 'private world.'" But the difference between neurosis and art is the difference between a private and a public world. If we think of such words as *culture* or *civilization*, we can see that we do in fact live in the world created as an artistic image. It is because of its clear reference to two orders of nature in human life that Aristotle's word *mimesis* seems to me a safer guide than even the most cautious use of *illusion* or *semblance*.

Reservations about Mrs. Langer's arguments do not add up to anything like a rejection of them. *Feeling and Form* was obviously never designed to be monumental and definitive, but to explore and search and raise new questions. In this it succeeds admirably: it is a thoroughly likeable and candid book, and as far as its appearance in the contemporary critical scene is concerned, a reviewer has nothing to do but spread out a welcome mat.

FORMING FOURS

For some time now, the Bollingen Foundation has been producing a series of books on symbolism, the unifying theme of which would have puzzled anyone who did not realize that they were mostly Jungian documents. Now, as number twenty in the series, a complete English translation of Jung, in eighteen volumes, is announced, and the first two, volumes seven and twelve, have just appeared. One is a revision of *Two Essays on Analytical Psychology* (the phrase "analytical psychology" means Jung, just as "psychoanalysis" means Freud), and the other, *Psychology and Alchemy*, is a more systematic and erudite version, with a tremendous bibliography, of the desultory work previously known in English as *The Integration of the Personality*.

Jung's conception of human personality, or what he calls the psyche, is built on a Freudian foundation of a conscious ego, trying to be rational and moral and adjusted to the demands of society and nature, and a subconscious "shadow" (not far from Freud's "id"), formed of one's suppressed or ignored desires. If the ego insists on regarding itself as wholly good and the shadow as wholly evil, the way is open for neurosis and schizophrenia: for a healthy life the ego must come to terms with the shadow and recognize its essential continuity with it. The center of the psyche then shifts back from the ego to a balancing point between ego and shadow, a point of pragmatic wisdom. The outer and inner worlds then appear as a

Review of C. G. Jung, *Two Essays on Analytical Psychology*, trans. R. F. C. Hull (New York: Pantheon, 1953); and Jung, *Psychology and Alchemy*, trans. R. F. C. Hull (New York: Pantheon, 1953). Reprinted by permission from *The Hudson Review*, vol. 6, no. 4 (Winter 1954). © 1953 by the Hudson Review, Inc.

world of power and a world of love, respectively, which the pragmatic wisdom in the center of the human trinity tries to hold together. The outer psyche now becomes a "persona," or social mask, and the inner one a "soul," or focus of love. If the outward formation of the psyche is that of a man, the soul is a female "anima"; if it is a woman, the soul becomes a masculine and rationalizing "animus," often taking the form of a group. The problem now is to prevent the center of pragmatic wisdom from becoming absorbed into either persona or anima. If this happens, they will become autonomous "complexes" (a word of Jung's invention). A dominating persona, or superiority complex, is the natural danger of an extroverted temperament: it may turn one into a stuffed shirt with a bad temper, for the word *hypocrite* is really a synonym of persona, and the bad temper is the revenge of the neglected anima. Introverts (the words *introvert* and *extrovert* are also Jung's) are more in danger of an "inferiority complex," the anima-dominated life of a social craven.

But if persona and anima are kept in balance and each limited to its proper function, the natural result is the release of two deeper powers from the unconscious, which move up to reinforce them. These correspond approximately to the parental figures of Freud's later essays on the ego and id, and are called by Jung the Great Mother and the magician or wise old man. Here there is still a possibility of becoming absorbed in one function or the other, but on this third level the absorption would make one a leader or spellbinder ("mana-personality"), either of the sage type or of the hero type, depending on whether the absorption is inward into the mother or outward into the father (in a woman these directions would be reversed). If the psyche successfully navigates this third crisis, the center of the personality has finally been transferred from the ego to a "self" which is the real center. The four "archetypes," or semi-autonomous personalities which the psyche has partly created and partly evoked, now settle into the four functions of psychic life: thought, feeling, intuition, and sensation. (At least I think they do, but this point comes somewhere in between the two books, and Jung's argument here may be less symmetrical than my account of it.) The self is now the center of a circle with four cardinal points, and this fourfold circle appears everywhere in religion, art, and private dreams as the diagram called the "mandala." A simple Western example is a picture of Christ as the fourfold Word of God, surrounded by the four "beasts" of Revelation, later identified with the four Gospel narrators. The whole process of shifting the center to the true self Jung calls "individuation," or, sometimes, "transformation."

Of the differences between Jung's thought and Freud's, there are two that concern us just now. All modern scientific analysis of the psyche must, of course, be rooted in therapeutic techniques for helping the mentally ill to function at least normally, whatever normally means. Jung believes, however, that the ordinary medical analogies of diagnosis, treatment, and cure are not adequate for the psychologist. The physical body nearly always matures in about twenty years, but in most people the psyche remains largely undeveloped throughout life, though it possesses within it a force of growth toward the "individuation" which is its peculiar maturity. This growing force within the psyche is what Jung, in contrast to Freud, means by libido, and, being a biological force, it behaves teleologically, just as an acorn behaves as though it intended to become an oak tree. When a psychologist tries to help a neurotic, he is helping to release this power of growth, and he ought to realize that any "cure" is only one stage in the process he has started going.

Secondly, the drama of individuation does not take place entirely within the individual. The archetypes come into the individual from a "collective unconscious," inherited from our ancestors and extending over present-day society. Hence the dreams and fantasies of the individual should not be interpreted solely in relation to his personal life: they are also individual manifestations of a mythopoeic activity found in everbody; and private analysis should be supplemented by an objective study of the analogies between the patient's mythopoeia and that of the art, folklore, mythology, and romance of human beings generally. In Jung, as in Proust, the study of the psychology of the mind leads to the discovery that men are "titans in time" and that their creative powers rise from an essentially timeless world.

This at once raises the question: if the self is established at the center of the personality, and the center implies a circle, what and where is the circumference of that circle, if it is not to be confined to the individual? Of course by hypothesis nobody can establish the boundary of an "unconscious." But Jung is finally, in contrast to his former attitude, beginning to assert explicitly that "there could just as well be layers *above* consciousness." In this context his maturing psychic process latent in the "normal" mind has close analogies with Indian yoga and the Chinese Tao, and his conception of a self which is the opposite of the ego seems to lead logically toward the Hindu Atman or the Buddhist Citta, in which the self becomes fully enlightened by realizing its identity with a total self, an indivisible unity of God, man, and the physical world. This conception is the basis of Aldous Huxley's "perennial philosophy," the mystic's axiom "Thou art That."

In Christianity it would correspond to the final integration of man into the body of Christ, Christ being not simply God and the creator of nature but a God who is also Man. Jung gives a good deal of attention to the Oriental analogues to his thought, especially Taoism, but his attitude toward Christianity is more devious. The doctrine of an "immortal soul" he rejects, as the soul in his system is the anima, a part of the undeveloped ego which is eventually dissolved into a function of an obviously mortal individual. However, they told me at Sunday school that the Christian view of immortality was based on the conception of a spiritual body, not of a bodiless soul, and Jung may not have got this doctrine quite right.

Catholic theology supplies a set of existential or objective counterparts to the archetypes of the unconscious (the Father-God, the Mother Church, the Virgin, and the Son manifest in the world), and this enables the believing Catholic to project his archetypes, and so attain a pragmatic balance between his inner and outer worlds. For all those who feel compelled to regard these personal entities as psychological fictions, the archetypes have to be dealt with in the psyche itself. This is very difficult to do, and the upheavals of mass neurosis in the twentieth century are the result. The Catholic solution is, Jung feels, whether actually true or not, psychologically the easiest and for most people still the best, but Jung's own "individuation" is closer to a visionary tradition which runs through Meister Eckhart and after the Reformation is mainly Protestant, apppearing in Paracelsus, Boehme, Blake, and some of the Anabaptists and Quakers. But Lutheran and Calvinist Protestantism tend to rest on a simple contrast between a good God and a sinful man, and thus project, not the archetypes, but the original tension between ego and shadow which leads to neurosis. The idea of God as the "wholly other," in which regeneration becomes a kind of drama within the Trinity which man is somehow in but not of, is evidently regarded by Jung as his chief theological opponent.

This exposition ignores a few nonfunctional inconsistencies which seem to have an emotional origin. There is, to use his own term, a complex in Jung's mind that makes him balk like a mule in front of the final acceptance of the totality of the self, the doctrine that everybody is involved in the fate of everybody else, which the uncompromising charity of the great religions invariably insists on. His "collective unconscious" is actually the total mythopoeic power of humanity and has nothing to do with ancestor cults of "racial differentiation," or groping around in the windy bowels of Teutonic exclusivism. But the explicit affirmation of this obvious fact seems to stick in his throat like the *amen* in Macbeth's, although his intelligence has to proceed exactly as though it had been made anyway. We simply have to step over such passages as a footnote in the *Two Essays* in which he says he's not anti-Semitic: he just thinks "it is a quite unpardonable mistake to accept the conclusions of a Jewish psychology as generally valid. Nobody would dream of taking Chinese or Indian psychology as binding upon ourselves." Well, he does, and if by "Jewish psychology" he means Freud, he has certainly accepted plenty of its validity for his own system.

When Jung began to supplement the purely analytical

interpretation of dreams with a hermeneutic study of the analogies to dreams in myth and romance, the result was a most important study, soon to be republished in this series as volume five, *Symbols of Transformation*. It was previously known in English as *The Psychology of the Unconscious*, although its original title, *Wandlungen und Symbole der Libido*, gives a much better idea of its contents. Just as the "individuation process" became the informing principle of his psychology, so the mythopoeic counterpart to it, the hero's quest, became the informing principle that Jung, with some help from Frobenius, perceived in myth, folklore, and literature. The heroic quest has the general shape of a descent into darkness and peril followed by a renewal of life. The hero is confronted by a dragon or power of darkness who guards a treasure or threatens a virgin. He is often accompanied by a shadowy companion who seems to be a double of himself, and is given counsel by a magician, an old woman, or a faithful animal, the last being a regular symbol of unconscious powers. The hero kills the dragon, or sometimes, as in the story of Jonah and the Harrowing of Hell, disappears into its body and returns, often finding, as Beowulf does, that the most dangerous aspect of his enemy is a sinister female principle, whom Jung calls the "terrible mother" and links with the fear of incest and other erotic regressions.

In any case, the accomplishing of his quest gains him his bride, the dragon's hoard, or both. The double-edged power of the archetypes for good or evil is reflected in the stock black-and-white patterns of romantic characters: there is a wise old man and an evil magician, a solicitous mother and a wicked stepmother, a heroine and a siren or temptress, a hero and a traitorous companion. One can see in the quest-myth, too, not simply a psychic allegory but a kind of geotropism as well, as the heroic quest catches the cyclic rhythm of nature, the sun setting and reappearing from the body of a dark, monstrous underworld the next day, and, every year, transforming the sterility of winter and raising new life from underground. Thus, the salvation of the individual soul, the religious myth of a Messiah or redeeming God, and the renewal of energy in nature all seem to be contained in a single mythopoeic framework. At the same time there is a dialectic in the quest, not a passage from death to revival, but a transformation to a new and timeless life, which means that in the final analysis the dragon or enemy of the quest is the cycle of time and nature itself, symbolized by the ouroboros, or serpent with his tail in his mouth.

The themes and patterns of this book are strikingly similar to those of Frazer's *Golden Bough*. I think there is an explanation for the similarity, but I have first to explain my explanation. Literary criticism, as a science, is obviously a social science, but the social sciences are so recent in their development that they have not been clearly separated even yet. Thus *The Golden Bough* was intended to be a book on anthropology, but it was also a book on literary criticism, and seems to have had far more influence in literature than in its alleged field. Perhaps the reason is that, in extracting a single type of ritual from a great variety of cultures, Frazer has done what the anthropologist, with his primary interest in cultural pattern, cannot do—if I may speak under correction of a science I know very little about—but he has also done precisely what the literary critic, with *his* interest in ritual pattern, wants to see done. Similarly, Jung's book on libido symbols extracts a single dream type from a great variety of individuals, all except one unanalyzed and many of them not even identified. Again, he has done something which may be largely meaning-less to most therapeutic psychologists, but places the book squarely within the orbit of literary criticism. It has thus become, along with *The Golden Bough*, a cornerstone of archetypal criticism, and it appears to have made more stir among the literary critics who happen to be, like the girls in *Finnegans Wake*, "yung and easily freudened," than among psychologists—though again I speak under correction. At any rate, Jung seems to be leading Freud's great discoveries in the direction of a firsthand study of literature, whereas Freudian criticism iteslf, even Freud's own brilliant essay on Leonardo, tends to take us away from the works of art into the biography of the artist, and so, like many other forms of research, to neglect real criticism in favor of the peripheral darkness of "more light."

Archetypal criticism is that mode of criticism which treats the poem, not as an imitation of nature, but as an imitation of other poems. It studies conventions and genres and the kind of recurrent imagery which connects one poem with another. The archetype is thus primarily the *communicable* symbol, and archetypal criticism deals with literature as a social fact and as a technique of communication. To an Aristotelian critic, poetry exists, as Sidney says, between the example and the precept. The events of a poem are exemplary and general, hence there is a strong element of recurrence in them. The ideas are precepts, or statements of what might be or ought to be, hence there is a strong element of desire in them. These elements of recurrence and desire come into the foreground with archetypal criticism. From this point of view, the narrative aspect of literature is a recurrent act of symbolic communication: in other words, a ritual. The narrative content of a poem is studied by the archetypal critic as ritual or imitation of action, and not simply as a *mimesis praxeos* or imitation of *an* action. Similarly, the significant content is the conflict of desire and reality which has for its basis the work of the dream. Hence it is inevitable that the archetypal critic would find much of interest in the work done by contemporary anthropology in ritual and by contemporary psychology in dreams.

Archetypes are most easily studied in highly conventionalized literature, which means, for the most part, naive, primitive, or popular literature. It attempts to extend the kind of comparative study now made of folktales and ballads into the rest of literature and seizes on the primitive and popular formulas in great art: the formulas of Shakespeare's last period, or the book of Revelation, with its fairy tale about a damsel in distress, a hero killing dragons, a wicked witch, and a wonderful city glittering with jewels. We may distinguish two kinds of archetypes: structural or narrative archetypes with a ritual content, and modal or emblematic archetypes with a dream content. The former are most easily studied in drama: not, as a rule, in the drama of the educated audience and the settled theater, but in naive or spectacular drama: the folk play, the puppet show, the pantomime, the farce, the pageant, and their descendants in masque, comic opera, and commercial movie. Modal archetypes are best studied first in naive romance, which includes the folktales and fairy tales that are so closely related to dreams of wonderful wishes coming true and to nightmares of ogres and witches.

Frazer's *Golden Bough* is, as literary criticism, an essay on the ritual content of naive drama: that is, it reconstructs an archetypal ritual from which the structural and generic principles of drama may be logically derived. It does not matter two pins to the critic whether this ritual ever had any *historical* existence or not. Frazer's hypothetical ritual would inevitably have many and striking analogies to actual rituals, and such analogies are part of his argument. But the relation of ritual to drama is a relation of content to form, not of source to derivation. Similarly, the dream content of naive romance is the communicable dream content. It has no relation to psychoanalyzing dead poets, but it would have striking analogies to the fantasies dredged up during psychoanalysis. Jung's book on libido symbols is, as criticism, an essay on the dream content of naive romance, and Jungian criticism is always most illuminating when it deals with romance, like Zimmer's *The King and the Corpse*, an earlier volume in the Bollingen series. And the central dream in Jung is essentially identical with the central ritual in Frazer, though the hero is individual libido in one and social fertility in the other, and his enemies parental regressions in one and the wasteland in the other.

Soon after the publication of *Wandlungen und Symbole der Libido*, an associate in Jung's field, Herbert Silberer, made a study (known in English as *Problems in Mysticism and Its Symbolism*) of an alchemical tract in the Rosicrucian tradition, which he analyzed first psychologically and then in terms of its own cosmological, or, as he called it, anagogic meaning, and showed that the two interpretations ran parallel. Jung also soon discovered in alchemy another mythical parallel to his individuation process and plunged into a study of alchemical

symbolism, both Oriental and European, which has borne
fruit in this lavishly illustrated, exhaustively documented study
of *Psychology and Alchemy*. The structure and symbolism of
alchemy is here compared, not simply with Jung's own
psychological system, but with the archetypes of the heroic
quest as well. It should be said at once that most of its readers
will want to hold it up to a mirror, like Jabberwocky. That is,
the way that Jung has approached myth, working outward
from his own practice as a doctor, has had the result of turning
every mythopoeic structure he has studied into a vast allegory
of his own techniques of psychotherapy. It is doubtful that
anyone not a hundred percent Jungian can take the whole of
myth, including alchemy, in quite that form, but the parallel
mythopoeic structures that emerge from his study are not less
rewarding in themselves. Some of these parallels are suggested
by the admirably chosen illustrations, even when they are not
explicitly dealt with in the text.

Alchemy, at least in its fully developed Christian form, was
based on the idea of a correspondence between Scripture and
Nature, the *verbum scriptum* and the *verbum factum*. Its
religious basis is biblical commentary (*not* the "Church," as
Jung keeps saying). Repeating classical experiments is a normal
part of scientific training, and the idea of alchemy was to
repeat the original divine experiment of creation: "Lapidis
generatio fit ad exemplum generationis mundi," as one al-
chemist quoted by Jung remarks. One isolated, first of all, a
prima materia, corresponding to the chaos of Genesis; then
one extracted from this a spirit of life, called Mercurius and
associated with the *anima mundi*, which contained within
itself the potency of all life and was consequently hermaphroditic. This hermaphrodite then became the substance that had
to be redeemed or transformed; it changed from the chemical
analogy of the Holy Spirit to the analogy of the old Adam or
fallen nature (not Adam as first man, which would be the
homunculus). As such, this hermaphrodite corresponds to the
antagonist of the heroic quest: the dragon or monster, the
leviathan, the old man, the serpent or ouroboros, and it is
represented by these symbols.

From this the principle of complementary opposition was next evolved, associated with various symbolic pairings, male and female, sun and moon, odd and even numbers, red and white. It was often called the marriage of the red king and the white queen. The union or *coniunctio* of these (often thought of as some form of incest, because they sprang from a common parent) shifted the theater of operations from a hermaphroditic to a female principle, just as in the Bible it is shifted from fallen nature to the Church, or Bride of Christ. At this stage, a third principle, a son or divine child, regularly made his appearance. The final stages are full of associations with the number four, especially the four elements, as the final work of redemption brings with it the power of living in water and fire as well as earth and air—a symbolism familiar to us from a late and not overprofound Masonic treatment of it in *The Magic Flute*.

The philosopher's stone itself was the chemical or demiurgical analogy (or perhaps rather *aspect*) of Christ, the elixir being to nature what his blood is to man. The fourfold symbolism is based on the fact that both man and nature have an inside and an outside, a subject and an object. The center of nature (the gold and jewels hidden in the earth) is eventually to be united to its circumference in the sun, moon, and stars of the heavens; the center of the spiritual world, the soul of man, is united to its circumference in God. Hence, there is a close association between the purifying of the human soul and the transmuting of earth to gold, not literal gold, but the fiery quintessential gold of which the heavenly bodies are made. The human body and the *vas* or alembic vessel of the laboratory thus experience parallel phenomena. The power of Christ is, in Scripture, the teaching that gives man immortality, the fountain of eternal youth; in Nature, it is the healing power or panacea that will restore nature to its original innocence, or the Golden Age.

The relation of all this to the actual attempt to transmute base metals into gold was, and still is, the great mystery about alchemy. The unifying conception soon died out, presumably because the alchemists got nowhere with their experiment (although, as we really don't know what they were trying to do, many of them may, for all we know, have done it), and alchemists broke into straight chemical experimenters on the one hand and occult philosophers on the other, each group regarding the other as a rabble of self-deluded charlatans. The associations of alchemy were apocalyptic and visionary, but not necessarily heretical, as Jung tends to think: the notion of a redeeming principle of nature as an aspect of Christ is a quite possible inference from the conception of substance which underlies the doctrine of transubstantiation. The parallels between alchemy and the mass, worked out by some of the more zealous allegorists, are perfectly logical granted their premises, and there is no occasion for Jung's speaking of their "bad taste." The rejection of transubstantiation by Protestants, however, along with the Protestant minimizing of the value of works (which would, of course, include the alchemical *opus*), had a lot to do with hastening the decay of alchemy. The essential point to remember is that when alchemy loses its chemical connections, it becomes purely a species of typology or allegorical commentary on the Bible.

In Jung's book the symbolic structures of alchemy and the heroic quest are united on the Euclidean principle that things equal to the same thing are equal to one another. The "same thing" is Jung's own individuation process, whose general resemblance to the *great work* of alchemy, on its psychological side, is not difficult to demonstrate. But, centuries before Jung was born, the "same thing" to which alchemy and romance were equal was biblical typology. For the Bible was not only the definitive alchemical myth for alchemists, but the definitive grammar of allegory for allegorical poets. Its central structure is that of quest-romance: it tells the story of a progress from creation to recreation through the heroism of Christ in killing the dragon of death and hell and rescuing his bride the Church. Jung would perhaps have made this point clearer if his own literary experience, being German, had not given so central a place to Goethe.

For Goethe's Faust is already a chemist, ready to believe that St. John's *in principio* means "nothing but" (one of Jung's most effective phrases) "Im Anfang war die That." And Goethe himself does not follow the central structure of biblical typology: hence his treatment of symbolism, while it is brilliant, varied, and ingenious, is not scholarly, as Dante, Spenser, and Blake are scholarly. When we read the quest-myth in the first book of *The Faerie Queene*, with its elaborate red and white imagery, it seems loaded down with alchemical symbolism, but we don't need to assume that Spenser knew about alchemy, because we can derive all the symbolism from the biblical tradition anyway. True, when we meet the hermaphrodite and ouroboros in the temple of Venus in the fourth book, we realize that Spenser *did* know about alchemy, but by that time we have a better idea of the context of such symbols. As for Blake, there is hardly a page of *Psychology and Alchemy* without close analogies in the Prophecies. But that does not prove that Blake knew alchemy; it proves that he knew the Bible and how to use it in poetry. With this additional connecting link, we can see that Jung's book is not a mere specious paralleling of a defunct science and one of several Viennese schools of psychology, but a grammar of literary symbolism which for all serious students of literature is as important as it is endlessly fascinating.

MINISTRY OF ANGELS

The science of criticism, as distinct from its art, that is, the shape of criticism as a structure of knowledge, is undeveloped. What follows is Newman's principle, that when a genuine academic subject is not properly defined, it creates a vacuum and all its neighbors move in. We have critics assuming that the fundamental principles of criticism are to be found in religion, metaphysics, psychology, or social studies, but not many who are willing to find them in criticism itself. Such an attempt would return us to Arnold's conception of "culture," which is really the conception of criticism as the central division of the humanities, flanked by history and philosophy. (Literature and the other arts are, like nature, a *field* of knowledge, not subjects of study but objects of study.)

But developing a science of criticism would not do everything. Berdyaev begins one of his books by pointing out how anxious society is to make the philosopher do something more obviously useful than philosophizing. It is the same in history: there the way to attract attention is to be a determinist. We get determinism whenever a writer with a special interest, say in geography or economics or religion, expresses that interest by the rhetorical device of putting his favorite study into a causal relationship with whatever interests him less. Such a method gives one the feeling of explaining one's subject while one is studying it, thus wasting no time.

Review of Allen Tate, *The Forlorn Demon: Didactic and Critical Essays* (Chicago: Regnery, 1953); Herbert Read, *The True Voice of Feeling: Studies in English Romantic Poetry* (New York: Pantheon, 1953); and Francis Fergusson, *Dante's Drama of the Mind: A Modern Reading of the Purgatorio* (Princeton: Princeton University Press, 1953). Reprinted by permission from *The Hudson Review*, vol. 6, no. 3 (Autumn 1953). © 1953 by The Hudson Review, Inc.

Criticism today is largely occupied by determinisms of this sort.

Mr. Allen Tate is a religious determinist, and, apart from his intellectual honesty (he constantly makes a point of giving his own case away), a very astute one. If the reader is a little jaded with the taste of dogmatic tabasco sauce on modern literature, he will have no relief here: he gets a familiar mouthful on the opening page: "The saints tell us that confident expectancy of damnation is a more insidious form of spiritual pride than certainty of salvation." But Mr. Tate continually refers to his prejudices, and the modern liberal's attempt to escape from prejudice is nailed into its coffin with three resounding whacks: it is private, mantic, and willful. Normally, a prejudice in the mind is a major premise which is mostly submerged, like an iceberg. Mr. Tate's explicit prejudice is more like a loadstone mountain or a siren's island and is for a view of man which coordinates and limits the faculties of intellect and feeling. Such a view he finds in Catholic Christianity, particularly in the period before Descartes introduced the dualism of the "angel in the machine"—a dualism which splits man into a pure but proud intellect trying to know essences directly, like an angel, and an autonomous feeling trying to gain an equally direct possession of experience. Dante is thus at one poetic pole of Mr. Tate's critical system; at the other is Poe, the "forlorn demon" of the title, in whom both aspects of the Cartesian dualism coalesce.

With one exception (a rather irresponsible discussion of "Is Literary Criticism Possible?"), the essays in his book are excellent. Few critics can write with more sustained brilliance or employ the technical language of criticism with more assurance and dexterity. The incompetent critic has a delicate instinct for avoiding the center of his subject; Mr. Tate has an infallible instinct for finding it. In discussing Poe, he goes straight for *Eureka* and the "colloquies" and relates the speculative nihilism in them with the more obvious nihilism in the Usher story. In discussing Johnson, he puts his finger at once on Johnson's lack of sense for the dramatic or experiential aspect of literature. Even when his dialectic

seems merely ingenious, it still has the brain-softening plausibility that we used to find in the best Marxist criticism. There
is no question of finding in Mr. Tate himself what he calls the
pride that prevents the complete discovery of the subject.
Nothing is actually obscured: I get, rather, a sense of a
wrenched and astigmatic intensity of vision. The astigmatism
is due to what he calls "an ambitious assumption, about the
period in which we live, which I shall not make explicit."
There is an uneasy feeling of unwritten thus-we-see perora-
tions hovering around the conclusions of his essays.

I call Mr. Tate a determinist because he says and assumes
that literary standards, "in order to be effectively literary,
must be more than literary." That is, they have ultimately to
be religious. The theme of his essay on "The Man of Letters in
the Modern World" is that the profoundest view of the man of
letters is to take him as a lay preacher, revealing the apocalyptic dimensions of the contemporary scene. "There would
be no hell for modern man if our men of letters were not
calling attention to it." This determinism is then projected
historically as the Great Western Butterslide, the doctrine of a
coordinated synthesis in medieval culture giving place, at the
Renaissance, to a splitting and specialized schizophrenia
which has gotten steadily worse until it has finally landed us
all in that Pretty Pass in which we are today. His pages are
strewn with such remarks as "a society which has once been
religious cannot . . . secularize itself," or "there is no end, yet
in sight, to the fragmenting of the western mind," or "the city
of Augustine and Dante, where it was possible for men to
find . . . the analogue to the City of God" ("still visible,"
faintly, in eighteenth-century America).

In this theory, the Middle Ages becomes, like the moon in
Ariosto, a vast repository of all cultural acquisitions which we
have since lost. It has a miraculous supply of everything that
we need in our time. For such an Eden we ought to have,
somewhere in the Renaissance, a forbidden tree, or at least
an ideological clotheshorse on which to tie the fatal apple.
This lay figure used to be Bacon, now it is Descartes, or, in
more esoteric circles, Ramus. (Mr. Tate, who doesn't miss

much, says: "The demonology which attributes to a few persons the calamities of mankind is perhaps a necessary convention of economy in discourse." It seems to me necessary only for a deterministic organization of values.) We also need a type of argument that exaggerates to the limit the social and ethical consequences of contemporary beliefs, while taking an almost perversely intellectualized view of medieval beliefs. Dante told Can Grande that the aim of his whole poem was practical and moral, which means that his primary purpose in writing the *Inferno* was to scare the pants off his reader. This need not affect our appreciation of Dante, for we take his realities for fictions, just as we take our own fictions for realities. Still, a modern reader might well find Dante's motivation, in itself, quite as repulsive as the motivation of Berenice's lover, returning from her body with a greatly relieved mind and a fine set of teeth. But Dante has receded into a purely aesthetic distance; Poe, says Mr. Tate, is "our cousin," but Dante's cousins have all disappeared into the Wonderful Synthesis.

It takes a genuine effort, usually accompanied by genuine annoyance, to realize that the Great Western Butterslide is a myth, like the Golden Age or the Social Contract. Suppose it were examined as a problem within criticism, and not used as a grindstone for an extracritical ax. I think that then, as we studied medieval, Renaissance, Baroque, and later cultures impartially, suspending our value judgments, we should find ourselves revolving around the simple fact that one follows another in time. We should discover, in short, a process of cultural aging, and we should come to think of Western culture as having become, not better or worse or less unified, but simply older. And while aging may be reacted to emotionally as the working of a cruel fate or as a progressive deterioration or as a breakdown caused by a loss of innocence, all these are immature views.

The trouble is that the best statement of the problem of cultural aging is in Spengler, and nobody wants Spengler's maudlin hero-cult, his conscientious Philistinism, or the gloomy Wagnerian whinnies in his sound effects about the dark goings-on of nature and destiny. Still, value judgments founded on a theory of cultural aging, including Spengler's own, are more or less addled versions of Spengler; and if we are all Spenglerians today, we may as well be clear-sighted ones. From this point of view, trying to find everything we have "since lost" in the Middle Ages is another way of looking for the fountain of youth. But, as Samuel Butler says in *Erewhon*, there is no way of making an aged art young again; it has to work out its own salvation in fear and trembling. Fear and trembling is at least one thing that we can find in Poe. I imagine that Mr. Tate would concede most of this, because he does not need the historical projection of his argument at all: his real aim is to set the Church against the world in a present confrontation. That would still make him a determinist, but a much more difficult one to refute.

Sir Herbert Read deals with the romantic poets and their tradition. He is also a determinist, though a gentler one than Mr. Tate—a psychological determinist this time, with latent political implications. He finds the basis of romanticism in Schelling's conception of art as the conscious recreation of what appears in nature as organic form. Such a conception immediately drives a wedge between the real thing in art, the living and integrated organism, and the dead artifact. One is a form, the other a superinduced shape. The latter owes its existence to the notion of art as artifice, of poetry as a rhetorical playing with words. The essential feature of dead poetry is predictability, or mechanical regularity. Living poetry is unpredictable, hence irregular, and is the "true voice of feeling"—a phrase quoted from Keats. Wordsworth and Coleridge brought in the "cult of sincerity," of never being satisfied with anything less than the true voice of feeling, and their tradition was continued by Keats, Hopkins, Pound, Eliot, and others, all of whom are dealt with in separate essays. The real tradition is contrasted with its pinchbeck imitation in Whitman and Lawrence, where there is more talk about sincerity than practice of it. Here the irregular rhythm is not organic, and so in Whitman it is constantly collapsing into a facile biblical parallelism. (Incidentally, it is a little insular for Sir Herbert to remark that Whitman has had no disciples except Lawrence and Edmund Carpenter.)

Romanticism in poetry is thus an attempt, not to know essences like Mr. Tate's angels, but to create them, or rather to liberate them. To express the true voice of feeling is, in fact, one of the central liberating processes of human life, and it arises as part of our heritage of freedom, in opposition to the classical view of a prefabricated nature and an art which is merely "a grace added to life: a plaything." (Before long we meet the inevitable unhappy footnote saying that of course in these terms a great deal of Racine is really romantic, and a great deal of Wordsworth classical.) In true poetry, the poet and the man must be united in a state of psychological purity, for "all great poetry, as Keats realized, is born of a certain modesty and simplicity of heart." Through all his sensitive criticism and his very real erudition, Sir Herbert carries a most disarming simplicity of heart himself.

His main theme is essentially the same as the problem of *ecstasis* or "transport" in Longinus, very ably handled in one of Mr. Tate's essays. The problem is to locate the point at which rhetoric passes into poetry; persuasion, stimulus, and suggestion into the recognition of the true voice of feeling, of what the cult of sincerity produces. Sir Herbert is not careful to distinguish personal from literary sincerity or to keep in mind the principle that with the poet, as with Machiavelli's prince, the reality of such virtues is irrelevant: the simulation of them is everything. But then he attaches great importance to the biography of the poet, psychologically interpreted. There is a curious argument in his essay "In Defence of Shelley," to the effect that Shelley was a narcist suffering from hallucinations, which makes him abnormal, and consequently valuable to us, as the normal is so dull. There is much more said about Shelley's thought than his poetry, perhaps because there is undoubtedly a good deal of rhetorical playing with words in Shelley. Surely it would be equally possible to argue the question of sincerity the opposite way.

In some Elizabethan lyrics, for instance Campion's "When thou must home," it seems to me that it is the completely conventional nature of theme, structure, and technique that sets free the true voice of feeling. There is no organic place for preromantic poetry in Sir Herbert's book: he merely says: "I assume that in so far as the poetry of the past is sincere, to that extent it is organic in form." So two themes are mixed together, one the creative process itself, the other the manifestation of that process in the romantic movement.

Now, once more, suppose Sir Herbert's subject were approached from within criticism, instead of being externally determined by the psychological principle of sincerity. If we take a line of Shakespeare at random:

Ay, but to die, and go we know not where;

we can see at least three main rhythms in it. One is the running rhythm, the ten syllables of iambic pentameter; another, more important for this line, is the semantic or prose rhythm. There is also a soliloquizing, oracular rhythm, turning meditatively on its axis around its sound pattern:

> *Ay;*
> *but to die . . .*
>> *and go*
>> *we know*
>>> *not where . . .*

This, we may say, is the "poetic" rhythm, as distinct from the "verse" rhythm, and it is essentially irregular and discontinuous, in contrast to running rhythm, which can go on indefinitely.

The main technical experiments in the sixteenth and seventeenth centuries were with running rhythm and established blank verse, various stanza forms, and later the couplet. Prose was still half-metrical rhetoric. From the "Senecan amble" on, a series of technical experiments in prose, carried through mainly by Dryden, Addison, and Swift, set free the distinctive semantic rhythm of prose. Then, with the later eighteenth century, there begins a series of technical experiments designed similarly to set free the distinctive "poetic" or sound-pattern rhythm. Long poems were still written in running rhythm, but no new running rhythms were established, except the ones that ran too fast, like the anapests of Swinburne. In short, the technical discoveries of the last century or so, including Hopkins's sprung rhythm and *vers libre*, are best seen as discoveries within a genre. Such a view would logically account for a poet who merely baffles Sir Herbert—Byron, who, realizing that the perfection of running rhythm in Pope was a dead end, relapsed into *knittelvers*, which is also a parody of the conventions of running rhythm. It would also give central importance to Poe, whom Sir Herbert ignores, and Poe's theory that poetry is essentially discontinuous sound pattern. In this way we could separate the technical problem, confined to one genre and one historical period, from the larger implications of the creative process, and so the former would not become merely a loose allegory of the latter.

Mr. Fergusson's book on the *Purgatorio* appears not to be deterministic. Surely a book on Dante could not entirely forgo the vision of modern man coming out of the Middle Ages with everything in his pockets and dropping it all on the way, like Hansel and Gretel. Ah, yes: "I suppose it was in the 17th century . . . that . . . the *lumen naturale* of the Middle Ages was finally lost." But this is rare in his book, and he also avoids, more by instinctive good taste than by design, the graduate-school clichés about the *Commedia* as Thomism set to music. The result is that he has written a charming and eloquent book on the *Purgatorio*. It is primarily a teacher's book. Dante's poetry, like Bach's music, adopts bewilderingly complex means in order to produce an effect of massive simplicity, and Mr. Fergusson has concentrated on the simplicity. He adopts Dante's "the exposition of the letter is nought else than the development of the form" as an axiom, and so his form does not emancipate itself from being a running commentary.

Some things thereby are necessarily lost: the treatment of

recurring symbols, for instance, such as the sirens and especially the mirror, the subject of Mr. Tate's Dante essay. And perhaps we are referred a bit too often to the excellent notes in the Temple Classics edition for the details of the allegory. We get little sense of the incredible skill of Dante's allegorical counterpoint as it rumbles through the great stretto of the closing cantos, at every tercet taking our breath away with its ingenuity, yet inevitably right, and never manipulated. Mr. Fergusson does, however, catch the sense of suppressed excitement that we feel in these cantos: here we are in the center of the *Commedia*, and therefore at the center of our whole literary experience, and so the memories of other things near the center, late plays of Shakespeare and Sophocles, the Bible, some moments in Plato and in modern poetry, crowd into our minds, and we glimpse a mass of converging rays of significance, as though there were one great thing that the whole of literature had to say to us.

It is a self-effacing book, patiently linking Dante, as a teacher should, both with the "great tradition" coming down from Aristotle and with contemporary thought and his reader's own experience. He is content to throw out some of his most illuminating remarks parenthetically, almost apologetically, as when he says that Dante's "will" is closer to what we mean by "libido" than it is to our rationalized conception of will. He shows unobtrusively how Dante, not knowing Greek drama, was still able to pick the essence of the "Dionysiac" out of a couple of bad lines in Lucan, which to me implies that the real "great tradition" is not a curriculum but a habit of imaginative reading. He follows with great clarity and skill the central process of freeing the will through a series of progressive rebirths, until the pilgrim reaches the original unfallen childhood of the Golden Age. He shows how the pilgrim's climb is at once an effort of will and an effort to relax the will, like the creative process itself, a purification of everything that obscures the free creative spirit, until, as the pilgrim enters the innocent world on top of the mountain, he becomes one with the poet who watches him. Thus—and this I think is the distinctive feature of Mr. Fergusson's exposition

—one of Dante's themes is the liberation of his own liberal art of poetry.

Mr. Fergusson shows, I think correctly, that the *Purgatorio* illustrates in its development a progression up Dante's four levels of meaning. (Incomprehensibly, he inverts the second and third levels, contradicting Dante's express statements and the whole medieval tradition. I am not interested in his reasons: I think he has simply made a mistake, one that has to be corrected by the reader before his argument comes into focus.) The crisis of the *Purgatorio*, then, would be the passage from the allegorical (*quid credas*) to the moral (*quid agas*) as Dante passes from invisibly directed penance to the direct vision of the Word of God. As he goes through the ring of fire, he passes Kierkegaard's "either-or" dilemma, leaving his "aesthetic" dalliance with Casella far behind and moving into the sphere of ethical freedom, in the moment that the poet and the pilgrim begin to become the same man.

The relation of *quid credas* to *quid agas* is the center of the *Purgatorio*, and therefore of Mr. Fergusson's book. It is also the central theme of Mr. Tate, especially in his opening essay on the relation of communication to communion. It is also, in a way, the central theme of *The True Voice of Feeling*, which turns on a parallel distinction of external and internal creation. Sir Herbert is, naturally, bothered by Kierkegaard's identification of freedom with an ethical activity which rejects the aesthetic. He writes two essays proving that Wordsworth and Coleridge were early existentialists, which is hardly much of a point, though the essays are interesting enough. But Kierkegaard's "aesthetic" attitude is that of a detached spectator, not the artist: Galileo's view of man as a spectator of nature makes science equally a part of Bacon's "idol of the theater." The "either-or" is between two mental attitudes, not two subjects. One attitude says "this is" and contemplates whatever it is; the other says "let this be" and acts creatively. At the end of the *Purgatorio*, Dante is approaching (the *quo tendas* of anagogy) the presence of a God, who, when incarnate in man, spoke in parables rather than propositions, and taught, not a system to be admired, but aphorisms to be recreated in action. Hence, Dante does not renounce but emancipates his creative and poetic powers, for "let this be" is the axiom of the poet's craft as well. Dante thus claims for his poetry, as Mr. Fergusson says, an authority which cannot be overruled by any other aspect of human activity. Like Mr. Tate, I think it is very unlikely that Dante is predicting his personal salvation at the end of the *Paradiso*, but that he is asserting the salvation of the poetic vision I have no doubt. And that is why I feel that the critic, who follows the poet with a confidence in direct proportion to the poet's greatness, need not look for his guiding principles in any more authoritative field than his own.

THE RHYTHM OF GROWTH AND DECAY

It is curious, and probably significant, that two books by well-known Protestant theologians, on practically the same subject, should appear at practically the same time. They are based on the same essential facts, take quite similar attitudes toward them, and quote much the same authorities, an interpretation of the Bible being, of course, fundamental to each. But in spite of this parallelism, which extends to an identical number of pages, they complement rather than overlap each other. Dr. Niebuhr presents an argued thesis of his own; Dr. Löwith offers a series of studies of philosophical historians, beginning with Spengler and Toynbee and going backward through Marx and Hegel, through Vico and Voltaire in the eighteenth century, to the great medieval prophet of historical progress, Joachim of Floris, thence to St. Augustine, and finally to the Bible. This crablike movement is a little confusing to the reader until he gets used to it, in spite of the fascinating information to be picked up on the way. Dr. Löwith's book documents and supplies evidence for Dr. Niebuhr's thesis, and Dr. Niebuhr's thesis synthesizes and illuminates Dr. Löwith's erudition. Even their faults are complementary: Dr. Niebuhr's book has too many misprints, and Dr. Löwith's a bad index.

Both writers agree that there are three major views of history, the classical, the Christian, and the modern. The classical view is that history is a series of cycles: the same

Review of Reinhold Niebuhr, *Faith and History: A Comparison of Christian and Modern Views of History* (New York: Scribner's, 1949); and Karl Löwith, *Meaning in History: The Theological Implications of the Philosophy of History* (Chicago: University of Chicago Press, 1949). Reprinted from *The Canadian Forum*, vol. 29 (Sept. 1949).

things happen over and over (or, at any rate, the same kinds of things do), empires rise and decline and give place to other empires, and no one can look for anything in history but change and decay. The wise man, from the classical point of view, would do well to cut loose from history altogether and cultivate the life of reason, which is timeless and not subject to change.

This pessimistic view of history is, Dr. Niebuhr argues, an oversimplified identification of history with nature, and tends increasingly to identify the salvation of the soul with a withdrawal from contemporary reality. It was overthrown by Christianity because Christianity's central doctrine is the coming of God to the world at a certain time in history. It was partly because Christianity could give a religious meaning to history, while pagan philosophy could not, that Christianity conquered the intellectual world during the fall of the Roman Empire. (The evidence for this is set out in the late Charles Cochrane's book, *Christianity and Classical Culture*, one of the finest scholarly studies ever written by a Canadian.)

The Christian sense that there is meaning in history beyond just an endless series of cycles gave birth to the modern theory of progress. This theory is at the opposite pole from the classical one: it finds a redeeming force within history itself and thinks that man should become wholly absorbed in it. Both writers agree that the doctrine of progress, like the cyclic view, is inconsistent with Christianity, but Dr. Niebuhr devotes more attention to it. He gives some very melancholy quotations from apologists of progress, which indicate that nearly all nonreligious modern views of history, whether bourgeois or Communist, liberal or reactionary, are attempts to cheer ourselves up by saying that while most human problems are still unsolved, nevertheless man is going on and on and up and up to greater and better things. Just what these things are depends on the taste of the theorizer. Some people say that we're improving generally because we're getting more individual freedom; others say it's because we're getting more social order. Some say that the advance of science will fix everything, others that a change in our economy will do it.

The discovery of evolution in biology gave a lot of people a vague idea that science had now proved that there is progress in history—a notion that Dr. Niebuhr correctly identifies as "social Darwinism."

The views of the progressivists referred to by Dr. Niebuhr are a curious melange of half-baked liberal and half-baked revolutionary ideas, in which freedom and dictatorship are often treated as though they were interchangeable. Thus, says one writer, the management of human affairs requires a thorough knowledge of anatomy and physics, physiology and metaphysics, pathology, chemistry, psychology, medicine, genetics, nutrition, pedagogy, aesthetics, ethics, religion, sociology, and economics: that it would take about twenty-five years to learn all that, and that those who did learn it could start directing the "reconstruction of human beings" from the age of fifty on. This precious pearl of wisdom happens to come from Dr. Alexis Carrel's *Man the Unknown*, but Dr. Niebuhr quotes others equally depressing. His conclusion, which he feels is the only one possible to Christianity, is that man alone cannot arrive at a final judgment of value on human life, for all human judgments reflect some kind of class prejudice or special interest.

That is, you can't assume that whatever you happen to be most interested in is the key to everything. If you're interested in science, it doesn't follow that the advance of science will bring man freedom. Even if it does, it doesn't follow that freedom is the best thing for man to have, particularly if you don't know what you mean by freedom anyway. Even if it is the best thing for man, it doesn't follow that all history is a movement toward getting it. If you assume that it is, your "progress" is the automatic plodding of a donkey with a carrot in front of his nose. The donkey would do much better to stop and turn around and see who is driving him on and why that particular carrot is dangling there. All the evidence goes to show that the real driver of the progressive human donkey is the selfish, greedy, and tyrannical part of man himself. Once we realize that, we may get somewhere with a theory of progress.

It seems rather ironic, if not silly, to be talking in terms of progress when the world we actually live in is a world of dictatorships, global wars, and political persecutions of unprecedented fury. When an American intellectual looks out on such a world and sees that it is fundamentally very good, he really means that the enormous wealth and power of the American middle-class culture he belongs to make him feel, for the moment, very comfortable. When a Russian communist talks the same way, he means really that production of steel in the Soviet Union is up and things look good for the advance of Communism. After the last war and the atomic bomb, a lot of people began to realize that the express train to Utopia might be derailed, but were unable to turn from a frivolous optimism to anything but an equally frivolous despair. Dr. Niebuhr refers to H. G. Wells, who began by writing books with such titles as *A Modern Utopia* and *Men Like Gods*, who then began to talk in terms of scientific dictatorships, and whose last book was called *The Mind at the End of Its Tether*.

Neither writer, however, really brings out the moral horror of a progressive view of history or points to the consequences of the reckless sacrificing of means to ends which it entails. It is progressive to say: If we murder a hundred thousand farmers now we may get a more efficient system of collectivized agriculture in a hundred years. The arguments of the inquisitors in Koestler's *Darkness at Noon* are progressive arguments. The point is important, because our use of words is easygoing, and all the well-meaning people in the country describe themselves as progressive, including the writer of this article and most of his readers. It should be clearly recognized that the real dynamic of democracy is empiric and experimental rather than progressive in any metaphysical sense. Democratic action involves foresight and long-term planning rather than merely muddling through, but that is something very different from a belief that the real end of what we are trying to do now lies in the future. Such an attitude leads to despising the present generation for not being a hypothetically ideal posterity, which is a completely vicious state of mind.

Both writers are far better on negative than on positive criticism. Dr. Löwith is deliberately negative: he comes much closer than Dr. Niebuhr to Luther's complete separation of Church and world, and the main thesis of *Meaning in History* is that there isn't much meaning in history. He agrees that the classical view of history was cyclic and the modern one progressive, and that both are inconsistent with Christianity. But he also feels that every philosophy of history must be either cyclic or progressive and that, therefore, no Christian philosophy of history will work out. He feels that the Incarnation is something that cuts vertically across history, not a new historical principle. So for him a religious philosophy of history is possible only in Judaism, where the Messiah is believed to be still to come. A progressive view of history therefore strikes him as a kind of parody of Judaism. Of all the people he discusses, he is most interested in St. Augustine, precisely because St. Augustine was the least interested in secular history as such.

Dr. Niebuhr attempts a more positive view in the second half of his book, but his argument is still heavily overlaid by negative statements. The people he disagrees with make up quite a large company, and after reading that the Catholics are wrong because they absolutize the Church, the Lutherans wrong because they believe in a rule of saints, the modern liberals wrong because they are infected with progressivism, one begins to reflect rather irritatedly that everybody seems to be out of step but our Reinhold. It is possible to attack human complacency to the verge of being complacent oneself in refuting it, and Dr. Niebuhr often does not do full justice to the intensity and power of some of the modern thinkers he refers to: Marx, for instance, or Nietzsche.

It seems to me possible to say much more about a Christian philosophy of history than either writer does say. The modern cyclic theories of Vico and Spengler, and to a lesser extent Toynbee, are very different from the old classical view of the cycle. And it is too simple to say that St. Augustine refuted all cyclic views of history merely because he ridiculed the classical one. It is possible to look at St. Augustine in another way and find in his *City of God* a conception of the recurrent rise and decline of civilizations as central to his whole idea of the thing which stands over against the City of God, the *civitas terrena* or earthly city. The fall of the Roman Empire was the immediate occasion for, and the most impressive proof of, St. Augustine's thesis that anything man can erect will fall down sooner or later. In all human institutions, then, there is a rotary movement of rise and fall which goes back to the original fall of man. The affinity of this rhythm of growth and decay to that of the natural world, with its yearly vegetable cycle of death and revival, is the basis for the Vico-Spengler conception of history as showing a series of "civilizations" or "cultures" which behave more or less like natural organisms and go through much the same phases of growth, maturation, and decline. It is also possible that behind this organic rhythm, which, it seems to me, certainly does exist in history, there may be an evolutionary one, and, without vulgarizing this into a theory of progress, we may perhaps see in the Industrial Revolution the beginning of something that makes us, in the words of Wyndham Lewis, the cavemen of a new mental era.

However, as far as they go, Drs. Niebuhr and Löwith are sound enough. The serpent in Eden told Adam that if he would take a few bites out of the apple of the tree of knowledge, he would become like the gods and know clearly what good and evil were. When Adam listened to this, he got into trouble. Adam's descendants, we are told, once decided to get together and build a big tower that would reach heaven, but before they finished it they found that they were no longer speaking the same language. The preachers of progress have been handing out similar advice and planning similar projects for well over a century, and with much the same result. There are many today who, looking at the world before them, feel vaguely that this was where they came in, but don't know how to get out of the dark theater and back to the sidewalks of a real city. All Drs. Niebuhr and Löwith have tried to do is to indicate a possible exit.

NATURE METHODIZED

What is the point of literary history? It must be different from that of ordinary history. If one were to write the history of English literature from 1700 to 1740 simply as history, it might still be a fairly interesting book because this age happened to be one in which the major writers, Defoe, Swift, and Pope, were deeply involved with the events of their time. But even so, the main emphasis would fall on such works as Swift's *The Drapier's Letters* and Defoe's *Shortest Way with the Dissenters*. All really major works of the imagination—*Robinson Crusoe, Gulliver's Travels, The Dunciad*—take us into something that is not history, and even the relation to history that they still have is a curious one.

Mr. Dobrée, naturally, devotes much attention to the political events of his period and to his writers' involvements with them. But he also comments on the naiveté and the black-and-white melodrama of Pope's political satire, and remarks: "It is this very innocence which gives these satires their pure quality." A poet can hardly help being a bad politician: he must retain an imaginative simplicity that has little relevance to what goes on in party conflict. Milton saw the Restoration of Charles II as the giving up, by a people chosen by God for the gospel (as Israel was chosen for the law) of its Promised Land, and turning to "a Captain back for Egypt." Charles himself saw it as a sign that the powerful and wealthy class which had risen in revolt against his father had achieved its ends. Charles's view of it was shrewd and accurate, and Milton's was preposterous; but it was Milton's

Review of Bonamy Dobrée, *English Literature in the Early Eighteenth Century* (New York: Oxford University Press, 1959). Reprinted from *The Griffin*, vol. 9 (Aug. 1960). © 1960 by The Readers' Subscription, Inc.

apocalyptic fantasies that made him Milton. And if great literature is always out of historical focus, the literary careers of minor or more retired writers are hardly in history at all. Mr. Dobrée's book has a chronological table of the main literary events of his period—publications, birth and death dates of authors, and the like—and this useful but hardly fascinating apparatus is really all that literary history, considered as a branch of ordinary history, amounts to.

No: The point of literary history is not to articulate the memory of mankind by putting a mass of documents into an ordered and coherent narrative. Its documents are far better worth reading than any history of them could ever be. Its task is to reawaken and refresh our imaginative experience by showing us what unexplored riches of it lie within a certain area. In every age there is a large group of writers who all seem to be more or less the same size. Those who eventually turn out to be the greatest writers are seldom wholly ignored in their own day; but even more seldom are they regarded as greatly superior to their contemporaries. The tragedies of Webster remind us of Shakespeare at every turn because our imaginations are possessed by Shakespeare. But Webster himself lists his influences as first Chapman, then Ben Johnson, then Beaumont and Fletcher, then Shakespeare, Dekker, and Heywood, and we have no reason to suppose that he was being disingenuous. Many decades have to elapse before the final comparative standards emerge. Even Dryden, while writing with great accuracy about Shakespeare, could still say, "However others are now generally preferred before him." Comparative standards are established by what may be called the usefulness of the writer to the culture that follows and absorbs him, the slow and gradual discovery, in general cultural practice, that he is indispensable. They cannot be established by the value judgments of individual critics, which are the effects and not the causes of his usefulness.

Once they are established, the dilettante is apt to assume that any writer he has not heard of has been "forgotten" and that anyone who has been forgotten deserved to be because posterity, including himself, is infallible in such matters. The literary historian, trying to absorb himself into the period he is studying, finds himself recapturing some of its perspective and discovers at once that posterity is the laziest and most incompetent of critics. If, for instance (to switch to another art: the principles of every mode of cultural history are the same), he is writing the history of eighteenth-century music, it is no sign of his feeling for the period if he likes Bach and Mozart: it is merely a sign that he is not quite a fool. If Soler or Mattheson or Cimarosa also burst on him with astonishment and delight; if he has an insatiable zest for rediscovering the most obscure music and the most humdrum composers; if he can sympathize with (which does not mean agreeing with) the councillors of Leipzig in their desire to get Telemann or Graupner for their organist rather than Bach, then he has some claims to historical sense. For even the errors of an age are inseparable from its integrity. A critic who loves Keats may produce fine criticism on Keats; but he will not have a genuinely historical approach to Keats unless he can understand why Croker reviewed *Endymion* as he did, and feels that he might well have written much the same review in the same situation.

This is not to say that the literary historian should not use his hindsight, but merely that literary history does not consist entirely of hindsight. For bringing our imaginative experience of the past to life there can be no substitute for history. *The Rape of the Lock*, embalmed in a freshman survey course, may well seem to the freshman to be little more than a long poem in heroic couplets about airy fairies. There is a limit, in other words, to what a limited literary experience can get out of any poem. And if such a poem is removed from its historical context and presented as one of the few memorable works of its age, limited experience, gazing at itself in the mirror of the poem, may only conclude that the other works must be pretty dismal. If one has read, with gradually increasing relish and without worrying about any comparative standards, Gay's *Trivia*, Mandeville's *Grumbling Hive*, Philips's *Splendid Shilling*, and Matthew Green's *The Spleen*, then *The Rape of the Lock* will grow, with its reader's experience, into something more like its proper proportions. The literary historian is the man who has read everything in his field with equal interest: he has lost his sense of comparative values in order to find them again in their genuine form, when the greatest writers of an age are seen to be mountain peaks and not passing clouds. And mountain peaks should be reached by climbing and descent, not by dropping on and off in a twentieth-century helicopter.

The literary historian begins in the "background" which is the subject of the second part of Mr. Dobrée's book, in the buzzing gossip of letters and memoirs, the random impressions of travelers, the network of allusions and value judgments in criticism and history writing. The literary historian needs a sharp eye for the historical epiphany, as a student of Joyce might call it: for the kind of remark that sums up not only the expressed opinions but also the unconscious assumptions of an age. When Mr. Dobrée quotes Lady Wentworth as saying, in her aristocratic spelling, that "mony now adays is the raening passion," we can see the kind of social milieu out of which Pope's *Moral Essays*, with their stress on the "ruling passion," emerged. Again, Mr. Dobrée quotes the critic Gildon, who is echoing Dennis, as saying: "Poetry is an Art; for since it has a certain *End*, there must be some certain Way of arriving at that *End*. No Body can doubt of so evident a Truth, that in all Things, where there may be a Right and a Wrong, there is an Art, and sure Rules to lead you to the former, and direct you to avoid the latter."

Every age produces these "there must be" statements, full of the desperate pathos of the effort to find values that time and chance will not happen to. But only the eighteenth century could have grounded a defense of the "rules" in so uncertain a pun on "certain."

From "background," the literary historian goes on to the foreground, the periodicals and magazines like *The Tatler* and *The Spectator*, where the cultural tastes of the age are formed and reflected, where literary and critical issues are discussed and the thought of the time is absorbed into polite conversation. Addison, that round peg in the round hole of his time, is a storehouse of the kind of cultural aphorism that characterizes an age. The arts, says Addison, "are to deduce their Laws and Rules from the general Sense and Taste of Mankind, and not from Principles of those Arts themselves; or in other Words, the Taste is not to conform to the Art, but the Art to the Taste." Nothing could be more wrong, or more characteristic of the culture Addison is reflecting, with its confidence in its taste, its absence of any sense of the shaping power of tradition, its conviction that every artist starts all over again to grapple directly with Nature.

From this we go on to the intellectual issues of an age, as literature treats them. What Newton and Berkeley meant is important, certainly; but what their contemporaries thought they meant is at least equally important to the literary historian. Nowadays many people feel that there is something about "relativity" or the "principle of indeterminacy" that gives them the best of both worlds: an up-to-date scientific doctrine which enables them to preserve their moral and religious intuitions. But this is tame compared to the kind of excitement that Newton aroused, with his mathematical genius and his deep religious convictions, his irrefutable laws of motion and his suggestion that space was the sensorium of God. Hence, as one poet said, "Newton demands the Muse," the title of a lively study by Miss Marjorie Nicholson that Mr. Dobrée follows in his penultimate chapter, which deals with the great mass of philosophical poetry in the period, from James Thomson down. Such Newtonian poetry raises an interesting critical problem. Mr. Dobrée quotes several passages such as this:

> Let curious Minds, who would the Air inspect
> On its Elastic Energy reflect.

Why does this kind of writing not come through to us, when Pope's *Essay on Man*, certainly no better intellectually, does? To answer this, one would need a clear insight into the difference between poetry and discursive writing, between the poet's task of putting words into patterns and the philosopher's task of putting them into propositions, between the poetic language of analogy and identification and the scientist's language of accurate description.

All this is the literary historian's underpainting, so to speak, the tempering of tones and colors that makes the greatest achievements of an age shine in depth. Here the literary historian meets his real test. It is extremely easy to belittle writers by a historical treatment, through some such formula as this: "Swift and Pope are rationalistic writers in contrast to the Romantics, who put imagination and emotion in the ascendancy." Such formulas assume that a writer's age limits him to half a reality, however great he may be. There is no such blither in Mr. Dobrée's book, but there is plenty of it in the kind of pseudohistorical material that inexperienced students are afflicted with. To make a great writer gain rather than lose by a historical treatment takes a sense of the interlocking relevance of all the literature of his age, conceived as a unit of culture complete in itself. The true literary historian can see, under the surface, the conflict of party interests and of social and cultural clichés taking the form of an imaginative vision of life which the great masterpiece reveals.

Thus Defoe is an overworked journalist writing incessantly about free trade and inflation and the cost of living and the rise and decline of manufacturing. In his age, the stereotype of the middle-class Englishman was formulated in Arbuthnot's *History of John Bull*. The paradoxes of Mandeville's *Fable of the Bees* about public benefits depending on private vices showed that people were thinking seriously about the economic context of moral behavior. Voyages of discovery and the plantation of colonies were beginning to show what a modern French writer has remarked, that Teutonic empire builders impose their own cultural pattern wherever they go, in contrast to the Latin tendency to adapt to the "native" one after the initial massacres and enslavements are over. It was out of this milieu that Robinson Crusoe emerged: Robinson Crusoe who, once alone on his island, instantly opens a journal and a ledger, surrounds himself with pets (for an Englishman's home is his castle), catches his man Friday and promptly converts him to the true faith, which is his own brand of modified Calvinism, oblivious of the irony of Friday's innocent questions. It was out of this milieu that the even greater figure of Moll Flanders emerged. Hyprocrisy has been called the tribute that vice pays to virtue, but in Moll's two-way-stretch conscience there is something far more profound than hypocrisy. There is a deep respect for the proprieties, and yet an iron determination to go on living and not be martyred by them, which makes her as impressive a heroine as any in fiction. "Without my book I should mope and pine," said the applewoman in *Lavengro*, when George Borrow proposed to buy her copy of *Moll Flanders*, and the feeling that the book actually has enough vitality to sustain life is not wholly fanciful. The sense that the history of Defoe's time gives of being a growing point of social energy is confirmed by its greatest novel.

Just as the social life of the time grows into Defoe's fiction, so its intellectual life grows into *Gulliver's Travels*. The Newtonian universe and the researches of the Royal Society were not simple advances in knowledge—nothing is ever that —but also new modes of sharpening the conflict between civilization and its discontents. All the nightmares of science fiction about the destructiveness of technology and the death wish lurking in much of its progress are anticipated in Swift's Laputa, especially in such episodes as the Lindalinian rebellion. But even this does not kick us in our solar plexus like the Yahoo. Mr. Dobrée urges, somewhat plaintively, that Gulliver "is no Yahoo," that Swift "is not saying that man is a Yahoo," that Swift "is careful to make the distinction between civilized man and the Yahoos." The fact that he feels it necessary to say this shows how *Gulliver's Travels* can still make us wince and look away.

> When I thought of my family, my friends, my countrymen, or human race in general, I considered them as they really were, Yahoos in shape and disposition, perhaps a little more civilized, and qualified with the gift of speech, but making no other use of reason than to improve and multiply those vices whereof their brethren in this country had only

the share that nature allotted them. When I happened to behold the reflection of my own form in a lake or fountain, I turned away my face in horror and detestation of myself, and could better endure the sight of a common Yahoo than of my own person.

Swift is a Christian bishop in attitude if not in fact, and these measured words carry with them the whole weight of the Christian tradition. Man's nature is human nature, which is civilized; he has fallen into physical nature but cannot adjust to it as a gifted animal might do; he must either rise above it into humanity or sink below it into sin and filth; sin and filth are where he spends most of his time. So Gulliver returns to his people with a hatred, not of the human race, but of pride. In Swift this vision runs headlong into the new views of a "natural society," propounded tentatively by Bolingbroke in Swift's day, later developed by Rousseau, and now, on the other side of Darwin, one of our central preoccupations. Swift's blistering contempt for the notion that man is primarily a child of *nature* may be wrong, but in the age of Ionesco and Beckett it can hardly be called antiquated. Literary history fulfills itself by ceasing to be history when its great masterpieces enter our own age, not to be judged by us, but as themselves judges.

What I have outlined is, of course, an ideal literary history. Mr. Dobrée's book is not ideal, but it contains the kind of material that the reader in search of such a history would be looking for and could perhaps construct out of it to his own taste. Apart from the apparatus which all the books in the Oxford series have—a general bibliography, shorter bibliographies of the major writers arranged alphabetically, a chronological table, and brief biographical footnotes on the minor writers—the text itself contains a full and clearly written account of every writer of significance in the period. The overall arrangement may be somewhat confusing at first, with the three major writers, Defoe, Swift, and Pope, being split between the first and third parts, but everything essential is covered.

Mr. Dobrée's sense of proportion is sound: he knows that

clichés about the age of reason will not fit the English eighteenth century; he knows that such movements as Deism affected only a small fraction of the intellectual life of the time; his introductory chapter gives a good account of what is both distinctive and traditional in the social background of the age. What one misses, perhaps, is that final unification of material which is the mark of the completely realized history, in whatever field: what one has, however, is a most useful reference work in which there is also a great deal of sensitive criticism. I know of no other book which brings together so great a volume of material: from the philosophy of Berkeley to the poetry of Prior, from the incredible profusion of Defoe pamphlets to the spare and articulate paradoxes of Mandeville, any reader or student who loves the period will find it here in all its variety.

2

ORDERS OF POETIC EXPERIENCE

It is a central function of criticism to explain what is going on in the habit of reading, using "reading" as a general term for all literary experience. . . . Criticism which studies literature through its organizing patterns . . . rejects the evaluating hierarchy that limits us to the evaluator's reading list, and encourages each reader to accept no substitutes in his search for infinite variety.

The Critical Path

THE ACCEPTANCE OF INNOCENCE

A new translation of *Don Quixote*, the result of sixteen years of work, has now made its appearance, and it is, we are told, the first really good English rendering of the world's greatest novel. There have been fourteen English versions altogether, but two made in the eighteenth century, one by Peter Motteux, a naturalized Frenchman who also completed the Urquhart Rabelais, and one by Charles Jarvis, a friend of Pope, have held the field. The former is the better known in America, and the latter in England. Mr. Putnam's introduction is severe on Motteux, whom he accuses of having coarsened two of the subtlest characters in fiction into a couple of slapstick buffoons. This opinion of Motteux is endorsed by other Cervantes scholars and a number of reviewers.

Well, the scholars must know; but for vigor and the free play of a rough but spontaneous wit, there is a lot to be said for the earlier version. Mr. Putnam has perhaps reacted too strongly against it (after all there *is* some buffoonery in Cervantes), and sometimes his own sentences tinkle along rather languidly, the rhythms too carefully calculated, the English idioms and colloquialisms slipping a little too glibly into their Spanish context. But when one has said this, one hastens to concede that, both for its text and for its admirably terse notes, this is the translation that the modern reader would want. Certainly, wherever delicacy is required, Mr. Putnam is to Motteux as Pegasus to Rosinante.

Perhaps it would be fairer to say that Motteux represents what the eighteenth century, an age of solid intellectual and social values, saw in *Don Quixote*. The eighteenth century

Review of Cervantes, *Don Quixote*, trans. Samuel Putnam (New York: Viking, 1949). Reprinted from *The Canadian Forum*, vol. 29 (Dec. 1949).

could accept the folly of Quixote and the clownishness of
Sancho as simply as it accepted the cowardice of Falstaff, and
it saw them in the sharp light of the world of common sense
that gave them both so many hard knocks. From the point of
view of, say, Smollett (another translator of *Quixote*), hard
knocks are funny when they happen to people who ask for
them. In the romantic period, *Don Quixote* is read in a
romantic light and joins Hamlet, Byron, Werther, and the
noble savage in that gloomy and desperate band of idealists
who maintain the purity of their egoism in the teeth of a
scoffing society. Here we have passed from the squat, grinning
caricatures of Hogarth's illustrations to the haunting and
sinister paintings of Daumier, where the knight of the sorrow-
ful countenance looks like a pale horse riding on Death. "One
of the saddest books in the world," a Victorian critic asserts.
Mr. Putnam's translation belongs to the twentieth century,
which assumes that an author becomes great by virtue of
Saying Something Significant. He quotes Mr. Lionel Trilling
on Cervantes' treatment of the problem of appearance and
reality and puts references to the existentialism of Kierkegaard
and Sartre and the symbolic logic of Bertrand Russell into his
footnotes. These references are very unobtrusive, but they will
probably set the tone for the renewed criticism which his
translation will certainly inspire.

Cervantes' intention in writing *Don Quixote* was, no doubt,
to ridicule the stories of chivalry, with a result summarized in
the Dewey Library Catalogue as: "immense vogue of books of
chivalry despite legislation till publication of *Don Quixote*;
thereafter only one written." But great art comes from har-
nessing a conscious intention to the creative powers beneath
consciousness, and we do not get closer to the author's
meaning by getting closer to the book's meaning. The greater
the book, the more obvious it is that the author's consciousness
merely held the nozzle of the hose, so to speak. For instance,
we can see after the event what Cervantes can hardly have
seen during it, that the tale of the crack-brained knight is one
of the profoundest social parables in history. The feudal
chivalric aristocracy has been caught at the precise moment of

its departure from the European stage, caught with its armor rusty, its ideals faded to dreams, its sense of reality hopelessly lost. Elsewhere, in England, for instance, a new middle class not only seized its money and power but stole its ideals as well: the story of Quixote is the story of Spain, with its great culture destroyed by poverty and bigotry, with its weak middle class and its rabble of fanatically proud pauper-nobles. "And so, Sancho my friend," pleads Quixote, "do not be grieved at that which pleases me, nor seek to make the world over, nor to unhinge the institution of knight-errantry." But it's no use; the made-over world is already there.

However, the book has profounder levels than that of historical parable. Cervantes may be said to have defined a principle almost as important for fiction writing as charity is for religion: the principle that if people are ridiculous, they are pathetic; and if they have pathos, they have dignity. The Don is ridiculous chiefly when he is successful, or thinks he is: when he has routed a flock of sheep or set free a gang of criminals. But with every beating he gets, his dignity grows on us, and we realize how genuinely faithful he is to the code of chivalry. He is courteous, gentle, chaste, generous (except that he has no money), intelligent and cultured within the limits of his obsession, and, of course, courageous. Not only was the code of chivalry a real code that helped to hold a real civilization together, but these are real virtues, and would be if chivalry had never existed. It is this solid core of moral reality in the middle of Quixote's illusion that makes him so ambiguous a figure. As with Alice's Wonderland, where we feel that no world can be completely fantastic where such Victorian infantile primness can survive intact, we feel that the humanity of Quixote is much more solidly established than the minor scholastic quibble about whether the windmills are really windmills or not. So we understand the author's explanation of Sancho's fidelity very well: "Sancho Panza alone thought that all his master said was the truth, for he was well acquainted with him, having known him since birth."

If we want satire on martial courage we should expect to find most of it in the army, and nobody could have written

Don Quixote except an old soldier. But to satirize martial courage is not to ridicule it, but to show the contrast between the courage itself, which may be genuine and even splendid, and the reasons for its appearance—that is, the causes of war, which are usually squalid and foolish. And however silly the Don may look in his barber-basin helmet, the qualities that make him so haunting a figure are, in part, the qualities that make a lost cause glamorous. Yet a lost cause, even one so literally lost as Quixote's is pathetic as well as glamorous, and no one can miss the pathos in Quixote. Pathos arises when attention is focused on an individual excluded from a community. The child or animal whose affection is repulsed, the colored student whose offering of intelligence is rejected by a white society, the girl whose manners are laughed at by rich people because she is poor—these are the figures we find pathetic—and with them is the mad knight whose enormous will to rescue the helpless and destroy the evil shows itself in such blundering nonsense.

As humanity is always trying to find human scapegoats, it dislikes having its attention called to their human qualities, and besides, the fear of being oneself isolated is perhaps the deepest fear we have—a much deeper one than the relatively cosy and sociable bogey of hell. Whatever the reason, long-sustained pathos is intolerable, and the story of Quixote would be intolerable without the fidelity of Sancho, who enables the knight to form a society of his own. Even so, it would be hard going without the good humor and charity of so many of the people they meet. There must have been times when Cervantes wished he had not made Quixote so pathetic. In the second part, the Don is in charge of a duke who has read part one, and who is responsible for most of the adventures, going even to the point of allowing the knight and squire to live for a time in an external replica of their fantasy. He does this purely to amuse himself, but still, a fundamental act of social acceptance underlies part two. One gentleman has recognized another, however much he has turned him into a licensed jester.

Don Quixote is the world's first and perhaps still its greatest novel, yet the path it indicated was not the one that the novel followed. Imitations of his pedantic crackpot and simple companion, such as we get in *Huckleberry Finn* or *Tristram Shandy*, do not constitute a tradition. The novel is an art of character study, and character study is mainly a matter of showing how social behavior is conditioned by hidden factors. Realistic novels select mainly the factors of class and social status; psychological ones select those of individual experience. Very few have followed Cervantes in tackling the far deeper problem of private mythology, of how one's behavior is affected by a structure of ideas in which one thinks one believes. Flaubert (in *Madame Bovary*) was one such follower, and Dostoyevsky another; but the full exploitation of this field has yet to come. One hopes it will come soon, as the shallower fields are nearly exhausted.

I have hinted that Quixote does not so much believe his fantasy as think he believes it: an occasional remark to Sancho like "upon my word, you are as mad as I am" gives him away. His fantasy is the facade of a still deeper destructive instinct, for at one level of his mind, Don Quixote is one of the long line of madmen, ending in Hitler, who have tried to destroy the present under the pretext of restoring the past. It is at this level that we find the puzzle of reality and appearance. The physical world rocks and sways as Quixote explains that his valiant deeds are real, but appear ridiculous through the artfulness of enchanters. It is difficult to know where a man will stop who regards the creator of "reality" as a magician to be outwitted. One feels at times that Quixote rather enjoys the paradoxical clash of his inner and outer worlds, and that, like so many who have committed themselves to heroism, he finds that the damage he does is something of an end in itself.

But, the Don insists, he really has a positive mission: it is to restore the world to the Golden Age. In a passage of wonderful irony, he tells Sancho that the Golden Age would soon return if people would speak the simple truth, stop flattering their superiors, and show things exactly as they are. The childish element in Quixote, which breaks through in fantasy, believes that the Golden Age is a wonderful time of make-believe, where endless dreams of conquered giants and rescued maidens keep coming true. But then he comes across a group of peasants eating acorns and goat's cheese, who hospitably invite him to join them, and he suddenly breaks out into a long panegyric about the Golden Age, which, it appears, was not an age of chivalry at all, but an age of complete simplicity and equality. In such a kingdom, the social difference between himself and Sancho no longer exists, and he asks Sancho to sit beside him, quoting from the Bible that the humble shall be exalted. The bedrock of Quixote's mind has been reached, and it is not romantic at all, but apocalyptic. The childishness has disappeared and the genuinely childlike has taken its place, the simple acceptance of innocence.

This dream returns at the end, where Quixote and Sancho plan to retire to a quiet, pastoral life, and the author intends us to feel that by dying Quixote has picked a surer means of getting there. With this in our minds, we are not at all surprised that when Sancho, who has been promised the rule of an island, actually gets one to administer, he rules it so efficiently and wisely that he has to be yanked out of office in a hurry before he wrecks the Spanish aristocracy. We are even less surprised to find that Quixote's advice to him is full of sound and humane good sense. The world is still looking for that lost island, and it still asks for nothing better than to have Sancho for its ruler and Don Quixote for his honored counselor.

THE YOUNG BOSWELL

It is now well known that a great mass of Boswelliana, recovered from Fettercairn and Malahide castles, has been bought by Yale University and is in course of publication. The story is summarized by Mr. Christopher Morley in the introduction to the newly published journal kept by Boswell, then aged twenty-two, from November 1762 to August 1763, the year that he met Johnson. The journal is full of narrative and antiquarian interest, but it adds nothing startling to our present knowledge of the period. Its importance is rather that it illustrates a significant stage in the development of a writer of genius.

We may feel that Boswell had no right to be a great artist: that biographies should be factual and works of art fictional, and that they should be kept apart. But there it is. Without using a single faked or illegitimate device as a biographer, Boswell has given us a real person who is also a great fictional character, and who keeps obstinately getting mixed up in our minds with Falstaff and Micawber. When we talk about Johnson we still tend, even with Boswell to help us, to make him as dull and obvious as a face on a billboard, whether we adopt the "sturdy common sense" cliché or the approach of Churchill's "Pomposo, insolent and loud." To contrast either with the subtlety of Boswell is to get some idea of Boswell's achievement. The phrase "a Boswell" generally means a silent stenographer, but Boswell was anything but that, and when we turn to his life and character we are mystified. One of the things the Boswell papers should do is to give us some idea of

Review of *Boswell's London Journal, 1762–1763*, ed. Frederick A. Pottle (New York: McGraw-Hill, 1950). Reprinted by permission from *The Hudson Review*, vol. 4, no. 1 (Spring 1951). © 1951 by The Hudson Review, Inc.

how this strange creature with his spastic will managed to keep sprawling and shambling up to the top of one of the dizziest technical pinnacles of art.

In the art of Boswell's biography, two things are remarkable. One is the endless patience and skill with which he drew Johnson out through cunningly chosen questions and situations: Johnson comes to life as a result of what one can only call an exhaustive biographical dialectic, a Platonic dialogue in reverse. The other is his powerful grasp of the organic consistency of Johnson's character: his ability to show that the tenderness and the brutality, the outraged bellows and the flashing epigrams, the heartiness and the misanthropy, were inseparable parts of the same man. He saw the wistful Quixote behind the coffeehouse buccaneer, and he saw that Johnson's arrogance was really a high courage because of the loneliness it had to conquer. Boswell possessed a very rare kind of sympathetic *Einfühlung* which he applied to others besides Johnson. He succeeded in gaining introductions to both Rousseau and Voltaire by writing a Rousseauist letter, exclamatory and self-deprecating, to Rousseau and a Voltairean one, witty and *épatant*, to Voltaire. To call the motive for these letters snobbery gets us nowhere: we might as well call it original sin. It is at least fairer to Boswell to notice how well he understood the weaknesses of these men, and how uncynical and tolerant that understanding was. In his journal, after a day of letter writing he says: "I have touched every man on the proper key, and yet have used no deceit."

Tolerance, like charity, begins at home in self-tolerance, a quite different thing from self-indulgence or self-conceit, however much of either Boswell also had. The present journal gives one more respect for Yeats's "mask" conception of the psychology of the writer. The writer, says Yeats, compensates for his personal deficiencies by projecting an ideal self which is the exact opposite of his real self; his ability as a writer then crystallizes around and expresses this ideal self. Boswell, at twenty-two, noted in himself an infantile confidingness, a desperate urgency to be noticed, and a wit that seemed to come off best when the victim of it was himself. And so, being like other self-conscious young men much preoccupied with social rhythms, he tried to become as exquisitely poised and disciplined as Castiglione's courtier. He assumed that it was possible to grow into the character of "what God intended me and I myself chose" by an act of conscious will. Because his social defenses were apt to fall with a crash at the first moment of contact, he stresses the importance of being what he calls *retenu*. No one ever died for a backslapper: the magnetic personalities are those who can suggest by their manner that other people should come to them. "I am always resolving to study propriety of conduct," he says; and "I pride myself in thinking that my natural character is that of dignity." There follows a more rueful entry: "Dempster and Erskine breakfasted with me. . . . I said I wanted to get rid of folly and to acquire sensible habits. They laughed."

In this deadlock a third character takes over, cold, precise, and ruthless: the character of Boswell the writer. Boswell the writer works the same miracle of recreation on himself that he was later to work on Johnson, and he does it by the same process of inspired listening, except that here he is able to eavesdrop on thoughts as well. Boswell the writer listens to Boswell reflecting on a spasmodic act of charity: "The creature did not seem so grateful as I could have wished." He listens to Boswell contemplating his ideal image after telling off the mistress who gave him gonorrhea: "During all this conversation I really behaved with a manly composure and polite dignity that could not fail to inspire an awe." Then he records how he wrote her to get back his entrance fee of two guineas. And so on. The editor, Mr. Pottle, explains that the journal was, like Swift's *Journal to Stella*, sent to a friend as correspondence and hence written for a reader, and he notes that Boswell will often, writing several days after an event, build up narrative interest by excluding his later knowledge. Boswell noted his own selectivity, and remarks that he wants his journal "to contain a consistent picture of a young fellow eagerly pushing through life." But the sinewy narrative drive of the journal and its constant impression of being humorously aware and emotionally on top of all situations comes, not from the man, but from the mask that conceals the man and reveals the artist.

The result, as Mr. Pottle also remarks, is quite different both from Rousseau's (and Goethe's) factitious manipulation and from the almost inhuman self-extroversion of Pepys. It is quite different, too, from the only other English prose writer from the age of sensibility who ranks with Boswell: Sterne. Sterne, like Boswell, is a connoisseur of unstudied simplicity, and, though we know that Toby's reactions will always be military, each one is fresh and spontaneous. "Ilus," says Walter Shandy, rationalizing the disaster of little Tristram and the windowsash, "circumcised his whole army one morning.—Not without a court-martial? cry'd my Uncle Toby." But Sterne himself is cunning and artful. Boswell the subject is naive rather than simple, and Boswell the writer is correspondingly candid.

Naive, because, being prey to conflicting moods, he allows each mood to project its own image of himself and the world in turn. He tries to get a commission in the Guards, and remarks, "I do think my love of form for its own sake is an excellent qualification for a gentleman of the Army." He climbs into bed with Louisa and says, "I surely may be styled a Man of Pleasure." And candid, because he records all his moods and does not conventionalize himself. Aristotle remarks that morally there is little to choose between the boaster and the ironic or self-deprecating man, as they both lie about themselves. And, from a literary point of view, they both produce rather facile autobiographies. Boswell shows an uncanny knack of hitting a tone exactly in the middle, vain and ironic at the same time. "I have an honest mind and a warm friendship. Upon my soul, not a bad specimen of a man. However my particular notions may alter, I always preserve these great and worthy qualities." Or, perhaps with more obvious artfulness: "I really conducted this affair with a manliness and prudence that pleased me very much. The whole expense was just eighteen shillings." This kind of thing is the very essence of human self-revelation and is far above a mere willingness to tell the worst of oneself.

It is fascinating, too, to read the famous 1763 bits of the *Life* in relation to Boswell instead of Johnson. Like most people who struggle for impossible masks, Boswell had father trouble, and this journal polarizes him between his own father and a new father figure. We notice for the first time how Boswell's opening conversations with Johnson turn on the relation of father and son and on the limits of obedience and authority. Boswell's own father, Lord Auchinleck, was a provincial Scotch Presbyterian who despised literature in general and Boswell's writings in particular, and insisted that Boswell should go into law (which, Boswell observes, would force him "to be obliged to remember and repeat distinctly the dull story, probably of some very trivial affair"). Johnson was a Londoner, an Episcopalian monarchist, and a literary figure, who specifically encouraged Boswell to keep a journal. A letter to Boswell from his father is printed in an appendix: it is the first document of a long tradition, culminating in Macaulay's essay, which can see nothing in the man Boswell but a deplorable ass. Meanwhile, Boswell had been composing, with all his usual tact and skill, his letter of introduction to posterity, which has taken much longer to be delivered, but should give him the last word.

Most of us think of Coleridge, at least for a time as a writer of bits and pieces. I can still remember the nugget I had to memorize about him in grade eight: "A writer of great powers and promise, but incapable of steady work." There is a good deal of patronizing biography and criticism in the same tone, implying that if the critic had had Coleridge's genius and his Wedgewood pension, he would have laid off the opium, not married until he met the right Sara, finished his books and poems, and led a tidier life. But it is slowly becoming apparent that, while Coleridge certainly proposed more books than he ever disposed of, the impression of bits and pieces is not altogether due to Coleridge. Within the last twenty years, more and more of the vast bulk of what he actually did write has been coming into view. His letters, his table talk, his Shakespearean and other literary criticism, all form big collections, and Miss Kathleen Coburn, who has already edited his *Philosophical Lectures*, is now, as she says, "working towards an edition of Coleridge's note books," of which there must be at least fifty-four, the highest number in her references.

Preparatory to this, she offers us a collection of over three hundred numbered short notes and aphorisms, gathered partly from the unpublished notebooks and marginalia, partly from prose writings not reprinted in this century, such as *The*

Review of *Inquiring Spirit: A New Presentation of Coleridge from His Published and Unpublished Prose Writings*, ed. Kathleen Coburn (New York: Pantheon, 1951); *The Note-books of Matthew Arnold*, ed. Howard Foster Lowry, Karl Young, and Waldo Hilary Dunn (New York: Oxford University Press, 1952). Reprinted by permission from *The Hudson Review*, vol. 5, no. 4 (Winter 1953). © 1953 by The Hudson Review, Inc.

Friend and *Aids to Reflection*. It makes excellent reading, and though the editing is unobtrusive, the selection could not have been made without a complete and thoroughly well-proportioned knowledge of Coleridge. For the student of English literature, I should say it was practically indispensable, even though some of it can be found in other Coleridge collections. By the time all of Coleridge has been printed, we shall be unlikely ever to ask again, "Why couldn't he finish anything he started?" If we have a question of such a type, it is more likely to be, "Why did a man who may well have had a profounder mind than Goethe and was, at least intellectually, nearly as versatile, have failed so utterly to make Goethe's impact on modern culture?"

Coleridge's thoughts obviously came to him much as the images of *Kubla Khan* and *The Ancient Mariner* did, as a series of aphorisms crystallizing from his reading. Because these aphorisms contained his essential ideas, the process of translating them into a continuous prose narrative was, in theory, a mechanical piece of copying, to be done at any leisure time. In practice, of course, it turned out to be a deadly dull and painful drudgery, in which he found that he had, so to speak, no gear low enough to keep him moving. Hence, he would assert that books were finished because, in one sense, that was true; though in any sense that would interest a publisher, they had not been begun. His reputation has suffered from the fact that literature has not yet developed anything analogous to the sculptor's stonecutter.

Everyone is familiar with the way that he floundered through the *Biographia Literaria*. He hung a donkey's carrot in front of himself in the form of a great chapter on the imagination, to which the earlier chapters were the prolegomena. Eventually the chapter arrived, "On the Imagination, or Esemplastic Power," followed by three portentous harrumphs in English, Latin, and Greek quotations and a preliminary flourish on the history of philosophy. Then his will power digs its heels in and balks; his pen trails off: he writes a long letter to himself advising himself to postpone his chapter until he has time to write a supercolossal work on the

Logos, and then, as it is no longer necessary to go in one direction rather than another, he plunges into the critique of Wordsworth that he has had on his mind all along, and the rest of the book again is bits and pieces.

Miss Coburn's method of anthologizing is much fairer to Coleridge than he was to himself because she preserves the aphoristic quality of his real thinking. In continuous prose, even at his best, he is, as Chesterton says of Shaw, long-winded because he is quick-witted: he thinks of all the qualifications of his idea at once, hence his contemporary reputation for murkiness. In his discontinuous notes, we get the bite and the point of what he has to say because it is said in the rhythm of his thinking. Miss Coburn provides, up to a point, something that Coleridge badly needed as a discursive writer: an appropriate prose form.

Like Bacon, Coleridge was much preoccupied with tables of contents, methodological axioms, schemes for others to work out, and intellectual projects and agendas of all kinds. But unlike Bacon, he could not be complacent about this or about the possibility that his vast opus maximum might never be finished. He seems to have felt it imperative to write a long piece of continuous prose in the conventional treatise form. Writing continuous prose is (as I think Kafka says somewhere) an art of causality, in which the ideas form a linear progression. But when Coleridge got an idea, it became a center to which other ideas simultaneously attached themselves. His importance in the history of semantics is due to his ability to ask of common and significant words, like *mind*, *reason*, and the like, the same question that, according to Mill, made him the great seminal conservative mind of his age: "What does this word mean by being there, by having all the different associations which it actually does have in the language?" (See the fine aphorism numbered 73 in Miss Coburn's book.)

The Aristotelian treatise-book form, what he calls (no. 70) "the paideutic continuous form," was simply not his form. Still less congenial to him, however, was the method of the Platonic dialogue: whatever his opinion of Plato, he detested the whole dialectic either-this-or-that procedure and maintained that no argument could ever be refuted except by being contained in a more comprehensive system of thought, and so shown to be incomplete. The form that would best have suited his habits of thought was the intellectual auto-biography, in which there is no logical continuity, and yet no digression, because the essential informing power—himself—remains in the center, and everything radiates from it. The *Biographia Literaria* starts with this form, and that is why it is the most sustained of his writings. But it is too strongly attracted toward the systematic treatise to remain in the tradition of, say, Montaigne, or even of the Rabelais whom Coleridge, rather unexpectedly, admired. Carlyle's grasp of romantic ideas was not as secure as Coleridge's, but *Sartor Resartus* is a far better attempt at finding a form in which to expound them.

A great achievement results from the union of a great mind with a great idea: Coleridge had both, but some coagulating or—well—esemplastic power seems to be lacking. The failure to find a prose form is not the cause of this, but one result of it. The glib explanations of the cause, opium, weak will, unhappy love, and the like, clearly will not do, even if Coleridge himself offers them. I give my own guess, for what it is worth. Coleridge seems to have lacked the kind of detachment which is usually the product of a comfortable egotism (he says of Milton [no. 131], "The egotism of such a man is a revelation of spirit"). Miss Coburn is, rightly, impressed by Coleridge's many-sidedness, and has arranged his aphorisms in various divisions, psychology, philosophy, science, public affairs, linguistics, religion, and others. A certain remoteness from the subject seems to be an emotional advantage to Coleridge. He never claimed to be a man of affairs, and the political section is of an almost unvarying decency and good sense. He never claimed to know much about science and medicine, and he makes some fascinating speculations about them.

But in fields where he is more expert, a panting desire to teach and improve gives a bothered, blustery, self-conscious quality to his style. He can hardly write about the moral side of religion for very long without beginning to scream. In his literary criticism, one never knows when he is going to be seized by a moral spasm, and when he strikes a virtuous pose, he can be more pachydermatous than Johnson at his worst. As value judgments in criticism are largely based on moral metaphors, his sense of literary values suffers accordingly. In his careless denigration of everything French, he is little better than the culture blatherers of our own day who see everything in German thought from Luther to Nietzsche as potential Nazism. His remarks about Gibbon are embarrassing; his persistent undervaluing of Virgil is clearly derived from his moral disapproval of the second Eclogue, and so on.

Miss Coburn's only editorial appearance in the text is in the headings she gives to the aphorisms; and number 110, where Coleridge says, "It is still the great definition of humanity, that we have a conscience," she has headed "Conscience—Freedom to Will and Think." But a careful reading of the paragraph shows that while Coleridge may mean that too, he also means conscience in its unregenerate sense of a please-mamma moral compulsion—the conscience of which, Huck Finn complained, nagged him even when it knew no more about the situation than he did. In the same paragraph he distinguishes "the turbulent heat of temporary fermentation from the mild warmth of essential life." It is important to notice that when he expresses one of his major literary ambitions, his mood is usually turbulent and fermenting. (Compare the project for six hymns in the Gutch Memorandum Book: "In the last Hymn a sublime enumeration of all the charms or Tremendities of Nature—then a bold avowal of Berkeley's System!!!!") One can get becalmed not only through failing to love God's creatures, but through being too anxious to help them hatch their eggs.

Miss Coburn also emphasizes the modernity of Coleridge in her introduction, and in expressing it she favors the rhetorical question. "Was he not groping toward a *Gestalt* psychology before the gestaltists? . . . had he not a glimmering of freudianism before Freud? . . . would he not have recognized in Jung's doctrine . . . "—and so on. True, no doubt, and one could fall into the same rhythm almost *ad libitum*. Does he not anticipate Newman when he distinguishes positiveness from certainty (no. 110); Kierkegaard in his note on Dread (no. 37); Schopenhauer in his conception of will and reason (no. 235); the logical positivists when he stresses the necessity of "criterional logic" (no. 88); perhaps even Wittgenstein's opening aphorism when he says "The phrase, *true in all cases*, is preferable to *universal*" (no. 92); etc., etc.? I am not one of those, however, who feel that the ultimate justification of something great in the past is its relevance to the present, instead of its own greatness. For instance, in the *Biographia*, chapter 6, where Coleridge cites the case of a hysterical girl to prove that, taking in all levels of consciousness, we never forget anything, he does show "a glimmering of Freudianism before Freud." He goes on to suggest that this total recollection of experience may actually be the last judgment we experience as we pass from flesh to spirit—an idea that no Freudian would get a glimmering of in a million years. And I think the "seminal" quality in Coleridge's thought, the quality that will keep the reader of Miss Coburn's anthology finding good things in it for months after he buys it, can be explained in another way.

Miss Coburn remarks, "The more one reads Coleridge the more impressed one becomes with what can only be called a psychological approach to all human problems," and goes on to suggest that the whole shape of Coleridge's thought is psychological. Her opinion is authoritative, and she doubtless has reams of evidence for her statement in the notebooks of which I know nothing. But such an approach to Coleridge seems to me to be bound up with the indefensible view that in Coleridge, as in Blake, the central coordinating principle is the psychological one of imagination. The imagination is instrumental in Coleridge: it is the power that unifies, but not the thing to be unified, the real coordinating principle. The latter is the Logos, and every aspect of Coleridge's thought is an application of this conception. It leads him, in politics, to see human destiny as emanating from the Incarnation, in contrast to the "philanthropic" liberal humanism that starts by trying to improve human nature. It leads him, in religion, to the same perspective and to a theism which makes the knowledge of nature depend on reason, and reason on the presence of the Logos in the mind (see no. 99). It leads him, in philosophy, to hail the "second triumphant Coming" of medieval realism, after a reign of nominalism that ran through Bacon and Descartes to the French *philosophes* (No. 99, and compare the powerful analysis of Cartesianism in no. 52). It leads him, in criticism, to the conception of all literature as contained within an order of words identical with one personal Word—perhaps his greatest legacy to modern thought, and one still unexplored. It leads him, even in science, to a type of speculation aimed at restoring the system of analogies and correspondences on which medieval symbolism was based (compare no. 185). And although Coleridge's thought remains fragmentary, the fragments are priceless, not because they are imaginative, but because they are logia. Just as Blake urges us to see the world in a grain of sand, so in Coleridge we have to see the vast, ramifying body of the Logos in all the brilliant facets and prisms of these aphorisms, as they come tumbling over one another in a wonderful sweep of mental richness, like the drops in the Cumberland waterfalls that he loved so much to watch.

The reader unacquainted with *The Notebooks of Matthew Arnold* should be told immediately not to expect anything like Miss Coburn's "basket of plucked plums and windfalls," as she calls it. There is hardly anything by Arnold in them; they are not strictly his notebooks, but his commonplace books, lists of sentences quoted from his reading. They are in Greek, Latin, French, German, Italian, and English, the first five being left untranslated "By the wishes of the members of Arnold's family and of the publishers," according to the preface. Such lists of *adagia* or *sententiae* are a normal part of the training of a humanist scholar: they help him to see his reading as a program of life and focus in his mind the best that has been thought in the way in which it has best been said. They throw a light, too, on Arnold's stylistic habit of repeating a thematic phrase all through a book. Along with the supplementary lists provided by the editors at the end of the book, it forms a valuable guide to Arnold reading. Otherwise it is difficult to know what to say about this book, which has been edited with great pains and erudition, and is clearly the product of a touching personal devotion to Arnold. The long series of sentences in Greek from the New Testament and Marcus Aurelius, for instance, do not seem to illustrate the way Arnold read them as his published writings do. One can, perhaps, build up a picture of a harassed nineteenth-century contemplative, turning eagerly to Senancour and à Kempis, but forced to listen also to Goethe bellowing into his other ear about the vast and vague merit of getting something done. The conclusion of the main part of the book, a series of quotations dated a week after his death, has in it the melancholy withdrawing roar of the sea of faith, leaving beached a number of shored fragments like those at the end of *The Waste Land*:

When the dead is at rest, let his remembrance rest; and be comforted for him when his spirit is departed from him. (*Ecclus.*)

> Ipse suas artes, sua munera, laetus Apollo
> Augurium citharamque dabat celeresque sagittas.
> Ille, ut depositi proferret fata parentis,
> Scire potestates herbarum usumque medendi
> Maluit, et mutas agitare inglorius artes. (*Aeneid* xii)

Society is a sort of organism on the growth of which conscious efforts can exercise little effect. (Karl Marx)

Si est gaudium in mundo, hoc utique possidet puri cordis homo. (*Imitation of Christ*)

Mr. Wagner's book is an excellent study of one of the "men of 1914," as Wyndham Lewis styled the group of Joyce, Pound, Eliot, and himself. The approach is critical rather than biographical, although one important biographical detail does emerge: Lewis was born in the same year as Joyce, a fact which he seems to have concealed, but which must have been known to Joyce when he made Lewis the basis of his Shaun figure. Much has still to be done on Lewis's biography: Mr. Wagner could not have done it without writing a different kind of book, but he clearly feels that the key to the contradictions in Lewis's character and thought is biographical rather than critical. The book is divided into four parts. The first, "Politics," obviously put first in order to get *that* out of the way, deals with such things as the Hitler book and its recantation; the second, "Art," with Lewis's critical journalism; the third, "Time," with his larger cultural reflections; and the fourth, with his work as a satirist. Lewis is studied throughout as a literary figure, and it is his opinions about art rather than his practice as a painter that Mr. Wagner stresses.

The disadvantage of such an approach is that it deprives Mr. Wagner of a center of gravity. Lewis's painting usually makes sense; much of his writing does not, partly because writing with Lewis was a hobby, as painting was with D. H. Lawrence, though a hobby which he cultivated with such energy that it came to overshadow the main art. Many features of his writing are those of the amateur. He never mastered—never tried to master—the art of expository prose,

Review of Geoffrey Wagner, *Wyndham Lewis* (New Haven: Yale University Press, 1957). Reprinted by permission from *The Hudson Review*, vol. 10, no. 4 (Winter 1957–58). ©1958 by The Hudson Review, Inc.

and the insincerity in his journalism is mainly due to the fact that he does not have the technical equipment to be sincere. He cannot make words express a precise meaning: he showers his reader with a verbal offensive, with what the accurate schoolboy phrase calls shooting a line. A passage quoted by Mr. Wagner reminds us how much of Lewis's prose is couched in the huff-snuff rhetoric which is a nonoccult form of automatic writing:

> Ours has been in the West a generation of hypocrites . . . a generation that has shown less care for men in the mass than any for a great many centuries, combining this demonstrable indifference to the welfare of the generality with never-ceasing hosannas to the Common Man: a generation of power-addicts who put on a red tie with a smirk, climb upon the back of the Working Class and propose to ride it to a new type of double-faced dominion . . .

In reading even the best of expository works, one feels in contact with an acute, witty, and erudite mind, yet these books are unusually difficult to finish. There are two reasons, I think, for this. One is their inconclusiveness: they never seem to make a memorable or rounded point except when they are attacking some other writer. The other is their lack of rhythm: one bores one's way along a deafening, unaccented clatter of words until one can stand the noise no longer.

Such a style, though largely useless for exposition, has its points as a style for satire, founded as it is on invective and parody, and Lewis's theory of writing is chiefly a rationalization of his satiric style. The theory is that his approach is external and spatialized, in contrast to that of Joyce (whom he considers only as a stream-of-consciousness writer) and, more particularly, Gertrude Stein, who writes "like a confused, stammering, rather 'soft' [bloated, acromegalic, squinting, and spectacled, one can figure it as] child," and who is "just the german musical soul leering at itself in a mirror, and sticking out at itself a stuttering welt of swollen tongue." The difference in kind from his own style implied by such remarks does not, of course, exist: his is simply another highly mannered rhetoric, and it would be easy to think up similar epithets for it. Lewis maintains that his own approach is consistently concerned with the outsides of people, paying attention only to the visible "ossatures," in contrast to the emotional and temporal fumblings for a dark and soft interior. His definitions of his own aims, however, in the flat, antithetical form in which they are presented in *Men Without Art*, are sheer idiocies: space is better than time; the outside is better than the inside; painting is better than music, and so on, and so on. Besides, the human body not being crustacean, its ossature is inside anyway.

Even Lewis, however, can hardly be unaware of the badness of his metaphors: he adopts them because they give a general idea of his tradition. This is the line of intellectual satire represented by Petronius (one of the nearest to him technically), Rabelais, certain aspects of Dickens, and the Flaubert of *Bouvard et Pecuchet*, which he imitates to some extent in *The Human Age*. Satire is based on a moral attitude—there is a halfhearted effort in *Men Without Art* to argue that satire need not be moral, but it soon breaks down—and the basis of this attitude is frequently an assumed contrast between a moral norm that is pragmatically free and flexible, and behavior that appears grotesque because it is obsessed, or bound to a single repeated pattern of action, like Jonson's "humor." The obvious metaphor for the latter is the machine or puppet, and Lewis's characterization deliberately reduces his characters to mechanisms. Mr. Wagner has an interesting table of the number of mechanical and crustacean images Lewis uses for his characters: there are certainly more than enough to make the point. In the light of this, the image of the external ossature makes more sense: a machine does have such a thing, and, in studying a machine, only its external behavior need be examined; it has no inner essence or soul stuff. Lewis, in contrast to Lawrence, associates mechanical behavior with the primitive, the "wild body" which cannot attain the disciplined freedom of civilized man.

When we compare Lewis with other satirists in his tradition we notice that his metaphor has in one respect led him astray.

One element in writing is the rhythm of narrative, the inner pulsation and continuity in the style that keeps one turning the pages. Lewis's theory would doubtless oblige him to condemn this as an internal or temporal quality in writing, but unfortunately for the theory, structural rhythm is the real skeleton or inner ossature of writing. His neglect of it brings the defects of his expository style into his satires. If we look at *The Apes of God*, we see a use of catalogs and set repetitive passages, like the splitman's litany, that remind us of similar things in Rabelais. But in Rabelais there is a sweeping rhythmical power that carries them off, and Lewis has no power of rhythm. Words merely cover and congeal one scene after another; his writing is the opposite of his painting, a kind of literary pointillism. For this reason, even his best satires seem to me books more likely to be admired than read. Anybody can see that they are remarkable, even astonishing books; but they give a not wholly unjustified impression of being themselves the kind of clever mechanical imitation that they present as grotesque. The exuberance of Rabelais (and Swift and Joyce) results from a rigorous discipline which is also a professional competence in their art. Lewis has this discipline as a painter, but writing he has approached externally; and when his theory extends from a technique of satiric presentation to a technique of writing satire, caricature becomes self-caricature, and the book as a whole resembles a Cartesian ghost caught in its own machine, trying to break out of a closed circle of parody. Lewis speaks of D. H. Lawrence's painting as incompetent Gauguin: partisans of Lawrence might retort that much of Lewis's writing reads like delirious Dickens. For one is often reminded of the way in which Dickens allows his facility in caricature to take over the style of writing and produce the prodigies of unplausible melodrama that mark his lapses.

The same contradiction exists in Lewis's personal publicity. Lewis appears to think of the role of the artist in terms of an anti-Communist redefinition of a proletariat, anti-Communism being one of the few attitudes that Lewis has consistently maintained. The genuinely declassed person, for Lewis, is the detached or withdrawn observer. Such an observer has a continuity in his attitude that most people, stampeded as they are by the pressures of news and propaganda, lack; he is more radical than the crowd, yet he is deeply conservative too, for the crowd, being plunged into the time-spirit, is restless for constant change, this being what Lewis calls the attitude of the "revolutionary simpleton" in the arts. The crowd wants the kind of art that reflects itself: art which glorifies the primitive, the child, or the ordinary or inarticulate common man, as in the Chaplin films and in Hemingway's "dumb ox" characters; art which follows the endless associative burble of the inner consciousness, as in the interior monologues of Joyce and Stein; art which tends to approximate, in one way or another, the communal dance, the art which encourages a sense of participation by the untrained, or of what Lewis calls the "dithyrambic spectator." All this is in contrast to the detached contemplation necessary for the Egyptian and Chinese art that Lewis (like Gauguin) prefers to the modern West, where we realize that art is not self-expression but the expression of something disinterested, a "not-self." Such views are common to an antiromantic or "neoclassical" group of artists, both English and French, whose precepts and personnel Mr. Wagner ably outlines. The true artist thus becomes the "enemy" of society, for he must either declare war on it or be crushed by its hostility.

We seem to be close here, Mr. Wagner suggests, to a theory of a creative elite. Lewis says he holds no such view, and Mr. Wagner has got to the point of feeling that this is fairly good evidence that he does. Still, Lewis's denial points to some uncertainty in his mind. The real meaning of *elite* is "people like me," and nearly everyone believes in an elite, in the sense that nearly everyone with any social function at all will tend to think of that function ideally, as something on which society as a whole depends. For artists, the conception of an elite normally begins in the establishing of schools and trends and manifestoes aimed at waking society up to the importance of their art. But with the artist, the conception of "people like me" changes, as he becomes less fond of rival artists and more attached to the people who buy and appreciate his work, into the political question of what kind of public would make *his* art elite. The change for Lewis is accelerated by his insistence that most people have no right to participate in the arts and by his increasing jealousy of almost every widely acclaimed contemporary. Finally, the conception "people like me" modulates into "people who like me," a society recreated in one's own image, which at least has the advantage of permitting a more authentic form of creative life.

All three phases are clearly marked in Lewis. The first phase is the period of "vorticism" and the *Blast* manifestoes. Lewis was clearly fascinated by Marinetti's use of the new techniques of advertising and publicity stunts in an art movement. He sent a copy of *Blast* to a friend, with a letter, quoted by Mr. Wagner, apologizing for its noise but asserting that the artist cannot exist at all without such things—a statement one may beg leave to doubt. The second phase compels Mr. Wagner to deal with the shoddy story of the flirtation with fascism by British and French intellectuals. The "neoclassical" group favored a type of relatively unpopular art, and such art could win its place only through some kind of established authority, hence their speculations were largely concerned with what kind of authoritarian government would be most useful to them. The result was a series of self-contradictions (matched, of course, by similar ones in the Communist camp) unparalleled in the history of the arts, and Lewis's writings afford an excellent area for observing them.

In Lewis, as in others of the neoclassical group, antiromanticism seems to be a late romanticism fouling its own nest. The romantic decadence glanced at in Lewis's *Diabolical Principle* seems merely to expand into a more political form of experimenting in sadomasochism. The genuine statements in neoclassical theory are mainly of romantic origin. Mr. Wagner shows that Lewis's theory of satire is lifted almost bodily from Bergson's *Le Rire*—an excellent place to go for a theory of satire, except that Bergson is one of the two philosophers most violently attacked in *Time and Western*

Man. In any case, the contrast between organism and mechanism is a romantic commonplace, going back to Goethe and Coleridge. The other target of *Time and Western Man* is Spengler, and the framework of Lewis's pronouncements on contemporary culture comes straight out of Spengler. Lewis's polemical writings are in a relatively modern genre—Spengler calls it the diatribe—which was largely created by Victorian romanticism, though Milton and Swift had practiced the form earlier. It was romanticism that brought in Lewis's notion of a special type of creative man, superior to others not simply in his particular expertise, but·in general, in his whole attitude to life. This conception of the superior person is expounded particularly in Carlyle, whose Teufelsdröckh is a professor of things in general.

Our own age has inherited from this the conception of the "intellectual," who produces, in the line of duty, the "calling-for" book, the pseudopolitical treatise that "calls for" various shifts of attitude in society and is the modern form of Spengler's diatribe. It is based on the romantic assumption that if one's expertise is in, say, poetry or fiction, one's reaction to the morning paper will show an infinitely more searching insight than the reaction of one whose expertise is in greasing cars or curling women's hair. I imagine that this assumption has still to be substantiated: in any case, Lewis's political writings provide little evidence in its favor. Of the four men of 1914, Joyce, after his adolescence, remained almost entirely aloof from this kind of intellectualized journalism; Pound fell for it hard, which is one reason why he reads so like a late Victorian. Eliot has also yielded to the temptation to write the odd diatribe, but has had the literary tact to keep the musings of *After Strange Gods* and *Notes Towards the Definition of Culture* at least overtly out of his poetry and drama. But even in this addled century, there are few phenomena more strange than Lewis's fanatic addiction to the diatribe.

Mr. Wagner speaks of the influence on Lewis of Benda's *Trahison des Clercs*, yet his diatribes are a flagrant example of what Benda means, an artist deliberately vulgarizing criti-

cal and philosophical ideas, deliberately deserting the field of
his expert knowledge for a field where nobody knows anything
because there are no facts. Lewis condemns the "dithyrambic
spectator" in art only to become one himself in society. Lewis
thinks of art as aloof, unpopular, exact, and difficult: his
diatribes are slovenly, cliché-ridden, confused, and embar-
rassingly personal. Lewis is anti-Communist, yet if we ask
what is wrong with Communism, one of the most decisive
answers is that it adopts Lewis's technique of communication.
Lewis speaks of continuity as the feature that makes for
dignity in life: his polemics shift ground so often that it
becomes almost uncharitable to remember what he said last
Tuesday. The assumption in most of the political writings is
that the one form of society which makes such writing
possible—a tolerant bourgeois democracy—is the most con-
temptible of all social structures. But when we find Lewis
urging in 1936 that Germany be allowed to rearm (and urging
the opposite in 1942, Mr. Wagner notes), we feel less grateful
for the tolerance that allows him to write than for the
indifference that makes him relatively harmless.

Again, as a satirist, one would expect Lewis to lampoon the
popular ideals of the English, their devotion to sport and fair
play, their pride in having a sense of humor, and so on. The
villain of *The Human Age* is a cliché expert known as the
Bailiff, whose appearance, recorded on Michael Ayrton's
jacket design, recalls *Punch*. Yet this attitude exists beside
another which is its direct opposite, apparently motivated by
some feeling of guilt at being declassed by art, and which at
every stage has followed a Colonel Blimp line. *Tarr* reflects the
popular anti-Germanism of the First World War; in the
twenties Lewis is explaining that Stein, Joyce, and *transition*
are really "shams," that there are too many homosexuals in
modern art, and that cubism is largely humbug; as the
political situation darkens, he becomes pro-fascist and ridicules the color cult which is part of the reaction against white
supremacy; in 1939 he abruptly takes a democratic line on
Nazis and Jews; in 1941 he completes the circle by writing
Anglo-Saxony: A League that Works. Even in religion, on

which he says little, we still find him sucking his own blood, like the Ancient Mariner. He believes in Something Upstairs, rejects Catholicism with some respect, and treats Protestantism with great contempt, as was usual in diatribes of his generation. But the dead end of Protestantism is not capitalistic exploitation or bourgeois prudery or any of the things that intellectuals' lay sermons say it is; the dead end of Protestantism is the intellectual's lay sermon.

If these diatribes formed, as Lewis is not unwilling to suggest, a deliberate masquerade, behind which the serious writing of the "Not-Self" takes place, or if the diatribes could in any other way be separated from the serious writing, their inconsistencies would not matter. They cannot—*The Childermass*, in particular, is a diatribe in fictional form—and the inconsistencies of the one become a kind of split creative personality in the other. The masquerade theory ascribes an impossible degree of subtlety, in any case, to a most unsubtle writer. Lewis ridicules the archetypal approach to fiction, yet his most memorable characters are culture-myths, some of them, like Kreisler in *Tarr*, largely of newspaper origin. He nags at homosexuals, yet shows a curious distaste for the normal relation, and his women resemble Asiatic mothergoddesses as they might have been described by the prophet Elijah. One would expect his "external" approach to have some affinity with realism, as in Flaubert; but anything like a setting in a Lewis satire becomes a fantasy of Grand Guignol proportions. The Parisian left bank in *Tarr*, the Bloomsbury-Chelsea London of *The Apes of God*, the Toronto of *Self Condemned* (if the reader will accept the opinion of a reviewer who lives there) are all as far out of this world as the limbo of *The Human Age*.

What is one to make of a writer who hates everything, with the unvarying querulousness of a neurotic, that his own writing represents? The easy way out is to decide that Lewis must be some kind of phony. Even Mr. Wagner has twinges of wondering whether his subject has really been worth his pains, and speaks of Lewis's "constant, almost paranoid, lust for destruction." Certainly one cannot study Lewis in detail without exasperation, but that is true of many writers, and though he has uniformly substituted cleverness for wisdom, still no one can read *The Human Age* carefully and feel that its author has no real place in literature. The better solution is to take all Lewis's theories as projections, realizing that he is an almost solipsistic writer, whose hatreds are a part of him because he understands nothing of what goes on outside his own mind. As Stephen Spender pointed out in a hostile but shrewd critique of Lewis, that is what his external approach really amounts to. No one better manifests Yeats's dictum that we make rhetoric out of the quarrel with others, poetry (read satire) out of the quarrel with ourselves. Lewis's temporary admiration for Hitler thus becomes intelligible: here was someone else lost in a dream, yet with a medium's power of animating and imposing his dream. We come back to our figure of the Cartesian ghost caught in its own machine, which I have partly borrowed from Mr. Wagner. Lewis is the satirist of an age whose drama is a flickering optical illusion in a darkened room, whose politics is an attempt to make clichés into axioms of automatic conduct, whose spiritual discipline is a subjective exploring of the infantile and the perverted. Such books as *The Apes of God* or *The Human Age* can hardly be written without a personal descent into the hell they portray, and Lewis has made that descent, and taken the consequences of making it, with a perverse but unflinching courage.

INTERIOR MONOLOGUE OF M. TESTE

The second volume of a projected complete translation of Paul Valéry in the Bollingen series is a collection of Valéry's essays on the theory of criticism. In any such collection, there is bound to be a good deal of repetition, but it is instructive to see how few ideas Valéry really had on the subject. The earliest essay, dated 1889, checks off the standard objects of *symboliste* devotion like beads on a rosary: the "extremely original theory of Edgar Poe," the leitmotiv in Wagner, the symbol (referred to as vaguely as possible), the analogy of music, the technique of oblique suggestion. Even what sounds more distinctive of Valéry, the remark that the poet "is a cool scientist, almost an algebraist, in the service of a subtle dreamer," is reconstructed from Poe, who did his subtle dreaming in "The Raven" and his algebra in *The Philosophy of Composition*. The latest essay is the preface to the translation of Virgil's Eclogues, done in the year of the poet's death in 1945. But the form of the present book is, somewhat accidentally, one of Valéry's favorite forms: variations on a single theme.

There are traditionally two main centers of interest in the theory of criticism, sometimes described by the words *poesis* and *poema*. The former, or Longinian, center is primarily an interest in the psychological process of poetry and in the rhetorical relation (often arrived at by indirection) set up between poet and reader. The latter, or Aristotelian, center is primarily an interest in the aesthetic product and is based

Review of Paul Valéry, *The Art of Poetry*, trans. Denise Folliot (New York and London: Routledge and Kegan Paul, 1958). Reprinted by permission from *The Hudson Review*, vol. 12, no. 1 (Spring 1959). © 1959 by The Hudson Review, Inc.

on a specific aesthetic judgment, detached by catharsis from moral anxieties and emotional perturbations. Any complete theory of criticism needs both, but in a complete theory the aesthetic judgment must take precedence, for the Longinian interest is in enthusiasm, or what "carries us away," in other words, in what uncritical feelings we may trust to afterward. Europa needs to know whether the agent of her rapture is a god in disguise or merely a remarkably undiscriminating brute. Of course, scholarship, in its turn, has priority over judgment, but that is not our concern here.

Valéry is a Longinian critic, concerned with the poetic process. As T. S. Eliot points out in his very useful introduction, he has no sustained theoretical interest in any poetry except his own, not because he is egocentric, but because he is the only poet whose processes he can watch. And as he is a very good poet, the prior aesthetic judgment is taken care of. The book has a typically Longinian opening: Valéry begins, not like Aristotle, with what poetry is and what species it has, but with the reader in a receptive mood. There are two contexts, he tells us, to which the term *poetry* belongs. One is the context of the "poetic," a vague sense, in the mind of the reader, of the enormous significance that could be given to words and of their power, when properly handled, of expressing the reader's feelings. The other is poetry in the technical sense, as the specific supply of this general demand. The better the poem, the more precisely and inevitably it expresses the inarticulate need for articulation.

Longinian, too, is Valéry's conception of inspiration as meaning, not a state of mind that the poet is in, but a state of mind that he induces in his reader. The reader feels permeated with a sense of significance not coming from himself, so he projects this on the poet and assumes that the poet is a kind of medium for some hypothetical creative spirit. But while it is true that "poetry and the arts have sensibility as beginning and end," the process of creating it may involve any amount of purely conscious and voluntary effort, as in revision or the following out of a complex metrical form. It is probably an advantage to a medium to be slightly stupid, but it is difficult to see what advantage stupidity can be to a poet, or what use the uncritical inhaling of some kind of oracular nitrous oxide would be to someone who has to work out a sestina or canzone. There are superficial resemblances between the poem and the dream, but the poet and the dreamer are even more distinct for Valéry than for Keats: nobody is so wide awake or consciously alert as the person who has to *observe* a dream.

While Valéry is primarily concerned with the theoretical element in poetry, he is not, like Longinus, concerned with direct rhetoric or oratory, but with its opposite, the indirect, disinterested rhetoric of verbal elaboration. Whenever we read anything, we find our attention moving in two directions at once. One direction is outward, from the words themselves to their remembered conventional meanings. The other is inward, and is directed toward building up a unified apprehension of the structure of words itself. Where the outward direction is the primary one, we have signal language. Here words are used for the sake of what they mean, and when the meaning is grasped, there is no further need for the words. Meaning here, Valéry says, results from the "rapid passage over words," like a hand passed quickly through a flame. "Shut the door": as soon as the door is shut, the words vanish, having fulfilled their function. Even a long book, if written simply to give information, survives only as a convenience of reference, or until it is superseded by fuller information.

But where the inward direction is the primary one, we have poetry, a structure of words made for its own sake. Poetry does not tend to disappear when its meaning is grasped, but to repeat itself in the same form, whereas repetition in signal language merely means a failure in response. (For example: "Shut the door." "What's that?" "I said, 'Shut the door.' ") The difference between poetic and signal language may be compared to the difference between dancing and walking. Walking is purposeful, and its end or fulfillment is determined externally, when we get to where we're going. Dancing is movement for its own sake, and its end is determined only by the logic of its form.

The presence of signal meaning in words makes poetry an unusually complex art. In music, for example, there is no signal meaning at all, or if there is, nobody understands it. The chord of C major does not "mean" anything except in a musical context, and "program" music is mainly humorous in reference, the source of the humor being precisely the ineptness of music for descriptive meaning. Music, or the world of significant sound, turns its back sharply on the world of aural impressions, or noise. A noise in the middle of a concert, or the sound of a violin in a city street, is an interruption from another order of things. Similarly, mathematics, considered as an art, gets along with a minimum of signal meaning. The conception *pi* does not mean anything except another mathematical formulation of it. In ordinary experience, the shortest distance between two points may not be a straight line, as the shortest way to get to the other side of a wall is around by the door, but geometry knows nothing of such existential untidiness.

The poet, however, has to use the same dissolving words that we use for ordinary speech, where we are attending not to them but to what they point to. "Shut the door" is signal language, and in one of the most terrifying moments in literature, the close of the second act of *King Lear*, the operative phrase is only "shut up your doors." It is almost as though the art of painting consisted in making collages out of old dollar bills. One has to make a special, conscious effort to recognize, in poetry, a significant and organized world of words ("poetic universe," as Valéry calls it) corresponding to the world of significant sound in music or significant measurement in mathematics. Hence poetry is esoteric, in the sense that poetic meaning is a contrast to ordinary or signal verbal meaning. It is no more esoteric than music or mathematics, but the necessity of discarding our accustomed habits of response to words in poetry creates a peculiar psychological barrier.

The distinction between inward and outward meaning, and its corollary, that verbal structures can be divided into those made for their own sake and those made to serve other purposes, is, almost certainly, the basis of all practical criticism. It is, however, a distinction between the literary and the nonliterary verbal structure. Having made the distinction, Valéry muddles it again by calling the literary structure "poetry" and the nonliterary one "prose," thus confusing it with the technical distinction in rhythm between prose and verse. But while it is true that prose is, unlike verse, used for nonliterary purposes, the enormous bulk of literary prose makes nonsense of any attempt to equate prose with the extraliterary. (One may add for completeness, though the point is of minor importance, that nonliterary verse is also possible, as in mnemonic rhymes of the "Thirty days hath September" type.) Valéry is often forced by his own confusion of terms to treat literary prose as something to be explained away. True, he does not particularly like prose, and his references even to Flaubert and Proust are somewhat disparaging. In the most systematic statement of his theory, the essay called "Remarks on Poetry," he draws a distinction between the pure poetic universe and the mimesis of actual life in prose fiction that illustrates the essential affinity of prose with signal language. But his statements would apply equally well to many other genres.

The basis of Valéry's theory is in Poe: it would be difficult to get closer to Poe than Valéry does when he says: "What we call a *poem* is in practice composed of fragments of pure poetry embedded in the substance of a discourse." This means, among other things, that the difficult part of writing a poem of any length is the problem of poetic continuity. Poetic necessity, he says, can reside only in form, and "form demands a continuity of felicitous expression." But, like Poe, Valéry regards the standard narrative and didactic conventions of continuity as nonpoetic. Of Lucretius, he remarks that the attention given to following the ideas competes with the attention given to the poetry and that "the *De Rerum Natura* is here in conflict with the nature of things." He reverts over and over to the limited degree of tolerance that poetry has for conceptual language, to the equal importance of sound and sense in the poetic process, to the necessity of subordinating thought in poetry. "An intimate alliance of

sound and sense ... can be obtained only at the expense of
something—that is, thought." The poetic process of putting
words into patterns can never coincide entirely with the
conceptual process of putting ideas into words.

No one could agree less than Valéry would with Kafka's
remark that writing is an art of causality. "The sequence of
our feelings has no longer a chronological order, but a kind of
intrinsic, instantaneous order, which is revealed step by
step." A causal or sequential writer, such as a novelist, is
faced with the Leibnitzian problem of making actual the best
of a number of possibilities, but Valéry tells us that when he
reads continuous prose, he tends to reconstruct some of the
other possibilities. For an Aristotelian critic, tragedy is often
the central form of poetic experience, but Valéry's remarks
on tragedy are aimless and uncomprehending and end in the
reflection that "the tragic genre is completely opposed to
producing in the soul the most elevated state that art can
create there: the contemplative state." Similarly with narrative: he speaks of "the prosiness, even the platitudes, inevitable when any story is put into verse," and, in his delightful
essay on La Fontaine's *Adonis*, he sums up his whole attitude
by saying: "in poetry everything which *must* be said is almost
impossible to say well." Valéry is, as we have noticed, deeply
concerned with the reader, and feels that what has value only
for oneself has no value. But he will have nothing to do with
persuasive or confronting rhetoric: he abhors all forms of
proselytism and considers it rather vulgar even to be "right"
in any difference of opinion.

We soon realize that by "poetry" Valéry means his own
kind of poetry, that is, *symbolisme*, and what *symbolisme* is
able to absorb from the poetic tradition in general. The germ
of truth in this identification is the fact that the different
genres of literature may (up to a point) be arranged in the
order of their distance from signal meaning. Literary prose is
relatively close to it; narrative and didactic verse within sight
of it; but *symbolisme* stands at the greatest possible distance
from it and does its best to turn its back on it. But, as with all
selective traditions, even *symbolisme* breaks down, or up,

into a group of conflicting heresies. The tradition of Laforge and Corbière, from which Eliot derives, is, as Eliot points out, quite different; so is the disintegrative tradition that derives from Rimbaud and Jarry. Valéry as critic is simply the disciple of Mallarmé (his relation to Poe is through Mallarmé), and it is Mallarmé's great idea of the poetic universe (*le Verbe*) that informs all his criticism.

As the poetic universe, toward which the poet turns, is in the opposite direction from the marketplace, it would be convenient if there were an absolute "poetic diction," a language peculiar to poetry and used only for it, as there is a language of sounds used only in music. "All literature which has passed a certain age reveals a tendency to create a poetic language apart from ordinary speech." For poetic language ought to be "the language of the gods," or at least a language of magic or charm, spoken only within a spellbound, closed circle. Such poetic diction as we have, however, falls very far short of being a "Paradise of Language," and so various correlatives or equivalents for a separate language emerge. Among these are the conventions of form, such as the sonnet and chant royal, or the rules governing the rhyming and cadencing of alexandrines. There is a theory of games in poetry, as there is in economics; and poetry, like chess, makes a virtue of arbitrary rules, or at least of "considered arbitrariness." Such rules have the great virtue of interfering with the half-automatic flow of "natural" or nonpoetic speech.

Poetry as close to verbal organization and as far from signal meaning as possible is what Valéry means by "pure poetry." As long as words are employed in poetry at all, of course, pure poetry cannot exist except as an ideal. But its ideal existence is very important, for it means that the creative activity of the poet is not hitched to his ego. The poet uses all the resources of skill and intelligence in the interests of an impossible demand for integrity, not in the interests of self-expression. The pure poem is really the perfect poem, and "perfection elminates the person of the author." The minor artist impresses us as a sensitive and cultivated person; the major artist is simply speaking with the voice of his art.

When we hear a musical sound in the middle of ordinary noise, we hear something that reminds us, not of any specific piece of music, but of music itself and the whole range of its possibilities. That is why Valéry speaks of the "musical universe." Every poem, similarly, is a manifestation of poetry, or a total order of words. As Valéry remarks in a patriotic address, it is obvious that the greatest French poet is France. "I make one mighty poet from all our poets, forming a single being," he says in the same context. The sense that the background of every poem is the whole order of poetic experience is constantly present in Valéry, but is nowhere developed, partly because Valéry's sense of tradition is so limited. Consequently, the question of poetic meaning, of the poem's significance, not in terms of ordinary meaning, but as a phase of poetic experience, is left in the air.

The relation of a poem to poetry as a whole raises the question of the structural principles of poetry, and in particular the problems of convention and genre. Valéry largely ignores the problem of genre and is curiously selective in his approach to convention. Conventions of external form and of meter he accepts; conventions of narrative and of poetic concepts (*topoi*) he rejects out of hand; conventions of theme and imagery leave him with nothing to say, although he observes them in practice. He speaks of the content of the poem as its myth; *Le Cimetière Marin* and *La Jeune Parque* are clearly mythopoeic poems, and conventionally mythopoeic at that. Yet he seems to have no interest in discussing their myths or images—in short, he is not concerned to give any suggestion of what these very difficult poems are about. His attitude toward a critical explication of *Le Cimetière Marin* by someone else is one of delighted surprise that a poem of his should really have meant all that.

We naturally feel that it is not a poet's business to explain what his poems mean, even granting that "meaning" here is poetic meaning, or structural analysis. But the fact that we feel this way is significant in determining the role of the poet as critic. Valéry takes a rather sardonic view of the academic study of literature and writes with much pungency about its unreality, the pointlessness of all the "interpretations" of poets that cancel each other out. As he says: "these simulacra of thoughts take on a kind of existence and provide reason and substance for a mass of combinations of a certain scholarly originality. A Boileau is thus ingeniously discovered in Victor Hugo, a romantic in Corneille, a 'psychologist' or a realist in Racine. All these things are neither true nor false—in fact they could not possibly be either." The inference is that it is the poets themselves who are the trustworthy critics: of Victor Hugo, Valéry makes the unlikely remark that "Hugo, like all true poets, is a critic of the first rank."

Yet if the present volume proves anything, it proves that all a poet can do as critic is tell us those things of which he has special knowledge, and which belong to autobiography rather than criticism. Meaning in poetry, like inspiration, is a conception that relates primarily to the reader, not the writer. In the kind of poetry that Valéry writes this means a highly trained or critical reader. For Valéry's is a post-Kantian type of poetry in which the theme or organizing form of the poem remains invisible to the poet himself, and everything in the poem is an epiphany or manifestation of some aspect of it. The poet himself knows that everything he has written belongs in his poem; he does not necessarily know why. If we are to take Valéry seriously as a poet, we cannot afford to take him too seriously as a critic.

PHALANX OF PARTICULARS

Ezra Pound is not exactly unread, or even neglected, but he is, so to speak, unidentified. Criticism has not yet fitted him into his cultural milieu as it has fitted Joyce, Eliot, and Yeats; and our perspective on our culture is bound to be astigmatic until he comes into focus. The delay is due to certain prejudices against Pound, which fall into three main groups. Some feel that Pound's reputation ought to wait until a time when a man with his political record can be more calmly appraised. Others feel that, while Pound has obviously been an enthusiastic, generous, and often discerning man, he has not obviously been a wise man, and a glance at his work seems to confirm the impression of an exuberant crank. Still others are willing to concede his importance, but are simply not enough attracted to his idiom to grapple with all that Provençal and social credit and Chinese. All three groups do not so much reject Pound as postpone him, and are waiting for someone to begin the critical organization of his work.

It is fortunate for everyone concerned, including Pound, that the first full-length critical study of Pound should be written by Mr. Kenner, and not by the sort of punk who is more usually first in a new field. Mr. Kenner has accomplished his primary task of making it impossible for any serious reader of poetry to dismiss Pound out of mere petulance or suspicion. He has had the vision and the ability not only to argue for Pound on the proper grounds, but to present him in something like his proper context. He shows how clearly Pound grasped the essential fact about poetry, that it is a

Review of Hugh Kenner, *The Poetry of Ezra Pound* (Norfolk, Ct.: New Directions, 1951). Reprinted by permission from *The Hudson Review*, vol. 4, no. 4 (Winter 1952). © 1952 by The Hudson Review, Inc.

structure of images and that its structural principle is the
juxtaposition of images. This is linked with Pound's interest in
imagism, with Aristotle's conception of metaphor and with
the Chinese development of the ideogram or image-cluster as
the basis of language. Next comes the repudiation of the
Cartesian-Lockean view that knowledge is primarily of clear
and distinct ideas, a view which reduces poetry to rhetoric,
or rather to false rhetoric, which is the figuration of ideas, an
attempt at teaching or self-expression by means of loading
ideas with emotional charges of analogy and illustration. This
develops in literature the central principle of false rhetoric,
which is "style," the art of making all parts of a verbal
structure sound alike, and like the author. Pound's attitude
toward language replaces the false rhetoric of style with the
true rhetoric of decorum, of making every part of a verbal
structure sound like what it is.

The implications of this go far beyond literature. To base a
technique of poetry on the conviction that there is no such
thing as a clear and distinct idea is to restore to philosophy a
theory of knowledge founded on the perception of particulars. This, in turn, reacts on literature and gives poetry,
which is the definition of images, its true place as the central
act of creative vision and knowledge. Poetry thus becomes,
for the reader, revelation, and, for the poet, discovery. The
essential technical innovations in the ability of poetry to
express emotions and unite images can, Pounds says, be
identified by a sufficiently astute critic.

To distinguish the poet from the compulsive babbler is an
act of fateful social and political importance. It is the central
form of the distinction between the free act which proceeds
from self-knowledge, and the act which proceeds from
mysterious compulsion. Those who are slaves to the latter are
so because they have never articulated their emotions, but
have allowed them to remain passions, or secret masters of
the soul. The free society, of which the pattern is in Confu-
cius, springs from the activity of free men, who, like Jefferson
and John Adams, are self-disciplined and articulate men. The
form of compulsive action is cupidity, and in a slave state, the
great men are parasites or usurers, whose function it is to

adulterate the currency, whether of words or of coins. The connection between accuracy in poetry and freedom in life Pound calls *ching ming*, the ideogram of which appears to mean something like "rule by the word." In the West, *ching ming* was at its height throughout the tradition of courtesy (the only word I know in English that unites the disciplines of speech and social art) which runs from the Provencal poets through the great Italian writers and painters to the Neoplatonics and Castiglione of Medicean Florence. After that, an advancing wave of cupidity debased all currencies alike, muddied the lines of art, and forced words into the slough of jargon (which, as Orwell has shown more incisively than Pound, is the result of a passion for lying).

All this and much more is in Mr. Kenner's book. If I have made it clear that the reader cannot afford to pass it up, I can be frank about my opinion of its faults. The superficial faults, which do not affect the book's virtues, may be summed up in the remark that Mr. Kenner is not very good at polemic. There is too much labored irony directed at a number of hollow men, some of them straw. "Consideration of these facts may engender some *a priori* suspicion that the man who devotes a lifetime to the amelioration of poetry does not necessarily incur the limiting connotations of 'aestheticism.'" That sentence is not an example of *ching ming*. The author runs to ellipsis and allusion, and, like a bad lecturer, dribbles quasi-facetious asides out of the corner of his mouth, which are only audible to a front row, and interfere with the exposition. One doesn't mind his having crotchets and saying that Freud "remains hopelessly old-fashioned, a model-T Mephisto smelling of *Trilby*," even if one finds the remark rather silly, but it is confusing to meet it in a discussion of Pound's use of Propertius. Nor should he deprecate source hunting, nor talk about schematic commentary on a difficult and complex poem as though it were a regrettable necessity, like excretion, to be pushed into the backhouse of a third appendix. Criticism, like poetry, is either precise statement or blather. There is no need to distrust any kind of precise statement.

Above all, I am sorry to see the anti-Milton and anti-roman-

tic clichés of thirty years ago carried on into this book.
"Pound is a far more important figure than Browning or
Landor, Eliot than Tennyson or Shelley." "Milton's blank
verse, punctuated almost entirely by enjambed or caesural
thumps, is largely remarkable for what it excludes; com-
munications from Jonson, Marvell, Chaucer, do not pass
beyond that 'Chinese wall.'" Time has deprived such value
judgments of the only meaning they ever had, which was a
specific tactical meaning, a regrouping of critical forces
between 1915 and 1930 designed to get new kinds of poetry
accepted and obscurantist conventions thrown out. Thus,
Pound, working out his conception of technical discovery in
poetry, depreciates Milton's achievement on the ground that
something that sounds like Milton can be detected in Jaco-
bean drama a few years earlier. This should not be taken as a
serious critical dictum, as Mr. Kenner urges, but as a quite
funny parody of the sort of pedantic nonsense that historicism
unchecked by taste will fall into. Nemesis follows such hubris.
It is clear that Mr. Kenner is a little resentful of the way in
which the sensibilities of contemporary readers of poetry
have been monopolized by Eliot's rhythms and cadences. It
looks as though Eliot's "Chinese wall" remark were coming
home to roost.

There is far more than a difference of opinion involved
here. When Mr. Kenner comes to fit Pound into his tradition,
he writes—very helpfully—about the way that the technical
discoveries of French prose, notably in Flaubert, ran through
Laforgue and Corbière into the English cultural milieu out of
which imagism and the prose of Ford Madox Ford and
Wyndham Lewis emerged. He does not say that the structure
of Pound's thought, especially the way he unites art and
economics, is thoroughly Ruskinian. It was Ruskin, too, who
popularized the romantic, or butterslide, view of history:
everything seemed to be going all right in the Middle Ages,
but something awful happened with the Renaissance, and
things have gotten steadily worse until a new light has
dawned with the present generation, which is every generation from Gothicists of the eighteenth century to us. Mr.

Kenner takes Pound at his own valuation as the true neo-medieval Messiah, and so does not see that Pound the critic is a late pre-Raphaelite sniffing eagerly along the trail of the English romantics, of Blake's minute particular, Coleridge's esemplastic power, and Keats's life of sensations. Pound the propagandist, on the other hand, was caught in the rubble of the fascist terminal moraine that continental romanticism helped to push into our time. For Ruskin derives from Carlyle, and Carlyle has his roots in Fichte.

I can see why Mr. Kenner refuses as far as possible to discuss the personal tragedy of Pound, but I am not sure that he is right in doing so. Mauberley is warned by the vulgarian Nixon against repeating the lost cause of the nineties, and there is much in Pound's career that reminds us of Oscar Wilde. There are not many genuine examples of the "Hero as Poet," but Wilde was certainly one of them, and his trial and imprisonment was the climax of a life which was one long act of disciplined but desperate courage, a super-quixotic courage that hurled itself straight into the flailing arms of the windmill of Philistinism, knowing quite well that it was nothing but a damned old windmill. And the dream of Ezra Pound is a heroic dream, whatever else it is. To rescue the revolutionary energy of America from the cant of avarice, and the cultural tradition of Europe from the cant of pedantry, and then to unite the real humanity of the one with the real liberality of the other—this may be a grandiloquent ambition, but it is not cheap. When we think of this, and then think of the road that led to the cage in Pisa and to further cages beyond, it is clear that some response, beyond pity as well as beyond Mr. Hillyer's terror, is demanded from us.

I am left still wondering whether Pound, like Wilde, is not more significant as a martyr or witness to the poetic vision than as a shaper of it. If the units of poetry are particular images, it follows that the substance of poetry, the thing that we look for, is not anything relayed from the area of ideas, but the total image which the particulars compose. This total image is the myth or archetype which informs the poetry, and the presentation of myth gives a poet the only impersonality he can have. Poets who have nothing to construct are the ones who have everything to *say*, inspiring messages, great thoughts, rich experiences, and so on. Such poets address their readers directly: no separate poetic form evolves that the reader can contemplate instead. The existence of this separate form is what gives a great poet serenity, urbanity, stabilizing balance, and the ability to forget and to respect his audience at the same time.

What Pound seems to me to lack is the thing that Milton and the romantics preeminently had—the faculty of mythopoeia. He has plenty of what he calls logopoeia, verbal cleverness and subtle rhythm, wit and craftsmanship, deftness at building up a theme out of a mass of disparate materials. One may dislike the texture of his work—I find it, all too often, as harsh and gritty as a pile of dirty spinach—and still be continually fascinated by the "particulars" in it. But as one reads, the sense of an enveloping body of vision does not come, and one continues to slither along the surface, never out of reach of the excited, hectoring voice of direct address. In the *Cantos*, the structural and recurrent themes, the organizing images, the "ground bass" or controlling rhythms, seem to lead, not toward a great epic image of life, but toward clear and distinct ideas in Pound's mind. This being the contrary of Pound's own views, the *Cantos*, at their best, give the impression of brilliant rhetoric trying to persuade us of the desirability of being the opposite of what it is. When Mr. Kenner says "Pound's impersonality is Flaubertian: an effacement of the personal accidents of the perceiving medium in the interests of accurate registration of *moeurs contemporaines*," he is saying what I suppose a sympathetic critic of Pound ought to say; yet it seems to me fantastically untrue. I see in the *Cantos* a structural myth broken down into a pastiche of harangue and exempla. When Pound says:

> Go, song, surely thou mayest
> Whither it please thee
> For so art thou ornate that thy reasons
> Shall be praised from thy understanders,
> With others hast thou no will to make company. . . .

he seems to me to be telling the whole truth about himself as a poet.

I sincerely hope that all of this is quite wrong: it is, after all, the kind of thing that used to be said, and can no longer be said, about Joyce. Mr. Kenner will doubtless convince others that it is wrong, and, in any case, much more work on Pound has yet to be done. And whatever is done will look back with gratitude and admiration to Mr. Kenner's study, and will follow the broad lines of the course he has charted.

George Orwell's satire on Russian Communism, *Animal Farm*, has just appeared in America, but its fame has preceded it, and surely by now everyone has heard of the fable of the animals who revolted and set up a republic on the farm, how the pigs seized control and how, led by a dictatorial boar named Napoleon, they finally became human beings walking on two legs and carrying whips, just as the old Farmer Jones had done. At each stage of this receding revolution, one of the seven principles of the original rebellion becomes corrupted, so that "no animal shall kill any other animal" has added to it the words "without cause" when there is a great slaughter of the so-called sympathizers of an exiled pig named Snowball, and "no animal shall sleep in a bed" takes on "with sheets" when the pigs move into the human farmhouse and monopolize its luxuries. Eventually there is only one principle left, modified to "all animals are equal, but some are more equal than others," as Animal Farm, its name changed back to Manor Farm, is welcomed into the community of human farms again after its neighbors have realized that it makes its "lower" animals work harder on less food than any other farm, so that the model workers' republic becomes a model of exploited labor.

The story is very well written, especially the Snowball episode, which suggests that the Communist "Trotskyite" is a conception on much the same mental plane as the Nazi "Jew," and the vicious irony of the end of Boxer the workhorse is perhaps really great satire. On the other hand, the satire on

Review of George Orwell, *Animal Farm* (New York: Harcourt, Brace, 1946). Reprinted from *The Canadian Forum*, vol. 26 (Dec. 1946).

the episode corresponding to the German invasion seems to me both silly and heartless, and the final metamorphosis of pigs into humans is a fantastic disruption of the sober logic of the tale. The reason for the change in method was to conclude the story by showing the end of Communism under Stalin as a replica of its beginning under the Czar. Such an alignment is, of course, completely nonsense, and as Mr. Orwell must know it to be nonsense, his motive for adopting it was presumably that he did not know how otherwise to get his allegory rounded off with a neat, epigrammatic finish.

Animal Farm adopts one of the classical formulas of satire, the corruption of principle by expediency, of which Swift's *Tale of a Tub* is the greatest example. It is an account of the bogging down of Utopian aspirations in the quicksand of human nature which could have been written by a contemporary of Artemus Ward about one of the cooperative communities attempted in America during the last century. But for the same reason, it completely misses the point as satire on the Russian development of Marxism, and as expressing the disillusionment which many men of goodwill feel about Russia. The reason for that disillusionment would be much better expressed as the corruption of expediency by principle. For the whole point about Marxism was surely that it was the first revolutionary movement in history which attempted to start with a concrete historical situation instead of vast, *a priori* generalizations of the "all men are equal" type, and which aimed at scientific rather than Utopian objectives. Marx and Engels worked out a revolutionary technique based on an analysis of history known as dialectical materialism, which appeared in the nineteenth century at a time when metaphysical materialism was a fashionable creed, but which Marx and Engels always insisted was a quite different thing from metaphysical materialism.

Today, in the Western democracies, the Marxist approach to historical and economic problems is, whether he realizes it or not, an inseparable part of the modern educated man's consciousness, no less than electrons or dinosaurs, while metaphysical materialism is as dead as the dodo, or would be if it

were not for one thing. For a number of reasons, chief among
them the comprehensiveness of the demands made on a
revolutionary by a revolutionary philosophy, the distinction
just made failed utterly to establish itself in practice as it did in
theory. Official Marxism today announces on page one that
dialectical materialism is to be carefully distinguished from
metaphysical materialism, and then insists from page two to
the end that Marxism is nevertheless a complete materialist
metaphysic of experience, with materialist answers to such
questions as the existence of God, the origin of knowledge, and
the meaning of culture. Thus, instead of including itself in the
body of modern thought and giving a revolutionary dynamic
to that body, Marxism has become a self-contained dogmatic
system, and one so exclusive in its approach to the remainder
of modern thought as to appear increasingly antiquated and
sectarian. Yet this metaphysical materialism has no other basis
than that of its original dialectic, its program of revolutionary
action. The result is an absolutizing of expediency which
makes expediency a principle in itself. From this springs the
reckless intellectual dishonesty which it is so hard not to find in
modern Communism, and which is naturally capable of
rationalizing any form of action, however ruthless.

A really searching satire on Russian Communism, then,
would be more deeply concerned with the underlying reasons
for its transformation from a proletarian dictatorship into a
kind of parody of the Catholic church. Mr. Orwell does not
bother with motivation: he makes his Napoleon inscrutably
ambitious and lets it go at that, and, as far as he is concerned,
some old reactionary bromide like "you can't change human
nature" is as good a moral as any other for his fable. But he,
like Koestler, is an example of a large number of writers in the
Western democracies who during the last fifteen years have
done their level best to adopt the Russian interpretation of
Marxism as their own world outlook and have failed. The last
fifteen years have witnessed a startling decline in the prestige
of Communist ideology in the arts, and some of the contemporary changes in taste which have resulted will be examined
in future contributions to this column.

The theme of *Across the River and into the Trees* is death in Venice, with Colonel Cantwell, a reduced brigadier and a "beat-up old bastard," as a military counterpart to Mann's beat-up old novelist. The colonel is a lonely man. Around him is an impersonal hatred directed, like a salute, at his uniform; behind him is the wreck of a marriage and of the career of a good professional soldier; in front of him is his next and last heart attack. He meets all this with a compelling dignity, and there is pathos in his struggles to control his temper, to be "kind," and to avoid boring other people with his bitterness. It is not that he wants to be liked, but that he senses the rejection of humanity which is involved in every real breakdown of human contact. He has reached the rank in the army at which his superior officers give their orders in terms of a hideous "big picture" in which strategy is based on politics and publicity stunts instead of on fighting. He cannot cope with this because he cannot relate it to his job of leading men into battle; and when the war is over, he feels his kinship with those who have been maimed and victimized by war, as he knows that no one has profited from it except profiteers. But he has gone far past the stage at which the word failure means anything to him.

Review of Ernest Hemingway, *Across the River and into the Trees* (New York: Scribner's, 1950); Budd Schulberg, *The Disenchanted* (New York: Random House, 1950); William Goyen, *The House of Breath* (New York: Random House, 1950); Alberto Moravia, *Two Adolescents*, trans. Beryl de Zoete and Angus Davidson (New York: Farrar, Straus, 1950); Charles Williams, *Shadows of Ecstacy* (New York: Pellegrini and Cudahy, 1950); Marcel Aymé, *The Barkeep of Blémont*, trans. Norman Denny (New York: Harper, 1950); and C. Virgil Gheorghiu, *The Twenty-Fifth Hour*, trans. Rita Eldon (New York: Knopf, 1950). Reprinted by permission from *The Hudson Review*, vol. 3, no. 4 (Winter 1950–51). © 1950 by The Hudson Review, Inc.

His approaching death gives a bitter intensity to the ordinary events of his life: to the food and drink of his last meals, to his last look at the violated beauty of Italy, and, above all, to his love for a nineteen-year-old contessa who comes to him, a dream girl out of a dream city, to offer him an unconditional devotion. Everything that remains for him in life he accepts, simply and without question. The girl loves him, we are told, because he is never "sad": there is no self-pity which rejects life by clinging to the ego. On the contrary, he has some tenderness for braggarts and charlatans who respond to the exuberance in life, and if there is a desire that still holds him, it is for children to continue his own life, which may be one reason why he calls the contessa "daughter." It is a great theme, and in the hands of someone competent to deal with it—say, Ernest Hemingway—it might have been a long short story of overwhelming power.

It is pleasant to dwell on the idea and postpone the fact. In the opening scene and in the curt description of the colonel's death, there is something of the old Hemingway grip. In between, however, the story lies around in bits and pieces, with no serious effort to articulate it. The colonel is entitled to rancorous prejudice—the reader doesn't expect him to be a Buddhist sage—and in his political and military reflections one wouldn't mind the clichés of a commonplace grouch if they built up to something bigger, but they don't. We expect to find the love scenes stripped of eloquence, but not to encounter a cloying singsong of "I love you truly" and a repetitiousness that looks like padding. The role of the contessa is that of a more attractive version of a deferential yes-man. The colonel wanders in an empty limbo between a dead and an unborn world, at no point related to other human beings in a way that would give his story any representative importance. As far as anyone can be, he is an island entire of itself.

The last, of course, is part of Hemingway's point. His story is intended to be a study in isolation, of how the standards of a decent soldier are betrayed by modern war. The colonel is not a writer, and the things that are happening to him he assumes to be incommunicable, because he has found them so. And he dominates the book so much that something of his distrust of communication seems to have leaked into the author and paralyzed his will to write. In this kind of story, the hero's loneliness must be compensated for by the author's desire to tell the story and, to adopt one of his own cadences, tell it truly. But this involves the total detachment of author from character which comes when sympathy and insight are informed by professional skill. This detachment has not been reached, and the book remains technically on the amateurish level in which the most articulate character sounds like a mouthpiece for the author. Hence all the self-pity and egotism which have been thrown out the door reappear in the windows between the lines. The reader is practically compelled to read the story the wrong way, and the result is a continuous sense of embarrassment.

Budd Schulberg's *The Disenchanted* adopts a scheme not unlike Hemingway's. The story is the final, macabre souse of an American novelist, Manly Halliday, fabulously rich and successful in the twenties, now (the book is dated around 1938, so that the bender decade is recollected, not in tranquility, but during the hangover) ridden by debts, compulsive memories, a wrecked wife, diabetes, alcoholism, neglect, and self-neglect. The role of Hemingway's heroine is played by a younger writer, Shep Stearns, who is of the depression generation, and whose harassed solicitude is less uncritical than hers and more touching. Instead of the big picture of strategy, we have the big pictures of Hollywood, where a producer named Victor Milgrim is giving the ex-genius his last chance.

That the prototype of Halliday is Scott Fitzgerald is not, to put it mildly, much of a secret, but the author has begun with a quotation from Henry James asking us not to make too much of this. I myself forgot it entirely as soon as I recognized in Schulberg's wistful, genteel bum the outlines of a more familiar figure. All the well-loved conventions follow in his wake. The same dapper-seedy, timid-jaunty appearance; the same juxtaposition of luscious dreams (here presented as memories of a wonderful past that we can't quite believe in) and a miserable reality; the same crazy plot that lurches from one nightmare to another until it explodes in a crescendo of slapstick and tragedy. The only time Halliday reveals a mind superior to that of any other educated drunk is when he makes some acute remarks on Chaplin films. No, the book is far closer to *City Lights* than to *The Great Gatsby*.

Halliday rose to success by brilliant satire on the phony society he saw around him. It was not important, as Stearns at first thought, that he should understand the real significance of his satire. It was important that he should detach himself from the society he described, that in his success he should consistently bite the hands that fed him, which seems to be the only personal rule imposed by art on the artist. Failing in this, he became, as Blake says, what he beheld, and was swept into a noisy and vulgar inferno where he got a hot glare of publicity, but never any privacy. The society happened to be the America of the twenties, but there is nothing peculiar to that age about the situation itself, as the author comes near to suggesting—the second postwar era's attitude to the first occasionally gets a shade prissy. Henry James long before had shown how society sits like a fumbling, witless sea anemone waiting for someone with genius, beauty, freshness, or whatever else permits free movement to come within reach of its tentacles. It caught Halliday, and here the Chaplin parallel breaks down. Halliday retains his dignity because he makes society look as ridiculous as himself. But not, as in Chaplin, far more so—he has lost his innocence, as the Chaplin hero never does, and the best he gets with society is a split decision.

The story is well written, in spite of its unvarying *martellato* style, and the dialogue—a soft gilding of wit over a paste of wisecracks—is admirable. Yet, to make it more than a *Lost Weekend* with cultural overtones, Halliday needs to be tragic rather than pathetic, and he has to be heroic to be tragic. The heroic dimension in him could come only from his genius: we should see not only the destruction of the man, but the blinding of the vision that was presumably in the man. The discovery that his final bit of writing is a masterpiece sounds like a contribution to the plot by Victor Milgrim—again, I am taking the story as it stands, and not as fictional biography. Halliday's wife is forever trying to translate the *Saison en Enfer*, and somewhere in his flashbacks (called "Old Business," which I dislike) we should have caught a glimpse of the demon whispering into his ear those fatal, lying words that end "dérèglement de tous les sens."

William Goyen's *The House of Breath*, a first novel, begins with a rather dismaying rush of words and some self-conscious mannerisms, notably a kind of nudging parenthesis, but it soon settles down and becomes a style of some power as well as readability. The title refers to a house in an East Texas village, the past life of which is evoked, partly through a narrator who spent his boyhood there, and partly through the reflective monologues of the people who have lived in it. The pervading tone of the book is thus one of nostalgic reminiscence. This would normally be discouraging, because the emotional urgency of nostalgia is so often mistaken for inspiration, and yet it is one of the hardest moods to communicate. But here is one author who has boldly faced material that dozens of writers have failed with and made something of it. There is some fine and sensitive description of the woods and the river and the farm animals and the changing seasons, and an intricate but clearly developed pattern of themes and symbols is built up somewhat after the manner of Virginia Woolf. The house is thought of as haunted by its memories, and the monologues are extracted from it as though Yeats were right, and it was possible to sink into an *anima mundi* where one could tune in on a psychic ether of memory and points of brooding return. It sounds ectoplasmic, but it has been skillfully done, and when we finish this remarkable book, we have a panorama of a dozen interconnected and brilliantly summarized lives.

The author has an acute ear for the slurred elisions, agglutinative syntax, and somnolent rhythms of vernacular speech, and he is particularly successful with females and the female mood of querulous patience. He has also discovered that when East Texas lifts up its voice in complaint, the result is very suggestive of a banshee wail, which adds point to his scheme. He appears to be a little afraid that his characters will not get enough sympathy from the reader unless he insists on their claims to it. At any rate, his genuine humor seems a bit furtive, and some of his symbolism is over-italicized—the village the house is in is called Charity, for instance, which evidently means something, and there are other traces of portentousness. But these are trifles in a book that gets an extraordinary amount said in its hundred and eighty pages, a book which, if it remains something of a stunt, is an outstandingly clever and successful one.

Each of Moravia's stories of Italian schoolboys deserves the higher compliment of being called a story that you can put down. One pursues a clumsy and faked narrative as one gets through a crowd on a sidewalk, in haste to be rid of it—a point often overlooked by those who sit up all night over mystery stories. Moravia fits normal life: one can drop his Agostino or Luca anywhere with a coherent structure already in one's mind, secure in the writer's ability to continue it properly. Nothing happens to Agostino except that boredom, bad company, and ambiguous feelings toward his widowed mother fill him with a typically adolescent misery. Nothing happens to Luca except that he gets sick and recovers, his nurse climbing into his bed during his convalescence. The virtuosity of the born storyteller then goes to work. The story of Luca takes us deep into the death-wish that caused his illness, and shows how acts that outwardly seem only perverse or petulant really belong to an inner sacrificial drama. And as Luca recovers, the archetypal significance of what he has done takes shape. His story is a humble but genuine example of what the great religions are talking about: of losing one's life to find it, of gaining charity through renunciation, of becoming free by cutting oneself loose from everything that attaches and motivates. Symbols, ordinarily as hard to make convincing in fiction as jokes, drop into the right places, from the very adroit use of the *Purgatorio* to the final sentence about a train coming out of a tunnel into daylight. It is characteristic of such a story that a quiet word like *nausea* or *absurdity* (neither likely to be the invention of the unobtrusive translator), simply because it is the right word for its context, can bring into focus more of what Sartre and Camus, respectively, are trying to say than a good many pages of Sartre's metaphysics.

In the background of Moravia's stories is a solid sense of bourgeois Italian society, its values, its folklore, and its class conflicts. There is something oddly old-fashioned about this solidity: it is like finding good carpentry and seasoned lumber in a flossy new bungalow, and one feels that the swaying Venetian backdrops of Hemingway or the dissolving pan shots of Schulberg are unfortunately more up to date. Moravia still clings in technique to the old traditions of novel writing in which those who had a sense of established society, like Austen and Dickens and Trollope, wrote with authority in the center of tradition, while those who lacked it, like Scott and Lytton and Wilkie Collins, had to depend on plot formulas for support. This kind of novel is disappearing with the society that produced it, and a new approach has become necessary. Society is not a containing unit for characters any more: it is too nomadic and too much an open arena of clashing personalities and ideologies. Even in *The House of Breath*, the emphasis is thrown on the centrifugal movement away from the community. One can see the new plot formulas of the successors of Lytton and Collins shaping up in modern middlebrow thrillers, and the question naturally arises of what central vision has replaced the social vision of Austen and Trollope.

My guess is that it is a vision based on the sense of moral autonomy. The plot formulas of today's thrillers are solutions to problems. Why did A murder B? Because of narcissist conflicts resulting from a mother fixation—psychological thriller. Because the romanticism of a privileged class led him to make a scapegoat of a personal enemy—class-conscious thriller. Because the act of sin breaks out of the intolerable suspense of moral indifference—theological thriller. All these use dialectics and treat a condition as a determining cause. I call them thrillers because the characters are propelled by the

movement of the extraneous dialectic, instead of simply acting
out what they are. I think that the central tradition sees man
as conditioned at every point, but self-determined, so that all
these dialectics are contained, so to speak, with none of them
allowed to dominate the novel or dictate its resolution. Thus
Schulberg's first novel, *What Makes Sammy Run?*, would have
been a dialectic formula with some Marxist or Freudian
solution if the author had concentrated on trying to answer the
question instead of on the irreducible fact of Sammy's running.
If I am right, then the existential doctrine of moral freedom
has a good deal of historical and literary point, though so far it
seems to me to have produced only a fourth thriller formula.

Charles Williams's *Shadows of Ecstasy* is an intellectual
thriller, and its ancestors are Lytton and Rider Haggard—it is
by *Zanoni* out of *She*, if my grammar is right. The hero, or
villain, Nigel Considine, has, by a super-yogi discipline,
enabled himself to live indefinitely (two hundred years and
going strong), and has begun an attempt at a "second evolution of man," politically the resurgence of Africa, and psychologically the calling up of the unawakened powers of passion
and will, which has as its ultimate goal the return from death.
Because this program is the result of a human will to power,
Considine is a kind of Antichrist, and we are supposed to pick
up a great variety of allusions to different aspects of Antichrist
as we go on. If we get them all—they include the Bible,
Caesar, Constantine (whose name the hero echoes), Yeats's
Byzantium, Dante's Emperor, Milton's Satan, and the super-
man of Nietzsche and Shaw—we get quite a liberal education.
It is a good thriller, written with humor and relaxation,
with more respect for the art of fiction, more tolerance of
irony, and less didactic hectoring than are usual with Williams. The fantasy has its own logic, and the characters and
setting are studied carefully enough to give us the comfortable
sense of a familiar world taking a holiday from routine. It is
not giving anything away to say that the Galilean conquers,
but though the author's Christian dialectic determines the
solution, it does not try to force the reader's assent, and so

avoids the disadvantages of melodrama. The losing side gets our sympathy and a chance to put on a good show: we do not feel pushed around, nor do we get claustrophobia from a closed system of thought. In all these respects, *Shadows of Ecstasy* offers a remarkable contrast to a better known but far cruder version of the same story, *All Hallows Eve*, where the Aunt Sally epithet "morbid" seems to me for once appropriate.

On the other hand, Marcel Aymé's very able satire, *The Barkeep of Blémont*, is what I mean by fiction in the central tradition. Blémont is a small provincial town, and the kind of intrigue that goes on there is the same old intrigue, love affairs, political jockeying, graft, and the screening of self-interest by humbug. But the time is 1945: the humbug is the exposure of "collaboration"; the graft is profiteering; the jockeying is in terms of Communist tactics which have the police terrorized and the middle class almost resigned to defeat; and the love affairs are engaged in by people who have, or are trying to get, political influence. The individual who tries to mind his own business in such an environment merely creates a power vacuum. The attaching of individuals to pressure groups is as though the children of a tough and badly run school had been supplied with rubber truncheons. There is a brutal lynching, watched and approved by the whole town; there is a vicious beating in public ignored by the police; a hunted Nazi gives himself up to certain death; the police lock up people without influence at the bidding of people who have it; and a barkeep, an amiable gorilla who loves Racine and is trying to sweat out hexameters himself, is shot, quite unnecessarily, while resisting the arrest of his muse. One pole of the book is represented by a Vichyite collaborator and a war profiteer named Monglant, who is adroit enough to keep his money and become equally influential in the new regime, besides being in cahoots with the Communists. But a fear of public opinion makes him as unable to enjoy his possessions as any other miser, and he finally discovers that his only pleasure is in watching and causing pain. This, of course, is the cancer of Nazism, still uncured after its defeat.

In spite of all this, the tonality of *The Barkeep of Blémont* is
one of balanced and unstampeded maturity. When the characters have political ideologies, they patter glibly through the
gramophone records that we expect to hear; but we are shown
with great clarity how the ultimate use of such apparatus is
always to rationalize essential human activities, like bearing
false witness or coveting one's neighbor's wife. The psychological drives coincide with the political ones: brutalities not
only demonstrate political strength but give sexual pleasure,
and a Nazi can get that way because he needs love. But the
author sees no logical determining force in social behavior.
Society may at any time be caught in the bondage of fear and
hypocrisy, and the freedom of the individuals in that society
suffers accordingly. But man himself, society as a whole, is
self-imprisoned, and the easy fatalism that externalizes the
imprisoning power is making an evil god out of the dark
shadow of humanity.

This, at any rate, is the doctrine of a character named
Watrin, who polarizes Monglant, and who seems to mean
something rather special to the author, as he gets the last
word. Watrin, for reasons too complicated to go into here, has
gained an innocent vision of life: the world is new created for
him each morning; he feels that not only nature but man can
be loved, if not admired, and he not only enjoys the present
but is hopeful of the future. It is reassuring to have him as a
spokesman, if he is that, for what is on the whole, apart from
some rather nagging irony, a wise and witty book. It is also
somewhat disconcerting to notice that the characters who are
better than "all too human," Watrin and the barkeep, are
touched with slightly sentimental fantasy, and are not quite
believable.

We now have to hear from Virgil Gheorghiu, who wrote
The Twenty-Fifth Hour to prove that man has lost his moral
autonomy for good. The two chief characters of this book are
Romanians, one a peasant named Johann Moritz and the other
an intellectual named Traian Koruga, and the story begins in
the Nazified Europe of 1938. The peasant's wife is coveted by a
sergeant who gets rid of his rival by accusing him of being a

Jew, and the peasant starts on a picaresque journey like those of Candide and Schweik, except that Gheorghiu's satiric touch is not light and his skill in character drawing is not up to giving us a real picture of innocent simplicity. Johann is imprisoned, tortured, sold as slave labor to Germany, declared to be one of the world's purest Aryans by a Nazi race pundit, dragooned into the S. S., and imprisoned again as a Nazi by the Americans. The intellectual is, in the now somewhat hackneyed *Faux-Monnayeurs* formula, writing a novel called *The Twenty-Fifth Hour*, and is persecuted by the Nazis for his Jewish wife, and by the Americans, under whom he eventually dies, as an enemy alien. The novel ends with Johann conscripted again to fight for the Americans in the third world war with Russia, which has just begun.

The thesis both of Koruga's book and of the one that encircles it is that all humane and individual values have been wiped out by a technological civilization that can deal only with quantitative units. Men have become the "apes of robots": their admiration for the efficiency of machines has led to the deification of mechanical values. Eliot, Auden, Northrop, Keyserling, and others are quoted in support, sometimes strangely out of context. It makes no difference what any modern power calls its ideology: its end product will be the same, a bureaucracy of officials who have authority but no freedom. The official can only act mechanically and function on a subhuman generalizing level; he wants the people in front of him to be filed and forgotten, and he gets angry and flustered whenever he is reminded that they are unique human beings. The title means that the human race has already had it: not even a Messiah can save us now. For though Gheorghiu sees much the same facts as Aymé, he is not sustained by the latter's belief in the permanence of society: he sees only the individual and the mass, and his outlook has all the hopelessness of his very common type of naive and introverted anarchism. Koruga, though called a saint, is not really even a martyr, for a martyr is a witness to another community: he is only a victim, and whatever he represents dies with him.

There is probably very little in this book which has not happened, and doubtless nothing which could not happen. It is difficult to know what to say for art when it is outstared by truth, or some kinds of truth. In the face of torture and humiliation, it seems almost pedantic to say that the fiction writing is perfunctory and the social theories slapdash. The book is humorless and preachy, but its subject is not amusing, and maybe we could do with a sermon. The "apes of robots" doctrine is as oversimplified as a dictator's oratory, but the facts it tries to explain are as grim as ever. The irony is contrived and overdone, but so is the irony of a refugee's life. As for the "too late" thesis, one may feel that the very existence of so earnest a book tends to contradict, if not the thesis itself, at any rate the author's belief in it. But one sympathizes with the shrillness of tone, with his anger at our easy boredom and short memories, at the Erewhonian in us who feels that nobody's suffering is undeserved if he makes us uncomfortable to hear about him. In any case, Gheorghiu's conviction that American democracy can bring nothing to Europe but a third invasion of stupid and brutal officals makes *The Twenty-Fifth Hour* a document of great importance: it reflects an attitude too frequent among non-Communist Europeans to be shrugged off, and whatever reasons and evidence it presents need to be carefully examined. The hatred of occupied countries for an alien uniform, which Hemingway's colonel discovers but fails to understand, is expressed here from its own point of view.

THE NIGHTMARE LIFE IN DEATH

In every age, the theory of society and the theory of personality have closely approached each other. In Plato, the wise man's mind is a dictatorship of reason over appetite, with the will acting as a thought police, hunting down and exterminating all lawless impulses. The ideal state, with its philosopher-king, guards, and artisans, has the corresponding social form. Michael explains to Adam in *Paradise Lost* that tyranny must exist in society as long as passion dominates reason in individuals, as they are called. In our day, Marxism finds its psychological counterpart in the behaviorism and conditioned reflexes of Pavlov, and the Freudian picture of man is also the picture of Western Europe and America, hoping that its blocks and tensions and hysterical explosions will settle into some kind of precarious working agreement. In this alignment, religion has regularly formed a third, its gods and their enemies deriving their characteristics from whatever is highest and lowest in the personal-social picture. A good deal of the best fiction of our time has employed a kind of myth that might be read as a psychological, a social, or a religious allegory, except that it cannot be reduced to an allegory, but remains a myth, moving in all three areas of life at once, and thereby interconnecting them as well. The powerful appeal of Kafka for our age is largely due to the way in which such stories as *The Trial* or *The Castle* manage to suggest at once the atmosphere of an anxiety dream, the theology of the Book of Job, and the police terrorism and bureaucratic anonymity of the society that inspired Freud's term "censor." It was the same appeal in

Review of Samuel Beckett, *Molloy, Malone Dies* and *The Unnamable* (New York: Grove Press, 1959). Reprinted by permission from *The Hudson Review*, vol. 13, no. 3 (Autumn 1960). © 1960 by The Hudson Review, Inc.

the myth of *Waiting for Godot* that, so to speak, identified Samuel Beckett as a contemporary writer.

As a fiction writer, Samuel Beckett derives from Proust and Joyce, and his essay on Proust is a good place to start from in examining his own work. This essay puts Proust in a context that is curiously Oriental in its view of personality. "Normal" people, we learn, are driven along through time on a current of habit-energy, an energy which, because habitual, is mostly automatic. This energy relates itself to the present by the will, to the past by voluntary or selective memory, to the future by desire and expectation. It is a subjective energy, although it has no consistent or permanent subject, for the ego that desires now can, at best, only possess later, by which time it is a different ego and wants something else. But an illusion of continuity is kept up by the speed, like a motion picture, and it generates a corresponding objective illusion, where things run along in the expected and habitual form of causality. Some people try to get off this time machine, either because they have more sensitivity or, perhaps, some kind of physical weakness that makes it, not an exhilarating joyride, but a nightmare of frustration and despair. Among these are artists like Proust, who look behind the surface of the ego, behind voluntary to involuntary memory, behind will and desire to conscious perception. As soon as the subjective motion picture disappears, the objective one disappears too, and we have recurring contacts between a particular moment and a particular object, as in the epiphanies of the madeleine and the phrase in Vinteuil's music. Here the object, stripped of the habitual and expected response, appears in all the enchanted glow of uniqueness, and the relation of the moment to such an object is a relation of identity. Such a relation, achieved between two human beings, would be love, in contrast to the ego's pursuit of the object of desire, like Odette or Albertine, which tantalizes precisely because it is never loved. In the relation of identity, consciousness has triumphed over time, and destroys the prison of habit with its double illusion stretching forever into past and future. At that moment we may enter what Proust and Beckett agree is the only possible type of paradise, that which has been lost. For the ego, only two forms of failure are possible, the failure to possess, which may be tragic, and the failure to communicate, which is normally comic.

In the early story *Murphy*, the hero is an Irishman with an Irish interest in the occult—several of Beckett's characters are readers of AE—and a profound disinclination to work. We first meet him naked, strapped to a chair, and practicing trance. He has, however, no interest in any genuine mental discipline, and feels an affinity with the easygoing Belacqua of Dante's *Purgatorio*, also mentioned in *Molloy*, who was in no hurry to begin his climb up the mountain. What he is really looking for is a self-contained, egocentric consciousness, "windowless, like a monad," that no outward events can injure or distort. He is prodded by the heroine Celia into looking for a job, and eventually finds one as a male nurse in a lunatic asylum. In the asylum, he discovers a kinship with the psychotic patients, who are trying to find the same thing in their own way, and his sympathy with them not only gives him a job he can do but makes him something rather better than a "seedy solipsist." To take this job he turns his back on Celia and other people who are said to need him, but in the airless microcosm of his mental retreat there is the one weak spot that makes him human and not completely selfish, a need for communication. He looks for this in the eye of Endon, his best friend among the patients, but sees no recognition in the eye, only his own image reflected in the pupil. "The last Mr. Murphy saw of Mr. Endon was Mr. Murphy unseen by Mr. Endon." He then commits suicide. The same image of the unrecognizing eye occurs in the one-act play *Embers* and in *Krapp's Last Tape*, where Krapp, more completely bound to memory and desire than Murphy, and so a figure of less dignity if also of less absurdity, looks into his mistress's eyes and says "Let me in." Another echo of this phrase will meet us in a moment.

The figure of the pure ego in a closed, autoerotic circle meets us many times in Beckett's masturbating, carrot-chewing, stone-sucking characters. A more traditional image of the consciousness goaded by desire or memory (an actual goad appears in one of Beckett's pantomimes) is that of master and servant. Already in *Murphy* we have, in the characters Neary and Cooper, an adumbration of the Hamm and Clov of *Endgame*, a servant who cannot sit and a master who cannot stand, bound together in some way and yet longing to be rid of each other. *Watt* tells the story of a servant who drifts into a house owned by a Mr. Knott, one of a long procession of servants absorbed and expelled from it by some unseen force. Technically the book is a contrast to *Murphy*, which is written in an epigrammatic, wisecracking style. In *Watt* there is a shaggy-dog type of deliberately misleading humor, expressing itself in a maddeningly prolix pseudologic. One notes the use of a device more recently popularized by Lawrence Durrell, of putting some of the debris of the material collected into an appendix. "Only fatigue and disgust prevented its incorpora- tion," the author demurely informs us. The most trivial actions of Watt, most of which are very similar to those we perform ourselves every day, are exhaustively catalogued in an elabo- rate pretense of obsessive realism, and we can see how such "realism" in fiction, pushed to so logical a conclusion, soon gives the effect of living in a kind of casual and unpunishing hell. Watt finally decides that "if one of these things was worth doing, all were worth doing, but that none was worth doing, no, not one, but that all were unadvisable, without excep- tion."

In *Waiting for Godot*, as everyone knows, two dreary men in bowler hats stand around waiting for the mysterious Godot, who never appears, but only sends a messenger to say he will not come. It is a favorite device of ironic fiction, from Kafka to Menotti's opera *The Consul*, to make the central character someone who not only fails to manifest himself, but whose very existence is called in question. The two men wonder whether in some way they are "tied" to Godot, but decide that they probably are not, though they are afraid he might punish them if they desert their post. They also feel tied to one an- other, though each feels he would do better on his own. They resemble criminals in that they feel that they have no rights:

"we got rid of them," one says, and is exhorted by a stage direction to say it distinctly. They stand in front of a dead tree, speculating, like many of Beckett's characters, about hanging themselves from it, and one of them feels an uneasy kinship with the thieves crucified with Christ. Instead of Godot, there appears a diabolical figure named Pozzo (pool: the overtones extend from Satan to Narcissus), driving an animal in human shape named Lucky, with a whip and a rope. Lucky, we are told, thinks he is entangled in a net: the image of being fished for by some omnipotent and malignant angler recurs in *The Unnamable*. In the second act, the two turn up again, but this time Pozzo is blind and helpless, like Hamm in *Endgame*.

When the double illusion of a continuous ego and continuous causality is abolished, what appears in its place? First of all, the ego is stripped of all individuality and is seen merely as representative of all of its kind. When asked for their names, one of the two men waiting for Godot answers "Adam," and the other one says: "At this place, at this moment of time, all mankind is us." Similar echoes are awakened by the biblical title of the play *All that Fall*, with its discussion of the falling sparrow in the Gospels and its final image of the child falling from the train, its death unheeded by the only character who was on the train. Other characters have such names as Watt, Knott, and Krapp, suggestive of infantile jokes and of what in *Molloy* are called "decaying circus clowns." The dramatic convention parodied in *Waiting for Godot* is clearly the act that killed vaudeville, the weary dialogue of two faceless figures who will say anything to put off leaving the stage. In the "gallery of moribunds" we are about to examine there is a series of speakers whose names begin with *M*, one of whom, Macmann, has the most obvious everyman associations. In this trilogy, however, there is a more thoroughgoing examination of the unreality of the ego, and one which seems to owe something to the sequence of three chapters in *Finnegans Wake* in which Shaun is studied under the names Shaun, Jaun, and Yawn, until he disappears into the larger form of HCE. It is the "Yawn" chapter that Beckett most frequently refers to. In reading the trilogy, we should keep in mind the remark in the essay on Proust that "the heart of the cauliflower or the ideal core of the onion would represent a more appropriate tribute to the labours of poetical excavation than the crown of bay."

Molloy is divided into two parts: the first is Molloy's own narrative; the second is the narrative of Jacques Moran, who receives a message through one Gaber from an undefined Youdi to go and find Molloy. The echoes of Gabriel and Yahweh make it obvious by analogy that the name "Godot" is intended to sound like "God." Youdi, or someone similar to him, is once referred to as "the Obidil," which is an anagram of libido. The associations of Molloy are Irish, pagan, and a Caliban-like intelligence rooted in a disillusioned sensitivity. Moran is French, nominally Christian, and a harsher and more aggressive type of sterility. Molloy, like many of Beckett's characters, is so crippled as to resemble the experiments on mutilated and beheaded animals that try to establish how much life is consistent with death. He is also under a wandering curse, like the Wandering Jew, and is trying to find his mother. There are echoes of the wandering figure in Chaucer's *Pardoner's Tale*, who keeps knocking on the ground with his staff and begging his mother to let him in. But Molloy does not exactly long for death, because for him the universe is also a vast autoerotic ring, a serpent with its tail in its mouth, and it knows no real difference between life and death. Overtones of Ulysses appear in his sojourn with Lousse (Circe), and the mention of "moly" suggests an association with his name. He is also, more biblically, "in an Egypt without bounds, without infant, without mother," and a dim memory of Faust appears in his account of various sciences studied and abandoned, of which magic alone remained. Like the contemporary beats (in Murphy, incidentally, the padded cells are called "pads"), he finds around him a world of confident and adjusted squares, who sometimes take the form of police and bully him. "They wake up, hale and hearty, their tongues hanging out for order, beauty and justice, baying for their due." The landscape around him, described in terms similar to Dante's Inferno, changes, but he is unable to go out of his "region," and realizes that he is not moving at all. The only real change is a progressive physical deterioration and a growing loss of such social contact as he has. The landscape finally changes to a forest, and Molloy, too exhausted to walk and unable, like Beckett's other servants, to sit, crawls on his belly like a serpent until he finally stops. He arrives at his mother's house, but, characteristically, we learn this not from the last sentence but from the first one, as the narrative goes around in a Viconian circle.

Just before the end of his account, Molloy, who hears voices of "prompters" in his mind, is told that help is coming. Moran sets off to find Molloy, aware that his real quest is to find Molloy inside himself, as a kind of Hyde to his Jekyll. He starts out with his son, whom he is trying to nag into becoming a faithful replica of himself, and he ties his son to him with a rope, as Pozzo does Lucky. The son breaks away; Moran sees Molloy but does not realize who he is, and gets another order to go back home. He confesses: "I was not made for the great light that devours, a dim lamp was all I had been given, and patience without end, to shine it on the empty shadows." This ignominious quest for self-knowledge does not find Molloy as a separate entity, but it does turn Moran into a double of Molloy, in ironic contrast to his attitude toward his son. Various details in the imagery, the bicycle that they both start with, the stiffening leg, and others, emphasize the growing identity. Moran's narrative, which starts out in clear prose, soon breaks down into the same associative, paragraphless monologue that Molloy uses. The quest is a dismal failure as far as Moran and Molloy are concerned, but how far are they concerned? Moran can still say: "What I was doing I was doing neither for Molloy, who mattered nothing to me, nor for myself, of whom I despaired, but on behalf of a cause which, while having need of us to be accomplished, was in its essence anonymous, and would subsist, haunting the minds of men, when its miserable artisans should be no more."

The forest vanishes and we find ourselves in an asylum cell with a figure named Malone, who is waiting to die. Here there is a more definite expectation of the event of death, and an awareness of a specific quantity of time before it occurs. Malone decides to fill in the interval by telling himself stories, and the stories gradually converge on a figure named Macmann, to whom Malone seems related somewhat as Proust is to the "Marcel" of his book, or Joyce to Stephen and Shem. Here an ego is projecting himself into a more typical figure (I suppose Malone and Macmann have echoes of "man alone" and "son of man," respectively, as most of the echoes in Beckett's names appear to be English), and Macmann gradually moves into the cell and takes over the identity of Malone. Malone dreams of his own death, which is simultaneously occurring, in a vision of a group of madmen going for a picnic in a boat on the Saturday morning between Good Friday and Easter, a ghastly parody of the beginning of the *Purgatorio*. Dante's angelic pilot is replaced by a brutal attendant named Lemuel, a destroying angel who murders most of the passengers.

In *The Unnamable* we come as near to the core of the onion as it is possible to come, and discover, of course, that there is no core, no undividable unit of continuous personality. It is difficult to say just where or what the Unnamable is, because, as in the brothel scene of *Ulysses*, his fluctuating moods create their own surroundings. One hypothesis is that he is sitting in a crouched posture with tears pouring out of his eyes, like some of the damned in Dante, or like the Heraclitus who became the weeping philosopher by contemplating the flowing of all things. Another is that he is in a jar outside a Paris restaurant opposite a horsemeat shop, suspended between life and death like the sibyl in Petronius who presides over *The Waste Land*.

Ordinarily we are aware of a duality between mind and body, of the necessity of keeping the body still to let the mind work. If we sit quietly we become aware of bodily processes, notably the heartbeat and pulse, carrying on automatically and involuntarily. Some religious disciplines, such as yoga, go another stage, and try to keep the mind still to set some higher principle free. When this happens, the mind can be seen from the outside as a rushing current of thoughts and associations and memories and worries and images suggested by desire, pulsating automatically and with all the habit-energy of the ego behind it. Each monologue in the trilogy suggests a mind half-freed from its own automatism. It is detached enough to feel imprisoned and enslaved, and to have no confidence in any of its assertions, but immediately to deny or contradict or qualify or put forward another hypothesis to whatever it says. But it is particularly the monologue of *The Unnamable*, an endless, querulous, compulsive, impersonal babble, much the same in effect whether read in French or in English, and with no purpose except to keep going, that most clearly suggests a "stream of consciousness" from which real consciousness is somehow absent. *The Unnamable* could readily be called a tedious book, but its use of tedium is exuberant, and in this respect it resembles *Watt*.

The Unnamable, who vaguely remembers having been Malone and Molloy, decides that he will be someone called Mahood, then that he will be something called Worm, then wonders whether all his meditations really are put into his mind by "them," that is, by Youdi and the rest, for his sense of compulsion easily externalizes itself. If he knows anything, it is that he is not necessarily himself, and that it was nonsense for Descartes to infer that he was himself because he was doubting it. All Beckett's speakers are like the parrot in *Malone Dies*, who could be taught to say "Nihil in intellectu," but refused to learn the rest of the sentence. All of them, again, especially Malone, are oppressed by the pervasive lying of the imagination, by the way in which one unconsciously falsifies the facts to make a fiction more symmetrical. But even Malone begins to realize that there is no escape from fiction. There are no facts to be accurately described, only hypotheses to be set up: no choice of words will express the truth, for one has only a choice of rhetorical masks. Malone says of his own continuum: "I slip into him, I suppose in the hope of learning something. But it is a stratum, strata, without debris or vestiges. But before I am done I shall find traces of what was."

In *The Unnamable*, as we make our way through "this sound that will never stop, monotonous beyond words and yet not altogether devoid of a certain variety," the Unnamable's own desire to escape, to the extent that he ever formulates it as such, communicates itself to us. The tired, tireless, hypnotic voice, muttering like a disembodied spirit at a seance, or like our own subconscious if we acquire the trick of listening to it, makes us feel that we would be ready to try anything to get away from it, even if we are also its prisoner. There is little use going to "them," to Youdi or Godot, because they are illusions of personality too. Conventional religion promises only resurrection, which both in *Murphy* and in the Proust essay is described as an impertinence. But "beyond them is that other who will not give me quittance until they have abandoned me as inutilizable and restored me to myself." That other must exist, if only because it is not here. And so, in the interminable last sentence, we reach the core of the onion, the resolve to find in art the secret of identity, the paradise that has been lost, the one genuine act of consciousness in the interlocking gyres (the Dante-Yeats image is explicitly referred to) of automatism:

> The attempt must be made, in the old stories incomprehensibly mine, to find his, it must be there somewhere, it must have been mine, before being his, I'll recognize it, in the end I'll recognize it, the story of the silence that he never left, that I should never have left, that I may never find again, that I may find again, then it will be he, it will be I, it will be the place, the silence, the end, the beginning, the beginning again . . .

Many curiously significant remarks are made about silence in the trilogy. Molloy, for example, says: "about me all goes really silent, from time to time, whereas for the righteous the tumult of the world never stops." The Unnamable says: "This voice that speaks, knowing that it lies, indifferent to what it says, too old perhaps and too abased ever to succeed in saying the words that would be its last, knowing itself useless and its uselessness in vain, not listening to itself but to the silence that it breaks." Only when one is sufficiently detached from this compulsive babble to realize that one is uttering it can one achieve any genuine serenity, or the silence which is its habitat. "To restore silence is the role of objects," says Molloy, but this is not Beckett's final paradox. His final paradox is the conception of the imaginative process which underlies and informs his remarkable achievement. In a world given over to obsessive utterance, a world of television and radio and shouting dictators and tape recorders and beeping spaceships, to restore silence is the role of serious writing.

GRAVES, GODS, AND SCHOLARS

The trouble with being a literary critic is that one gets filing cards in the memory, and one is continually having to fish them out and wonder if the clichés typed on them are really so very bright. I imagine a good many people roughly familiar with modern poetry have some sort of card in their memories reading in effect: "Graves, Robert. Does tight, epigrammatic lyrics in the Hardy-Housman tradition; closer in technique to Blunden and de la Mare than to Eliot, Pound, or Yeats; a minor poet, but one of the best of the post-Georgians." There is some factual basis for such a note, but in terms of "covering" its subject, it would hardly make an honest woman of Lady Godiva. Whatever one thinks of Mr. Graves as a poet, novelist, critic, translator, mythographer, editor, anthologist, collaborator, surveyor of modernist poetry, or restorer of the Nazarene gospel, there can be no reasonable doubt that Mr. Graves is big, and bigness is certainly one important attribute of greatness. He is not a minor poet; he is not a minor anything.

Of all evidences of bigness, one of the most impressive is a sense of the expendable. The present volume is as much selected as collected poems: Mr. Graves has written many fine poems that are not here, which indicates, not only that he is highly self-critical, but that he believes that the poet always knows what his essential poems are. I have some reservations about this latter view, but, on the other hand, every poet has the right to his own canon, and it is as an author's canon that the present collection should be read.

Review of Robert Graves, *Collected Poems* (Garden City, N.Y.: Doubleday, 1955). Reprinted by permission from *The Hudson Review*, vol. 9, no. 2 (Summer 1956). © 1956 by The Hudson Review, Inc.

Lyrical poetry normally begins in an associative process in which sound is as important as sense, a process much of which is submerged below consciousness. Such a process may go in either of two directions. It may become oracular, ambiguous in sense and echoic in sound, in which case it is addressed in part to an uncritical faculty, concerned with casting a spell and demanding emotional surrender. Or it may become witty, addressing itself to the critical intelligence and the detached consciousness. The ingredients of paronomasia and assonance are common to both, and it depends on the context whether, for instance, Poe's line "The viol, the violet and the vine" or Pope's "Great Cibber's brazen, brainless brothers stand" is oracular or witty.

Mr. Graves is an epigrammatic writer who remains in full intellectual control of his work. The meaning of his poem never gets away from him, never dissolves in a drowsy charm of sound. He is a poet to whom theme means a good deal: every poem is aimed directly at a definite human or mythical situation and usually hits it squarely in its central paradox. The technique corresponds. In the earlier pages, one watches him practicing forms with a sharp, rhythmical bite: Mother Goose rhythms, ballads, and eight-six quatrains, and, in the fine "In Procession," Skeltonics reminding us how much Mr. Graves has done to rehabilitate Skelton. The deep incision produced by exact meter and clear thought makes some unforgettably sharp outlines:

> Courtesies of good-morning and good-evening
> From rustic lips fail as the town encroaches:
> Soon nothing passes but the cold quick stare
> Of eyes that see ghosts, yet too many for fear.

Later in the book we get more unrhymed poems, where the metrical and mental discipline have to stand alone, and finally, in the poems that come from or are contemporary with *The White Goddess*, incantation itself. But as the poet has approached incantation from the opposite end, his enchanters speak in a curiously reasonable and expository voice. Thus the Sirens urge Cronos:

> Compared with this, what are the plains
> Of Elis, where you ruled as king?
> A wilderness indeed.

The poetic personality revealed in the book is one of sturdy independence, pragmatic common sense, and a consistently quizzical attitude toward systematized forms of experience, especially the religious. From this point of view, Mr. Graves's collected poems could hardly have come at a better time. We have had a good deal of ecclesiasticized poetry, full of the dilemma of modern man, Kierkegaardian *Angst*, and the facile resonance of the penitential mood. Mr. Graves is strongly in revolt against all this, and he is old enough to have the authority of a contemporary classic, carrying on a tradition that goes back to the nineteenth century through Henley and Housman; a tradition that has more in common with Clough than with Arnold. He writes not humbly but defiantly of "Self-Praise," and says:

> Confess, creatures, how sulkily ourselves
> We hiss with doom, fuel of a sodden age—
> Not rapt up roaring to the chimney stack
> On incandescent clouds of spirit or rage.

He is occasionally betrayed into cliché on this point, as in "Ogres and Pygmies," but the sense of candor and freshness remains the primary one.

Mr. Graves is becoming an influence on contemporary British poetry in such a way as to suggest that we may be ready to repeat, on a very small scale of decades rather than millenia, Yeats's pattern of progress from Christian humility to the tragic pride of Oedipus the riddle-guesser. Certainly no one can doubt that Mr. Graves is by far the greatest riddle-guesser of our time: all the Gordian knots of antiquity, from the song of the sirens to the number of Antichrist, fall to pieces at the swing of his sword. Readers who are still bemused by the oracular, still accustomed to think of poetry as Lenten reading and of the poet as a psychopomp, may put their hands confidingly into Mr. Graves's with the hope of being led, like Prufrock, to some overwhelming question, perhaps even an answer. And as they proceed, whether through this book or through the formidable series of mythological works, a central myth begins to take shape. This, of course, is the myth of the White Goddess, the mother-harlot, virgin-slut, "Sister of the mirage and echo," whose elusive and treacherous beauty has inspired poets from prehistoric times to the last whimpers of courtly love in Baudelaire. "It's a poet's privilege and fate" to fall in hopeless love with her: condemned by his genius to go on trying to screw the inscrutable, he must stumble groaningly around the four seasons of her adoration, from the rapture of spring to the reviling of winter:

> But we are gifted, even in November
> Rawest of seasons, with so huge a sense
> Of her nakedly worn magnificence
> We forget cruelty and past betrayal,
> Heedless of where the next bright bolt may fall.

That's it, then: "There is one story and one story only." The key to all myths, the answer to all riddles, the source of all great poems, is the story of Attis and Cybele, where a feminine principle remains enthroned and a masculine one follows the cycle of nature, a Lord of the May who is soon "dethroned" and turned into a doomed victim, like Actaeon, while the poet urges:

> Run, though you hope for nothing: to stay your foot
> Would be ingratitude, a sour denial
> That the life she bestowed was sweet.

The Attis-Cybele story is very important in mythology; it underlies a vast number of poems; its ramifications are nearly as widespread as those of poetry itself. All this no one would wish to deny. One feels, nevertheless, that there is something dismally corny about isolating a myth in this way and in this form; something of rotten-ripe late romanticism; something that suggests the masochism of Swinburne or some of the worst effects of Maud Gonne or Yeats, rather than anything typical of Mr. Graves. So we go back and run through his book again.

We notice that the central theme of a relatively early

poem, "Warning to Children," is that of the boxes of Silenus, the image with which Rabelais begins. In the next poem, a most important poem called "Alice," we read:

> Nor did Victoria's golden rule extend
> Beyond the glass: it came to the dead end
> Where empty hearses turn about; thereafter
> Begins that lubberland of dream and laughter,
> The red-and-white-flower-spangled hedge, the grass
> Where Apuleius pastured his Gold Ass,
> Where young Gargantua made whole holiday . . .

We begin to wonder if perhaps Mr. Graves does not after all belong, not to the solemnly systematic mythographers, not to the tradition of Apollodorus and Natalis Comes and George Eliot's Casaubon, but to the tradition of the writers who have turned mythical erudition into satire, to Rabelais and Apuleius, or to the exuberantly hyperbolic Celtic mythical poets. The combination of erudite satire and lyrical gifts is not uncommon: we find it in Petronius, in Heine, in Joyce, and (counting his lethal scholarly essays as erudite satire) in Housman. Perhaps Mr. Graves's oracle, too, is the oracle of the Holy Bottle: certainly the myths in his poetry, like the ghosts, seem to be not part of the objective system but a kaleidoscopic chaos of human fragments. As he says:

> Now I know the mermaid kin
>   I find them bound by natural laws:
> They have neither tail not fin,
>   But are deadlier for that cause.

He does not lead us toward an objective or systematic mythology: he leads us toward the mythical use of poetic language, where we invent our own myths and apply them to an indefinite number of human themes. He has several doppelganger poems, in which he develops the theme of the looking-glass world as this world looked at mythically; as, in short, the world constructed by love and imagination. This is the theme of "The Climate of Thought," of "The Terraced Valley," and of several other poems.

Perhaps, then, his attraction to the white goddess myth is

simply that it is an ironic myth, ambiguous in its moral values, and providing in its human incarnations what is essentially a heap of broken images. In contrast, the masculine protest myths of father-gods, introduced to our culture by the prophet Ezekiel, according to *The White Goddess*, stand for order, system, and the limiting of poetic themes by artificial standards of truth and morality. In such poems as the early "Reproach," where Christ appears as an accusing father, in "The Eremites," in "The Bards," and elsewhere, we see the perversion of life that results from enthroning a male god in the sky in place of a mother. Perhaps we may understand from these poems how we are to read such a book as *Wife to Mr. Milton*: less as biography or literary criticism than as a blow struck in defense of the white goddess, and one in the eye for the prophet Ezekiel. The ambivalence of Mr. Graves's attitude to myth reminds one of Samuel Butler, whom he curiously resembles in many ways. Butler was so subtle and poker-faced an ironist that some of his parodies, such as the Book of the Machines in *Erewhon*, take in the casual reader, who is apt to assume that it's a straight Frankenstein fantasy. Others, such as *The Fair Haven*, took in nearly the whole reading public in their day. And there are still others so *very* subtle that they seem to have taken in Samuel Butler himself. His account of the Resurrection, for instance, reads like a deadly parody of Victorian pseudorationalism going to work on the gospel narratives, but Butler appears to have taken it seriously, as he did his notions about the *Odyssey* (some of them shared by Mr. Graves) and about Shakespeare's sonnets. Similarly, *King Jesus* and *The Nazarene Gospel Restored* impress one primarily as mythical satire: that is, as constructs so obviously hypothetical that they suggest an indefinite number of other possible constructs, each as ingenious and plausible as the author's—or as the orthodox version. But Mr. Graves appears to take them "seriously," as in some way definitive or exclusive. But fortunately we can dodge that issue in reading the poetry, and find the central path to his mind through something like this:

> He is quick, thinking in clear images;
> I am slow, thinking in broken images.

He becomes dull, trusting to his clear images;
I become sharp, mistrusting my broken images . . .

He in a new confusion of his understanding;
I in a new understanding of my confusion.

POETRY OF THE TOUT ENSEMBLE

One of the most unfashionable poets in English literature, Charles Doughty, made the unfashionable remark: "The poet's task is not to meditate on human vanity, but to serve his country." Most of us would perhaps feel that such an observation was, first, quixotic (what country cares whether its poets want to serve it or not?), and, second, a recommending of what would in practice be a dismal bureaucratic flunkeyism, like the pseudoarts of totalitarian states. In any case, the social gestures of twentieth-century writers are mainly negative ones: gestures of defiance (Pound), of detachment (Valéry), of silence, exile, and cunning (Joyce), of suicide, of transferred allegiance (Eliot), of religious conversion (usually to Catholicism in countries where Protestantism is popular), and so on. It is chiefly in such contexts as the French Resistance, where the negative gesture is appropriate, that we feel how much real truth there is in Doughty's statement. Certainly it seems surprisingly reassuring to discover a poet, who, like René Char, is a man with a heroic personal record, and not less a poet for having it; who is both "engaged" in his life and yet exact and difficult in his art.

A new poet usually impresses his immediate contemporaries as "experimental," or some similar term meaning relatively unintelligible. By the time criticism has made an experimental poet intelligible, it has also made him traditional. If he resists this process, he drops out of sight, not because he was

Review of René Char, *Hypnos Waking*, trans. Jackson Mathews (New York: Random House, 1956); and Maurice Blanchot et al., *René Char's Poetry* (New York: Noonday Press, 1956). Reprinted by permission from *The Hudson Review*, vol. 10, no. 1 (Spring 1957). © 1957 by The Hudson Review, Inc.

experimental, but because he was superficially traditional, a member of a school who went along for the ride. The criticism of Char, as revealed by a recent little volume, is still in the first stages. What it says about Char is largely a series of amiable and enthusiastic gargles: we read sentence after sentence with no actual content, beyond a general emotional aim of deprecating analysis in favor of applause. Such writing results from an effort to convey the direct experience of reading the poet, an experience for which there are, of course, no words. One understands and sympathizes with it; but a glance at Char is enough to show that for him, as for Wallace Stevens, "poetry is the subject of the poem": he is intensely preoccupied with the theory and function of poetry. Besides, even in a straight evaluation one is still left with the question: is Char's present reputation based solely on his merits, or is it in some measure due to the fact that he corresponds so closely to what an educated Frenchman, brought up in the tradition of Rimbaud and aware of the tremendous spiritual potential of the Resistance, would expect the next great poet to be like?

Char's most obvious affinities are with the surrealists: like them, he emphasizes the contrast between logical thought, which operates discursively and descriptively, and poetic thought, which operates by the immediate metaphorical identification of images. The latter is a direct and primitive form of thought which impresses the logical thinker as illogical to the verge of lunacy, or, if he is forced to take it seriously, as incredibly difficult and esoteric. Ordinary prose, or poetry approximating the idiom of prose like Wordsworth's, comes to terms with the logical thinker, which is what John Stuart Mill meant by calling Wordsworth the poet of unpoetical natures. Ordinary meter also comes to terms with him, as usually it is easy to see what concessions have been made from reason to rhyme. Char writes a good deal of his best poetry in the form of aphorisms, sentences which have the rhythm of prose but the imagery and concentration of poetry. These sentences are oracular, like the aphorisms of Heraclitus, a philosopher who has deeply impressed Char. Linear reading, of the kind we apply both to ordinary prose and to meter, will not do for them. The aphorism works on the principle of the Bloody Mary: it has to be swallowed at a gulp and allowed to explode from inside. It makes possible a kind of concentration that puts a considerable strain on Char's translators, who nonetheless do a both accurate and eloquent job. "What I have to do is hell," for instance, renders what in Char is simply "Devoirs infernaux." *Le Poème Pulvérisé* shows in its title how constantly Char works in the tradition of "fragmentation," deliberately breaking down everything that is continuous into a series of epiphanies or *illuminations*.

Char's imagery is based on the principle of opposites, another Heraclitean conception. The center of this principle is expressed in the title of the English collection, *Hypnos Waking*. In ordinary life, we have a "real" world of waking consciousness and a submerged world of dream and desire. The latter is the source of poetry and of all creative effort: it struggles "against the real" to create a world that makes more sense in terms of desire. "The poet must keep an equal balance between the physical world of waking and the dreadful ease of sleep; these are the lines of knowledge between which he lays the subtle body of the poem." Poetry finds its fulfillment in a universe of its own, a universe symbolized by the term *Word* (*le Verbe*, as distinct from *le mot* or *la parole*), which is, of course, not another world from ours but another way of dealing with it. This verbal universe, a world of poetry rather than of poems or individuals, is also a human universe, a world of realized freedom, desire, and intelligence. "Man be my metaphor," says Dylan Thomas, and Char says, "The being we do not know is an infinite being; he may arrive, and turn our anguish and our burden to dawn in our arteries." Like Rilke, he calls this being an "angel" to keep it "free of religious compromise." Thus, again as in Rilke, the poetic vision is from the circumference, not the center. "Do not seek the limits of the sea. You contain them." For just as the poem finds its ultimate meaning in a total poetic universe, so man finds his own being in the corresponding human totality. "Imagination consists in expelling from reality several incomplete persons, and then using the magic and subversive powers of desire to bring them back in the form of one entirely satisfying presence." "Later," says the poet, "you will be identified as some disintegrated giant, lord of the impossible."

The conception of a verbal universe comes, of course, from Mallarmé: it is also in Valéry, but whereas Valéry tends to think of the poet's world in Platonic and contemplative terms, Char thinks of it existentially, as "engaged" in a redemptive death struggle with the kind of world that produces such things as the Nazi occupation. "In poetry, only when there is communication and a free ordering of the totality of things among themselves, through us, are we ourselves engaged and defined." Hence, he is obliged to struggle against the world of the "Hitlerian shadows," where there can be no such thing as a "dialogue between two human beings." Hence, too, fighters in the Resistance discover that "the language in use here comes from the sense of wonder communicated by the beings and things we live with in continual intimacy." The sense that there is no otherness, that the moment of time encloses the whole of experience, breeds the kind of desperation that allows tyranny to flourish. "Have nothing to do with those in whose eyes man is merely a passing shade of the color on earth's tormented back."

Thus, the conventional religious conception of a world of eternal life, from which the "real" world has fallen and to which it will some day return, becomes in Char, as it does in most poets, whether religious in temperament or not, an allegory of the poetic universe. There is a Fall: "When the dam of man broke . . . words were heard in the distance . . . struggling to resist the enormous pressure." Char's poems are "poems of the illuminated absolute, of the madly impossible resurrection." This latter pole is usually placed in the future: poetry is "life's future held in requalified man," and he asks whether the quest for a great being is "merely the finger of the chained present touching the future still at liberty." All through *Leaves of Hypnos*, a poetic diary of his fighting in the Resistance, we read of a new world dawning. Yet this feeling is not the usual donkey's carrot of people at war who hypnotize themselves into believing that the war is worthwhile because of all the wonderful things that will happen after it. Many of Char's associates in the Resistance entered the Maquis simply to be flattered by their own conscience: he will have nothing to do with this, and nothing to do with the future of the illusions to which it gives rise. The "real" world that produced the war is always here, and only poetry can do anything effective about it.

The total impression one gets of Char is of a powerful and somewhat humorless poet grinding and churning his way like a bulldozer through the jungles of emotional confusion in contemporary life. Reading him, we see chiefly a chaos of uprooted trees, flying rocks, and "pulverized" soil; retrospectively, we see an impressive sense of direction and a good deal of courage and perseverance in following it. We have mentioned Dylan Thomas: the contrast between them indicates how much difference in national temperament there still is even in this shrinking world. Char has nothing of Thomas's very British and Dickensian zest for absurdity: like Sartre and Camus, he can deal with the absurd only when he has got it established as a metaphysical principle, and can see at a distance that man's "head trails a wake through the galaxy of the absurd." Nevertheless, there is a more important issue which is common to both traditions. We have heard a good deal about the "dissociation of sensibility" in nineteenth-century poetry; we have naturally heard much less about a parallel dissociation in our own time between poets of genuine warmth of feeling easily carried away by rhetoric (Jeffers, Lawrence), and poets of great technical skill who set up ironic barriers against feeling (Auden, Stevens).

Turning again to Char's critics, we notice how much they seem to think of Char as a kind of antidote to such a dissociation. We learn that Char is "a giant—a real physical giant," who gives a sense of personal authority because he "is a poet who believes what he says, and whose word we can trust." His "poetry is a total gesture of revolution," looking for a bigger transformation of society than, say, Marxism could achieve: he "is not a Christian," but "Salvation is always on his mind." He sounds, in short, like an old-fashioned romantic liberal, and there are certainly many worse things to be than that. His references to Heraclitus and Georges de la Tour are in the height of intellectual fashion, yet his critics keep coming back to the same point: something which has long been neglected is being reasserted in Char. Rimbaud, Valéry, even Mallarmé—each seems to represent a dead end of some kind— they are all, in different ways, voices of silence, and Char, his admirers say, restores one's faith in both the present and the future of French poetry. None of them would mention Victor Hugo, yet one wonders whether in the welcome given Char there is not some sense of relief that there should finally be someone in France who knows all the tricks of twentieth-century style and still is not ashamed to echo the hoarse, uninhibited rhetoric of the great exile of Jersey who, both in literature and life, would, as Char says today of himself, "write no poem of acquiescence."

NOTES TO THE INTRODUCTION

The following abbreviations of Frye's works are used in the Introduction and in the Notes.

AC   *Anatomy of Criticism*
CP   *The Critical Path: An Essay on the Social Context of Literary Criticism*
EI   *The Educated Imagination*
FI   *Fables of Identity: Studies in Poetic Mythology*
FS   *Fearful Symmetry: A Study of William Blake*
NP   *A Natural Perspective: The Development of Shakespearean Comedy and Romance*
SeS *The Secular Scripture: A Study of the Structure of Romance*
SM   *Spiritus Mundi: Essays on Literature, Myth, and Society*
SS   *The Stubborn Structure: Essays on Criticism and Society*
WC   *The Well-Tempered Critic*

1. "The Search for Acceptable Words," *Daedalus* 102 (Spring 1973): 19–20; reprinted in *Spiritus Mundi* (Bloomington, 1976), p. 16. Hereafter cited as *SM*.

2. "Current Opera: A Housecleaning," *Acta Victoriana* 60 (October 1935): 12–14.

3. "Ballet Russe," *Acta Victoriana* 60 (December 1935): 5. The same concepts appear in "Frederick Delius," *Canadian Forum* 16 (August 1936): 17. See also "Music in Poetry," *University of Toronto Quarterly* 11 (1942): 167–79. Edward Said is one of the few readers who have understood the centrality of music as a structural analogy in Frye's thought. See *Beginnings* (New York, 1975), p. 376. Frye, incidentally, understood the "harmonic" (vertical) and "melodic" (horizontal) ways of visualizing literature some twenty years before Lévi-Strauss was to speak of reading the Oedipus myth paradigmatically as well as syntagmatically.

4. "Wyndham Lewis: Anti-Spenglerian," *Canadian Forum* 16 (June 1936): 21–22.

5. The essay in the present volume on "Toynbee and Spengler" is from the

1940s. See also "Oswald Spengler," in *Architects of Modern Thought*. 1st series (Toronto, 1955), pp. 83–90, and "New Directions from Old," in *Myth and Mythmaking*, ed. Henry A. Murray (New York, 1960), pp. 117–18; reprinted in *Fables of Identity* (New York, 1963), pp. 53–54. The most recent treatment, which Frye describes as "an effort to lay a ghost to rest," is "*The Decline of the West* by Oswald Spengler," *Daedalus* 103 (Winter 1974): 1–13; reprinted as "Spengler Revisited" in *SM*, pp. 179–98. *Fables of Identity* hereafter cited as *FI*.

6. *A Map of Misreading* (New York, 1975), p. 30. Bloom echoes Geoffrey Hartman's remark about Frye: "What we need is a theory of recurrence (repetition) that includes a theory of discontinuity." See "Structuralism: The Anglo-American Adventure," in *Beyond Formalism* (New Haven, 1970), p. 17.

7. *The Secular Scripture* (Cambridge, Mass., 1976), p. 163. Hereafter cited as *SeS*. As Frye points out, these words were written before the appearance of Bloom's *A Map of Misreading* (p. 193). On Frye's discussion of continuity in another context, see "The University and Personal Life," in *Higher Education: Demand and Response* (San Fransicso, 1970), pp. 35–51; reprinted in *SM*, pp. 27–48. This essay examines the positive and negative features resulting from the meeting of continuous and discontinuous views of the world. There can be no doubt about Frye's indebtedness to Eliot's ideas about the order of literature and about tradition and the individual talent, but *The Modern Century* (Toronto, 1967), to cite another example, is an entire book about the interplay between continuity and discontinuity.

8. "Expanding Eyes," *Critical Inquiry* 2 (Winter 1975): 200; reprinted in *SM*, pp. 100–101. Although *Anatomy of Criticism* is a book of the midfifties, it incorporates material published as early as 1942. See, for example, "The Anatomy of Prose Fiction," *Manitoba Arts Review* 3 (Spring 1942): 35–47; "Music in Poetry," *University of Toronto Quarterly* 11 (1942): 167–79; "The Nature of Satire," *University of Toronto Quarterly* 14 (1944): 75–89, which are incorporated into the third and fourth essays of the *Anatomy*.

9. "Anaesthetic Criticism," in *Psychoanalysis and Literary Process*, ed. Frederick Crews (Cambridge, Mass., 1970), p. 1. Crews's essay originally appeared in a slightly different form in *New York Review of Books* 14, no. 4 (February 26, 1970) and no. 5 (March 12, 1970).

10. See, for example, V. G. Hanes, "Northrop Frye's Theory of Literature and Marxism," *Horizons: The Marxist Quarterly*, no. 24 (Winter 1968), pp. 62–78, reprinted in *Man and the Arts: A Marxist Approach*, by Arnold Kettle and V. G. Hanes (New York, 1968), pp. 17–33; Fred Inglis, "Professor Northrop Frye and the Academic Study of Literature," *Centennial Review* 9 (1965): 319–31; Richard Poirier, "What Is English Studies . . . ," *Partisan Review* 37 (1970): 41–58, reprinted in *The*

Performing Self (New York, 1971), pp. 65–86; Brian Robinson, "Northrop Frye: critique fameux, critique faillible," *Revue de l'Université d'Ottawa* 42 (1972): 608–14; Robert Weimann, "Literarische Wertung und historische Tradition: Zu ihrer Aporie im Werk von Northrop Frye," *Zeitschrift für Anglistik und Amerikanistik* 21 (1973): 341–59; Eugene Goodheart, "The Failure of Criticism," *New Literary History* 7 (Winter 1976): 384–86.

11. (Ithaca, N.Y., 1970), p. x. Hereafter cited as *SS*.

12. (Bloomington, 1971). Hereafter cited as *CP*.

13. *Anatomy of Criticism* (Princeton, 1957), pp. 342, 344, 345, 343. Hereafter cited as *AC*.

14. *AC*, p. 113. This position is also anticipated in the Polemical Introduction: "Ethical criticism [is based on] the consciousness of the presence of society. As a critical category this would be the sense of the real presence of culture in the community. Ethical criticism, then, deals with art as a communication from the past to the present, and is based on the conception of the total and simultaneous possession of past culture. An exclusive devotion to it, ignoring historical criticism, would lead to a naive translation of all cultural phenomena into our own terms without regard to their original character. As a counterweight to historical criticism, it is designed to express the contemporary impact of all art, without selecting a tradition" (*AC*, pp. 24–25).

15. *AC*, pp. 347–48. In "Criticism, Visible and Invisible," Frye says that the end of criticism is "not an aesthetic, but an ethical and participating end: for it, ultimately, works of literature are not things to be contemplated but powers to be absorbed. . . . The 'aesthetic' attitude, persisted in, loses its connection with literature as an art and becomes socially or morally anxious: to treat literature seriously as a social and moral force is to pass into the genuine experience of it." *College English* 26 (October 1964): 8; reprinted in *SS*, p. 82.

16. *The Modern Century* (Toronto, 1967). Many of the essays which show how Frye has gone beyond formalism are collected in part 1 of *The Stubborn Structure* and in part 1 of *Spiritus Mundi*.

17. *The Well-Tempered Critic* (Bloomington, 1963), pp. 111–22. Hereafter cited as *WC*.

18. "Literary History: The Point of It All," *New Literary History* 2 (Autumn 1970): 184.

19. On the myths of freedom and concern, see also "The Instruments of Mental Production," *Chicago Review* 18, nos. 3–4 (1966): 30–46; "The Knowledge of Good and Evil," in *The Morality of Scholarship*, ed. Max Black (Ithaca, 1967), pp. 1–28; "Speculation and Concern," in *The Humanities and the Understanding of Reality*, ed. Thomas B. Stroup (Lexington, Ky., 1966), 32–54. All three essays are reprinted in *SS*, pp. 3–54.

20. This tripartite schema derives from Richard McKeon, "The Philosophic Bases of Art and Criticism," in *Critics and Criticism*, ed. R. S. Crane (Chicago, 1952), pp. 466-90.

21. Their ideas on the power of the imagination to create an ideal world are, however, similar. Compare, for example, Frye's views on anagogy in the second essay with Kant's statement that "the poet ventures to realize to sense, rational ideas of invisible beings, the kingdom of the blessed, hell, eternity, creation, etc.; or even if he deals with things of which there are examples in experience—e.g., death, envy and all vices, also love, fame, and the like—he tries, by means of imagination, which emulates the play of reason in its quest after a maximum, to go beyond the limits of experience and to present them to sense with a completeness of which there is no example in nature. This is properly speaking the art of the poet, in which the faculty of aesthetical ideas can manifest itself in its entire strength. But this faculty, considered in itself, is properly only a talent (of the imagination)" (*Critique of Judgment*, part 49, trans. J. H. Bernard [New York, 1951], pp. 157-58).

22. Published originally in *The American Journal of Psychiatry* 119 (1962): 289-98; reprinted in *FI*, 151-67.

23. *Fearful Symmetry* (Princeton, 1947), p. 27. Hereafter cited as *FS*.

24. *The Educated Imagination* (Bloomington, 1964), p. 23. Hereafter cited as *EI*.

25. On the imagination as a vital force, see *FS*, pp. 55, 83, 230, 235; and *FI*, pp. 80-81; as a unifying and synthesizing force, see *FS*, pp. 56, 88, and *EI*, p. 38.

26. "Myth, Fiction, and Displacement," in *FI*, pp. 29-30. See also "The Developing Imagination," in *Learning in Language and Literature* (Cambridge, Mass., 1963), pp. 37-38. In the essay on Coleridge reprinted in the present volume Frye says: "The imagination is instrumental in Coleridge: it is the power that unifies, but not the thing to be unified, the real co-ordinating principle."

27. *SeS*, p. 35. Frye has studied Stevens's understanding of the imagination in "Wallace Stevens and the Variation Form," in *Literary Theory and Structure*, ed. Frank Brady et al. (New Haven, 1973), pp. 395-414; reprinted in *SM*, pp. 275-294.

28. Ben Howard, "Fancy, Imagination, and Northrop Frye," *Thoth* 9 (Winter 1968): 31.

29. For a summary of Frye's views on the imagination as a perceptive faculty, see Iqbal Ahmad, "Imagination and Image in Frye's Criticism," *English Quarterly* 3 (Summer 1970): 15-24.

30. "Three Meanings of Symbolism," *Yale French Studies*, no. 9 (1952), p. 18. This essay was incorporated into the "Theory of Symbols" of the *Anatomy*. For an excellent treatment of Frye's theory of symbols, see

Alvin A. Lee, "Old English Poetry, Mediaeval Exegesis and Modern Criticism," *Studies in the Literary Imagination* 7 (Spring 1975): 47–73. See also my "Frye's Theory of Symbols," *Canadian Literature*, no. 66 (Autumn 1975), pp. 63–79.

31. The complete scale of the "human forms" of nature is developed in detail in the third essay of the *Anatomy*.

32. *SM*, p. 117. In *The Critical Path* Frye says: "Because I found the term 'archetype' an essential one, I am still often called a Jungian critic, and classified with Miss Maud Bodkin, whose book I have read with interest, but whom, on the evidence of that book, I resemble about as closely as I resemble the late Sarah Bernhardt" (p. 16).

33. "Literary Criticism and History: The Endless Dialectic," *New Literary History* 6 (Spring 1975): 507.

34. "Reflections in a Mirror," in *Northrop Frye in Modern Criticism*, ed. Murray Krieger (New York, 1966), p. 142.

35. Although Spengler sometimes gives the illusion of holding a cyclical view of history, he "has no theory of cycles at all" ("Oswald Spengler," in *Architects of Modern Thought*, p. 86). See also *SM*, pp. 113, 185. Frye does, however, use the word "cycle" to refer to Spengler's metahistory in "The Rising of the Moon: a Study of 'A Vision'," in *An Honoured Guest* (London, 1965), p. 15; reprinted in *SM*, p. 254; and he uses it to refer to his own theory of modes in an early version of the first essay, "Towards a Theory of Cultural History," *University of Toronto Quarterly* 22 (July 1953): 341. The word is not actually used in the first essay to refer to the modal paradigm, though Frye does observe that as ironic literature moves toward myth it is often accompanied by cyclical theories of history —as in Nietzsche, Joyce, and Yeats (*AC*, pp. 62, 65).

36. "Utopian History and the *Anatomy*," in *Northrop Frye in Modern Criticism*, pp. 32, 34.

37. Ibid., p. 56.

38. Ibid., p. 34. See also p. 43.

39. Ibid., p. 53.

40. *Historical Inevitability* (London, 1954), p. 14, as quoted by Fletcher, p. 52. In "Northrop Frye: The Critical Passion," *Critical Inquiry* 1 (June 1975): 741–56, Fletcher re-examines Frye's understanding of history, qualifying his earlier judgment about its Utopian character but still maintaining that the first essay is "based on a theory of literary history. Essay I is not a history of literature: it is a theoretical history of literature, that is, it presents the past of our literature under the guise of a hypothetical formation of a series of eventualities" (p. 753). The view that the first essay "gives a shape to history" is also argued by Bruce Bashford in "Literary History in Northrop Frye's *Anatomy of Criticism*," *Connecticut Review* 8 (1974): 48–55.

41. "Interpretation in History," *New Literary History* 4 (1973): 287.
42. Ibid., pp. 291, 295. Cf. Frye's remark in "Reflections in a Mirror": "The only shaping principles of history in literature itself I have ever dealt with . . . are those of displacement, the oscillating technique from the stylizing of form to the manifesting of content and back again, and of what I call existential projection, the attributing of poetic schematism to the objective world, which takes different forms in different historical epochs" (pp. 142–43). In *Metahistory* (Baltimore, 1973), pp. 7–11, 231–33, Hayden White draws upon Frye's theory of myths to identify four different modes of emplotment, which he then uses as a part of his framework for analyzing nineteenth-century historians. See also White's "The Historical Text as Literary Artifact," *Clio* 3 (1974): 277–303.
43. *The Fantastic* (Cleveland, 1973), pp. 8–23. The issues raised by Todorov are also treated by Robert Scholes in *Structuralism in Literature* (New Haven, 1974), pp. 118–27, and by Christine Brooke-Rose in "Historical Genres/Theoretical Genres," *New Literary History* 8 (Autumn 1976): 145–58.
44. *An Anatomy of Literature* (New York, 1972), the most fully developed application of Frye's theory of modes.
45. Practical criticism is often associated with the kind of activity begun by I. A. Richards in the 1920s—the close analysis of specific works considered as poetic wholes. Frye's approach usually assumes a much broader perspective. He is closer to Coleridge, whose studies of Wordsworth and Shakespeare have caused some historians to refer to him as the father of practical criticism, than he is to the various New Critics who have practiced close rhetorical analysis.
46. Toronto, 1971. The books on Shakespeare are *Fools of Time* (Toronto, 1967) and *A Natural Perspective* (New York, 1965); on Milton, *The Return of Eden* (Toronto, 1965); and on Eliot, *T. S. Eliot* (Edinburgh, 1963). *A Natural Perspective* hereafter cited as *NP*.
47. See part 1 of my *Northrop Frye: An Enumerative Bibliography* (Metuchen, N.J., 1974). A supplement to this listing of primary and secondary materials is in *Canadian Library Journal* 34 (June 1977): 181–97.
48. "I hold to no 'method' of criticism," Frye says, "beyond assuming that the structure and imagery of literature are central considerations of criticism. Nor, I think, does my practical criticism illustrate the use of a patented critical method of my own, different in kind from the approaches of other critics" (*SS*, p. 82). J. Wilson Knight seems to have influenced Frye's ideas about the "central considerations of criticism." See *SM*, pp. 12–13.
49. See especially "Blake After Two Centuries," in *FI*, pp. 138–50; "The Drunken Boat: The Revolutionary Element in Romanticism," in *SS*, pp. 200–217; and "The Romantic Myth," in *A Study of English Romanticism* (New York, 1968), pp. 3–49.

50. "Notes for a Commentary on *Milton*," in *The Divine Vision: Studies in the Poetry and Art of William Blake*, ed. Vivian de Sola Pinto (London, 1957), p. 107.

51. Ibid., pp. 106-7.

52. Ibid., p. 108.

53. "Blake's Treatment of the Archetype," in *Discussions of William Blake*, ed. John E. Grant (Boston, 1961), p. 8. On "apocalypse," see also *FS*, *passim*, and *FS*, p. 143. Frye's conception of radical metaphor can probably be traced back to Max Müller's treatment of the same topic in *Lectures on the Science of Language*. 2d Series (New York, 1874), pp. 371-402, and *The Science of Thought* (New York, 1887), 2: 481-86.

54. *Fools of Time* (Toronto, 1967), pp. 15-16.

55. *SeS*, especially chapters 4-6. On "identity" see also *A Study of English Romanticism* (New York, 1964), chapter 4; "The Rising of the Moon," *SM*, pp. 245-74; *SS*, pp. 98-99; and *FI*, pp. 32, 35.

56. *Criticism: The Major Texts*, enlarged ed. (New York, 1970), pp. xiv-xv, 597.

57. *Northrop Frye in Modern Criticism*, p. 1.

58. *American Scholar* 34 (1965): 484.

59. "Northrop Frye Exalting the Designs of Romance," *New York Times Book Review*, April 18, 1976, p. 21. Bloom's opinion is echoed by Gregory T. Polletta in *Issues in Contemporary Literary Criticism*, ed. Polletta (Boston, 1973): "Northrop Frye . . . is the foremost theorist of literature writing in English since the 1950's" (p. 6). While Frye's work is of course best known among English and American readers, the *Anatomy* has been translated into German, French, Italian, and Spanish, and there have been ten translations of his other books into these languages as well as Japanese.

60. Lawrence I. Lipking and A. Walton Litz, eds., *Modern Literary Criticism: 1900-1970* (New York, 1972), pp. viii, 180.

61. *Northrop Frye in Modern Criticism*, p. 27. More recently, Frye has said: "I have had some influence, I know, but I neither want nor trust disciples, at least as that term is generally understood. I should be horrified to hear of anyone proposing to make his own work revolve around mine, unless I were sure that that meant genuine freedom for him" (*SM*, p. 100).

62. Ibid., p. 29.

63. "What's the Use of Theorizing about the Arts?" in *In Search of Literary Theory*, ed. Morton W. Bloomfield (Ithaca, 1972), p. 25.

64. See, for example, Florence E. Bennee, "Selected Applications of Frye's Academic Criticism in the Senior High School Years" (Ed. D. dissertation, Columbia University, 1971); Robert D. Foulke and Paul Smith,

"Criticism and the Curriculum," *College English* 26 (1964): 23–37; Eli Mandel, *Criticism: The Silent Speaking Words* (Toronto, 1966); Glenna Davis Sloan, *The Child as Critic: Teaching Literature in the Elementary School* (New York, 1975); Kenneth W. Davis, "Demystifying Literature: Northrop Frye in the Classroom," *English Education* 3 (Spring 1972): 203–9; W. T. Jewkes, ed., *Literature: The Uses of Imagination*. 11 vols. (New York, 1973). Frye's manual for this last series of texts is *On Teaching Literature* (New York, 1972). See also Jewkes, "Mental Flight: Northrop Frye and the Teaching of Literature," *Journal of General Education* 27 (Winter 1976): 281–98.

65. See George Bowering, "Why James Reaney Is a Better Poet (1) Than Any Northrop Frye Poet (2) Than He Used To Be," *Canadian Literature*, no. 36 (Spring 1968), pp. 40–49; Desmond Pacey, *Essays in Canadian Criticism, 1938–68* (Toronto, 1969), pp. 202–5, 211; James Reaney, *Alphabet*, no. 1 (September 1960), pp. 2–4; Lloyd Abbey, "The Organic Aesthetic," *Canadian Literature*, no. 46 (Autumn 1970), pp. 103–4; and Frank Davey, "Northrop Frye," in *From There to Here* (Erin, Ontario, 1974), pp. 106–12.

66. "Criticism and Other Arts," *Canadian Literature*, no. 49 (Summer 1971), p. 4.

67. "I have long ceased to view the *Anatomy of Criticism*," he says, "as a handbook of real practical value to the critic."

68. *Review of English Studies* 10 (1959): 323.

69. Hough, *An Essay on Criticism* (New York, 1966), p. 154; Levin, *Why Literary Criticism Is Not an Exact Science* (Cambridge, Mass., 1967), p. 24; Wellek, *Discriminations* (New Haven, 1970), pp. 257–58.

70. "Reflections in a Mirror," p. 136.

71. G. C. Simpson, *Principles of Animal Taxonomy* (New York, 1961), p. 5, as quoted in Claude Lévi-Strauss, *The Savage Mind* (Chicago, 1966), pp. 9–10, 13.

72. *The Savage Mind*, p. 13.

73. "Myth and Interpretation," *New Literary History* 3 (1972): 341.

74. *SM*, p. 105. In *SM*, p. 24, Frye says that we too often assume "that creative people are the people who write poems or stories . . . and that such people ought to have a specially protected place in the community. . . . There is nothing wrong with this except the fallacy of attaching the conception of creativity to the genres of poetry and fiction rather than to the people working in them. This fallacy is worldwide, and extends, for instance, to the Nobel Prize Committee in Sweden, who search over the world for poets and novelists but never consider the claims of critical or expository writing." Although Frye does not go so far as some of the new French critics when they seek to nullify literary texts, he is like them in maintaining that any form of verbal culture can be creative. In this

respect, he comes close to Geoffrey Hartman's argument in *The Fate of Reading* (Chicago, 1975) that criticism is a genre of literature.

75. "Myth and Interpretation," p. 342.

76. "Anatomy of Criticism," *University of Toronto Quarterly* 28 (1959): 196. The analogies Abrams refers to are found in *AC*, pp. 183, 190, and 46, respectively.

77. Abrams, ibid., and John Holloway, "The Critical Zodiac of Northrop Frye," in *The Colours of Clarity* (London, 1964), pp. 159–60.

78. "The Future of Metaphysics," in *The Future of Metaphysics*, ed. Robert E. Wood (Chicago, 1970), pp. 304–5.

79. "The Critical Zodiac of Northrop Frye," p. 159.

80. "Toward a Theory of Cultural Revolution: The Criticism of Northrop Frye," *Canadian Literature*, no. 1 (Summer 1959), p. 58.

INDEX